Non - Governmental Organisations –

Performance and *Accountability*

Non - Governmental Organisations –

Performance and Accountability

BEYOND THE MAGIC BULLET

EDITED BY MICHAEL EDWARDS AND DAVID HULME

Save the Children **Y**

EARTHSCAN

Earthscan Publications Ltd, London

First published in the UK in 1995 by
Earthscan Publications Limited

Copyright © Save the Children Fund – UK

A catalogue record for this book is available from the British Library

ISBN 1 85383 310 X Paperback

Typeset by DP Photosetting, Aylesbury, Bucks
Printed and bound by Biddles Ltd, Guildford and King's Lynn
Cover design by Yvonne Booth

For a full list of publications please contact

**Earthscan Publications Limited
120 Pentonville Road
London N1 9JN
Tel: 0171 278 0433
Fax: 0171 278 1142**

Earthscan is an editorially independent subsidiary of Kogan Page Limited
and publishes in association with WWF-UK and the
International Institute for Environment and Development.

Contents

Foreword

In 1992 Save the Children-UK and the Institute for Development Policy and Management at Manchester University co-sponsored an international workshop on 'Scaling-up NGO Impact: Learning from Experience', the outcomes of which were published in book form under the title *Making a Difference: NGOs and Development in a Changing World* (Edwards, M and Hulme, D (eds) Earthscan/SCF, 1992). *Making a Difference* has since been reprinted three times, but increasing concerns have been expressed about the causes and consequences of NGO growth, and what appears to be a closer relationship between NGOs and official aid agencies. To investigate these concerns, SCF-UK and IDPM organised a second international workshop in Manchester in June 1994, entitled 'NGOs and Development: Performance and Accountability in the "New World Order"', which provided the basis for this volume.

When we re-read the papers which were presented to the second Manchester workshop, it became clear that there were two common themes of concern, albeit overlapping. The first concerned issues of NGO performance and accountability, and how these processes were being reshaped by changing roles and funding arrangements. *Beyond the Magic Bullet* presents a detailed review of these concerns. The second theme concerned the broader relationships between NGOs, governments and official donor agencies, and how these changing relationships were affecting state-society relations, the future of development co-operation, and the interests of poor people. These concerns are explored in the companion volume to this book, entitled *Too Close for Comfort?* (Hulme, D and Edwards, M (eds) Macmillan/St Martin's Press).

Inevitably, both works are the result of contributions from a large number of people, not all of whom are credited in the text. In particular, we should like to acknowledge the contributions of all the participants at the second Manchester workshop who presented papers and took part in plenaries and discussion groups. These have helped to shape our own thinking and the thinking of other contributors to the two books. We should also stress that none of the contributors speak 'on behalf of' or represent a constituency in their writing: all write as individuals with their own personal point of view. No collection of essays can claim to be truly comprehensive, but we have endeavoured to include as wide a range of views and experiences as possible, from different regions of the world, alternative viewpoints and contrasting organisations.

We should also like to acknowledge the financial support of a number of institutions that helped to make the workshop and the resulting publications possible. These include the NGO Unit of the Swedish International Development Authority (SIDA), the Government and Institutions Department and ESCOR in the UK Overseas Development Administration (ODA), Save the Children-UK, and the Institute for Development Policy and Management at Manchester University. A large number of other NGOs also sponsored participants at the workshop, and our thanks go to them, especially to SCF Field Offices in Sudan, Uganda, Bangladesh, Peru, India, Pakistan, Thailand, Ghana, Colombia and Honduras.

At the University of Manchester especial thanks go to Debra Whitehead and Jayne Hindle for sweating blood to make the workshop a success; Catherine Williams and Marcia Doyle undertook similar responsibilities for Save the Children-UK. The same teams spent long hours hunched over computer screens in order to prepare the manuscripts for the two books in record time. Our sincere thanks go to them and to all the other individuals and agencies who have helped us to see these books through to a successful conclusion.

MICHAEL EDWARDS   DAVID HULME
London   *Manchester*
March 1995   *March 1995*

Contributors

Suliman Ali Baldo is Director of Studies for the Al Fanar Centre for Development Services, an independent research and consultancy group based in Khartoum, Sudan. A founding member of a leading Sudanese NGO, the Sudanese Popular Committee for Relief and Rehabilitation, he was also the Country Representative for Oxfam (USA) between 1988 and 1992.

Hector Béjar is the Founder-Director of the Centre for the Study of Development and Participation (CEDEP) in Peru. He is also a member of the Board of 'EL TALLER' and a member of CIVICUS (the World Alliance for Citizen Participation). He is a consultant, analyst and writer in the areas of civil society, the reform of the state, rural development, people's participation and non-governmental organisations (NGOs). He attended the Copenhagen Social Summit Conference as a member of the Peruvian NGO delegation.

Kees Biekart is a political scientist and research fellow at the Transnational Institute (TNI) in Amsterdam (Netherlands), who works in its Latin America programme. He is currently involved in a TNI research project on Northern NGOs and democratisation in Central America. He is the co-editor (with Martin Jelsma) of *Peasants beyond Protest: Challenges for ASOCODE and Strategies towards Europe* (TNI 1994, Amsterdam).

Stephen Biggs is a Senior Lecturer at the School of Development Studies, University of East Anglia (UK). He has worked for the Ford Foundation in Bangladesh and for the International Wheat and Maize Improvement Centre (CIMMYT), based in Delhi. He has been a member of advisory committees in Oxfam, the Intermediate Technology Development Group (ITDG), the Overseas Development Institute (ODI) and the Overseas Development Administration (ODA).

Robert Chambers is a Fellow of the Institute of Development Studies at the University of Sussex (UK). He has worked on rural development in sub-Saharan Africa and south Asia and is currently concentrating on the development and spread of the approaches and methods of participatory rural appraisal (PRA). He is the author of *Rural Development: Putting the Last First* (Longman, 1983, Harlow), and *Challenging the Professions: Frontiers for Rural Development* (IT Publishers, 1993).

Jane Covey is Executive Director of the Institute for Development Research (IDR) in Boston (USA), an international research and education centre that works in partnership with NGOs to support just and sustainable development. Her consulting and research activities include NGO strategic planning, and NGO influence on national and international policy-making. She serves on the NGO-World Bank Committee and on the Executive Committee of InterAction, a consortium of US private voluntary organisations.

Vandana Desai is a Fellow at the Institute of Development Studies, University of Sussex (UK), where she is currently involved in research into community participation, urban problems, slum housing and evaluating the effectiveness of urban NGOs. She completed her doctorate in sociology at the University of Oxford and has extensive experience of working with NGOs in the slums and squatter settlements of Bombay. She is the author of *Community Participation and Slum Housing* (Sage Publications, 1995, Delhi).

Michael Edwards has spent the last 14 years working for development NGOs. From 1984 to 1988 he was OXFAM-UK's Regional Representative in Lusaka, and then spent two years as Director of the PRASAD Foundation in India. Since 1990 he has been Head of Information and Research for Save the Children Fund-UK, based in London, and is currently undertaking research on the future of external intervention in development, funded by Fellowships from the Leverhulme Trust and Simon Fund. He co-edited (with David Hulme) *Making a Difference: NGOs and Development in a Changing World* (Earthscan/SCF, 1992, London), and *Too Close for Comfort: NGOs, States and Donors* (Macmillan, 1996, London).

Alan Fowler is a consultant, analyst and writer specialising in non-governmental development organisations, with which he has worked for the past 17 years, mostly in sub-Saharan Africa. Co-founder, in 1991, of the International NGO Training and Research Centre (INTRAC) based in Oxford (UK), he has also been a Visiting Fellow at the World Bank in Washington DC, advising on people's participation. His present work focuses on NGO effectiveness and organisational change.

Zie Gariyo is a Research Fellow at the Centre for Basic Research in Kampala, Uganda. Since 1989 he has researched and written on appropriate technology in peasant agriculture, press freedom in Uganda, and NGOs and development in East Africa.

Murdoch Gatward is currently Director of Traidcraft Exchange's Africa programme (based in Newcastle, UK), with particular responsibility for developing activities in South Africa and Tanzania. The subject of his chapter in this book, social auditing, is rapidly becoming a key tool to enable Traidcraft Exchange to assess the social and ethical profile of its own work, as well as that of actual and potential partners in the South.

Syed M Hashemi teaches in the Department of Economics in Jahangirnagar University, Bangladesh. He received his Doctorate in Economics from the University of California (Riverside). Currently he is on leave from his university post as Director of the Grameen Trust's 'Programme for Research on Poverty Alleviation'. For the past several years he has been involved in research on targeted credit programmes and the transformation of the lives of poor women in rural Bangladesh.

Mick Howes is a social anthropologist and a Fellow of the Institute of Development Studies, Sussex (UK), where he has been concerned mainly with rural development issues. He has a particular interest in the participatory planning, monitoring and evaluation of NGO activities, and is currently engaged in research on the role of NGOs in strengthening membership organisations.

David Hulme is Professor of Development Studies, Reader and Director of the Institute for Development Policy and Management, University of Manchester. He has worked and researched in Papua New Guinea, Sri Lanka, Bangladesh, Malaysia, Malawi and Kenya, and has a particular interest in rural development, anti-poverty policies, microfinance and civil service reform. His publications include *Making a Difference: NGOs and Development in a Changing World* (Earthscan (with M Edwards)), *Too Close for Com-*

fort? Donors, NGOs and States (Macmillan (with M Edwards)), *Finance Against Poverty* (vols 1 & 2) (Routledge (with P Mosley)) and *Administration, Policy and Development* (Macmillan (with M M Turner)).

Mahbubul Karim has been working with the Bangladeshi NGO Proshika since its foundation in 1976. Currently, he is the Director (Programmes) of the organisation and Head of its Institute for Development Policy Analysis and Advocacy (IDPAA). Before joining Proshika, he worked with the Bangladesh Rural Advancement Committee (BRAC) for three years as a development journalist. Between 1992 and 1993, he served as Director of the Association of Development Agencies in Bangladesh (ADAB) on secondment from Proshika.

Arthur Neame is Senior Programme Officer (South-east Asia) at Christian Aid in London (UK), and a director of the Philippine Resource Centre, an NGO involved in development education in both the Philippines and the UK. He worked for NGOs in the Philippines for four years where he studied community organisation and was involved in socio-economic projects with trade unions, people's organisations and church-based communities.

Peter Oakley was a Senior Lecturer in the Agricultural Extension and Rural Development Department, University of Reading, from 1976 to 1991. Since 1991 he has been the Head of the Regional Office for Latin America and the Caribbean for Save the Children Fund-UK, based in Bogota (Colombia). He is the author of *Projects with People* (ILO, 1991, Geneva) and co-author (with David Marsden and Brian Pratt) of *Measuring the Process: Guidelines for Evaluating Social Development* (INTRAC, 1994, Oxford).

David Pratten works for SOS Sahel, an NGO based in London (UK). He co-ordinates the agency's research programme on rural-urban linkages and local institutional development in Sudan, Ethiopia and Mali. He is also conducting PhD research at the School of Oriental and African Studies, University of London.

Janaki Ramesh is the Manager of the Indian Co-operative Network for Women (formerly the co-operative arm of the Working Women's Forum). She holds a Masters degree in communication from the University of Madras.

Meera Kaul Shah has experience of working with governments and NGOs in the development of local, and specifically women's, institutions concerned with natural resource management. She is currently working as a trainer and consultant, and providing support for the development of participatory approaches among governments, NGOs and donors in India, Morocco and Zambia.

Parmesh Shah has worked with both government and NGOs in India promoting participatory processes, local institutions and development programmes related to the management of natural resources. He is currently based at the Institute of Development Studies in Sussex (UK), working on his doctoral thesis, and as a trainer and consultant in providing support for developing participatory processes and institutions in India, Zambia and Vietnam.

Ian Smillie, author of *Mastering the Machine: Poverty Aid and Technology* (IT Publications, London) is a founder of Inter Pares and a former Executive Director of CUSO (Canada). He is also the author of *The Alms Bazaar: Nonprofit Organisations and International Development* (IT Publications, London, 1995). He works as an Ottawa-based development consultant.

Rajesh Tandon is Executive Director of the Society for Participatory Research in Asia (PRIA), New Delhi, India; Chairperson of Voluntary Action Network India (VANI); President of the Asian/South-Pacific Bureau of Adult Education (ASPBAE); and a founder board member of CIVICUS (the World Alliance for Citizen Participation). He has written extensively on Participatory Research, Training, NGO Management, and the Role of Civil Society and Voluntary Development Organisations in development.

Norman Uphoff is Director of the Cornell International Institute for Food, Agriculture and Development, and Professor of Government at Cornell University, Ithaca, New York (USA). He has worked on problems of rural development for more than 25 years, with special concern for participatory approaches and local organisations, with most involvement in Ghana, Nepal, Sri Lanka and Indonesia. He is the co-author (with Milton Esman) of *Local Organisations: Intermediaries in Rural Development* (Cornell University Press) and author of *Learning from Gal Oya: Possibilities for Participatory Development and Post-Newtonian Social Science* (Cornell University Press, 1993).

Frits Wils is Associate Professor at the Institute of Social Studies in The Hague (Netherlands). Through teaching, advisory work and publications, he is involved in NGO work in Latin America, South and South-east Asia, with a focus on organisation, NGO-government relations, and economic development strategies. He helped to co-ordinate a series of studies by ISS on large NGOs in Asia and Latin America, and has worked extensively on NGO evaluations with the Dutch NGO NOVIB and the Netherlands Ministry of Development Co-operation.

Simon Zadek is the Research Co-ordinator of the New Economics Foundation in London (UK), and heads the Foundation's social audit work with community enterprises, non-governmental organisations, and in the corporate sector. Social auditing is one of a number of NEF programmes dedicated to promoting a more ethical and environmentally sane approach to economics and broader social processes. He is the author of *An Economics of Utopia: Democratising Scarcity* (Avebury Press, Aldershot, 1993).

Part I
Conceptual Frameworks

1
NGO Performance and Accountability: Introduction and Overview

Michael Edwards and David Hulme

By any standards, the 1980s and 1990s have seen an explosion in the numbers of non-governmental organisations (NGOs) and grassroots organisations (GROs) active in relief and development.[1] The number of development NGOs registered in the OECD countries of the industrialised 'North' has grown from 1,600 in 1980 to 2,970 in 1993 (Smillie and Helmich 1993), and over the same period the total spending of these NGOs has risen from US$2.8 billion to US$5.7 billion in current prices (OECD 1994). The 176 'international NGOs' of 1909 had blossomed into 28,900 by 1993 (Commission on Global Governance 1995)! Similar figures have been reported in most countries in the 'South' where political conditions have been favourable, with a particularly rapid increase over the last five years. For example, the number of NGOs registered with the government in Nepal rose from 220 in 1990 to 1,210 in 1993 (Rademacher and Tamang 1993, p 34); in Bolivia the figure increased from around 100 in 1980 to 530 twelve years later (Arellano-Lopez and Petras 1994, p 562); and in Tunisia there were 5,186 NGOs registered in 1991 compared with only 1,886 in 1988 (Marzouk, 1995).

Paralleling this increase in overall numbers has been the growth of some individual NGOs to cover the provision of health, education and credit services to millions of people in thousands of communities, especially in South Asia. For example, the Bangladesh Rural Advancement Committee (BRAC) now has more than 12,000 staff and has plans to work with over three million people (AKF/Novib 1993); in India, the Self-Employed Women's Association (SEWA) has over one million clients in its credit programmes; while Sarvodaya in Sri Lanka works in 7,000 villages (Perera 1995). The access of NGOs to decision-makers in both North and South is greater than ever before, as their advocacy role continues to expand and they are courted in debates over policy and practice. GROs have a lower public profile, but they have also experienced considerable growth over the last decade and are beginning to organise themselves much more at the international level (Korten 1990; CIVICUS 1994). Clearly, something significant is happening in the world of international development. Lester Salamon (1993, p 1) goes so far as to say that 'a veritable associational revolution now seems underway at the global level that may constitute as significant a social and political development of the latter twentieth century as the rise of the nation state was of the nineteenth century'.

Whether or not Salamon's conclusion is justified by current trends, the rise of NGOs and GROs on the world scene is an important phenomenon which has implications for the development prospects of poor people, for the future of these organisations themselves, and for the wider political economy of which they form a small but growing part. But what lies behind these trends? This book takes the view that the rise of NGOs is not an accident; nor is it solely a response to local initiative and voluntary action. Equally important is the increasing popularity of NGOs with governments and official aid agencies,[2] which is itself a response to recent developments in economic and political thinking. Over the last 15 years, and particularly since the end of the Cold War, development policy and aid transfers have come to be dominated by what Robinson (1993) calls a 'New Policy Agenda'. This agenda is not monolithic – its details vary from one official aid agency to another, but in all cases it is driven by two basic sets of beliefs organised around the two poles of neo-liberal economics and liberal democratic theory (Moore 1993).

First, markets and private initiative are seen as the most efficient mechanisms for achieving economic growth and providing most services to most people (Colclough and Manor 1991). Governments 'enable' private provision but should minimise their direct role in the economy; because of their supposed cost-effectiveness in reaching the poorest, official agencies support NGOs in providing welfare services to those who cannot be reached through markets (Fowler 1988; Meyer 1992). Of course, NGOs have always provided welfare services to poor people in countries where governments lacked the resources to ensure universal coverage in health and education; the difference is that now they are seen as the *preferred channel* for service-provision in *deliberate substitution* for the state.

Second, under the New Policy Agenda, NGOs and GROs are seen as vehicles for 'democratisation' and essential components of a thriving 'civil society', which in turn are seen as essential to the success of the agenda's economic dimension (Moore 1993). NGOs and GROs are supposed to act as a counterweight to state power – protecting human rights, opening up channels of communication and participation, providing training grounds for activists and promoting pluralism. The rise of citizens' movements around the world documented by Korten (1990) and crystallised most recently in the establishment of CIVICUS (1994) (the 'World Alliance for Citizen Participation'), is not just (or perhaps even primarily) a result of developments in official aid, but it cannot be separated entirely from the political ideals of the New Policy Agenda.

As a result of these developments, governments have been prepared to channel increasing amounts of official aid to and through NGOs. Although accurate and comprehensive data are hard to come by, there is a good deal of evidence to suggest that the rise and growth of NGOs (and less so, of GROs) is directly related to the increasing availability of official funding under the New Policy Agenda. NGOs are seen as effective vehicles for the delivery of the agenda's economic and political objectives, although these roles are potentially incompatible, at least within the same organisation (a proposition which is explored later). The proportion of total aid from OECD countries channelled through NGOs increased from 0.7 per cent in 1975 to 3.6 per cent in 1985, and *at least* 5 per cent in 1993–1994 (some US$2.3 billion in absolute terms). This figure is certainly an underestimate since it omits multilateral agency funding to NGOs and NGO funding from the US Government, which represented over half the DAC total in all previous years (OECD 1988, 1994, 1995). Figures vary greatly between countries, donors and NGOs, but in general bilateral agencies are spending a steadily increasing proportion of their aid budgets through NGOs (including most recently directly through NGOs in the South), and most NGOs (especially the largest ones in both North and South) depend on these donors for an increasing slice of their total budgets, partly as a result of a flattening out in voluntary income over the last year or two.[3] NGOs which are *not* dependent on official aid for the majority of their budgets are now the exception rather than the rule. As Smillie (this volume) says, 'when CIDA (the Canadian International Development Agency) sneezes, Canadian NGOs reach for their Vitamin C!'.

Although both the economic and political dimensions of the New Policy Agenda are important to official agencies, aid to NGOs has gone primarily to finance welfare services. Some authors have criticised what they see to be a fundamental change in the *function* of NGOs as a result of official funding, with service-delivery and contracting replacing support to GROs and institutional development (Arellano-Lopez and Petras 1994). The increasing numbers of NGOs in many countries, a growth in the size of individual NGOs, an increasing concentration on service-provision, and rising reliance on official funding, do all seem to be related to each other, but this is not universally true (Wils, this volume).

The overall picture is one in which NGOs are seen as the 'favoured child' of official agencies and something of a panacea for the problems of development. As Vivian (1994) puts it, official agencies (and the supporters of Northern NGOs) often see NGOs as a 'magic bullet' which can be fired off in any direction and, though often without very much evidence, will still find its target. Clearly, the increasing availability of official funding for NGOs, the popularity they enjoy and the increasing access they are offered to centres of national and international decision-making, represent both an opportunity and a danger. NGOs can scale-up their operations using official funds and use the New Policy Agenda to make their voices heard more loudly and more often through lobbying and advocacy; at the same time, by becoming more dependent on governments, NGOs run the risk of being co-opted into the agendas of others and seeing their independent social base eroded. As far back as 1988, Jan Pronk (in Hellinger et al 1988) warned that 'the corruption of NGOs will be the political game in the years ahead'. Pronk saw 'corruption' not simply in terms of financial scandal, but more broadly as the deviation of NGOs from their mission for social transformation. The only way in which NGOs can avoid 'corruption' in this sense is to develop systems for performance-monitoring, accountability and strategic planning which 'ensure that a line remains drawn between transparent compromise and blind co-option' (Eade 1993, p 161). That is why the central themes of this book – performance and accountability – are so important.

Strong accountability systems can help NGOs to take advantage of the opportunities offered by the New Policy Agenda while ensuring that any warning signals are identified, listened to and addressed. Of course, performance and accountability would be crucial subjects for debate whether or not NGOs were growing closer to governments. Performing effectively and accounting transparently are essential components of responsible practice, on which the legitimacy of development intervention ultimately depends. Moving 'beyond the magic bullet' means taking accountability much more seriously than has hitherto been the case among most NGOs, Northern or Southern. But the New Policy Agenda does complicate the issue of accountability considerably; as the chapters in this book demonstrate, there are real dangers that dependence on official aid and the models of planning and intervention which underlie it will make an already unsatisfactory situation significantly worse.

NGO performance

For reasons which are explained later in this chapter, assessing NGO performance is a difficult and messy business. In any case, the absence of a large body of reliable evidence on the impact and effectiveness of NGOs and GROs makes it very difficult to generalise about this subject, despite claims that NGOs are 'cost-effective' or that GROs 'are close to the poor' (Fowler 1988). Most studies of NGO and GRO impact are based on small samples and are often restricted to agencies working in a particular sector (often economic development) or context (usually favourable), which makes measurement easier. Internal evaluations are rarely released, and what *is* released comes closer to propaganda than rigorous assessment. Nevertheless, there is increasing evidence that NGOs and GROs do not perform as effectively as had been assumed in terms of poverty-reach, cost-effectiveness, sustainability, popular participation (including gender), flexibility and innovation.[4] In terms of service-provision, there is certainly evidence that NGOs are able to provide some services more cost-effectively than governments – for example, the Orangi Pilot Project in Pakistan has developed sanitation systems at less than one-third of the equivalent cost in the commercial or government sectors (Hasan 1993); similar cost advantages have been claimed for BRAC in primary education and credit provision (AKF/Novib 1993). However, evidence from other studies contradicts this conclusion (Tendler 1989) and there is no empirical study which demonstrates a general case that NGO provision is cheaper than public provision. Even where NGO service-provision is 'low cost', it usually fails to reach the poorest people, although it may still reach a wider cross-section of the population than government or commercial agencies (Hashemi and Schuler 1992; Farrington and Bebbington 1993; Hulme and Mosley 1995). The sustainability of large-scale service-provision by NGOs has also been called into question by those who cite the large subsidies granted to NGOs (and denied to governments) which make the gap between private and public provision a 'self-perpetuating reality' (Farrington and Lewis 1993, p 333). There are also worries about a 'patchwork quilt' of social services developing in which only certain regions are supplied by well-resourced NGOs, leaving others to fend for themselves under weak central oversight (Robinson 1993; Edwards and Hulme 1994). In all cases, very careful management is needed to avoid a fall-off in quality when NGOs scale-up service-provision to cover large populations, although as Howes and Sattar (1992) and Wils (this volume) show, there is no necessary trade-off.

Evidence on the performance of NGOs and GROs in democratisation is more difficult to come by, except in the area of 'micro-policy reform' where a growing number of case studies demonstrate that NGOs and GROs can influence governments and official agencies, especially where they come together to form a united front (Edwards and Hulme 1992). On occasion (as in Bangladesh with the fall of President Ershad or the Philippines in the case of President Marcos), such united action can exert an influence on the position of governments as a whole. However, there is little evidence that NGOs and even GROs are managing to engage in the formal political process successfully, without becoming embroiled in partisan politics and the distortions that accompany the struggle for state power. In both Latin America and Africa, evidence shows that NGOs have had little impact on political reform, partly because states are adept at containing such a possibility, and partly because NGOs themselves (as non-representative organisations) have failed to develop effective strategies to promote democratisation (Lehmann 1990; Fowler 1991; Bratton 1990). The failure of many NGOs, and even GROs, to democratise their own structures makes them less effective in this process and, as the chapters in this book show, poses a particular problem for 'downward' accountability to members and beneficiaries (Carroll 1992; Bebbington and Thiele 1993). Nevertheless, NGOs and GROs can be proud of their achievements in helping to cement human and political rights in many societies, and in democratising the informal political process by training grassroots activists, building stronger local institutions, promoting micro-policy reform, and undertaking education for citizenship (Friedmann 1992; Ghai and Vivian 1992).

A particular area of concern here is the contradiction which may exist between effective performance in the two dimensions of the New Policy Agenda – economic and political – an issue to which little attention has been paid thus far. Large-scale service-provision requires standardised delivery mechanisms (to reduce unit costs), structures which can handle large amounts of external funding, and systems for speedy, and often hierarchical, decision-making; effective performance as an agent of democratisation rests on organisational independence, closeness to the poor, representative structures, and a willingness to spend large amounts of time in awareness-raising and dialogue (Edwards and Hulme 1994). It is difficult to combine these characteristics within the same organisation, and there is little evidence that alliances of different organisations (which could enable the two to go together) have developed very far. The fear is that, because service-delivery tends to attract more official funding, there will be a growing rift between well-resourced service-providers and poorly funded social mobilisation agencies, a danger already identified by Pearce (1993) in Chile and Central America.

The tendency of Northern NGOs to base their strategic plans on the easy availability of funding for humanitarian emergencies poses similar problems for their longer-term work in institutional development and development education. Some critics (including Hashemi in this volume) cite the switch from 'conscientisation' to 'service-delivery' by NGOs such as BRAC in Bangladesh as evidence that they have retreated from any serious role in addressing structural constraints to poverty and injustice. However, recent attacks on BRAC and other large NGOs by religious fundamentalists citing their 'success' in 'empowering women' suggest that such pessimism is misplaced, or at least that the real situation is more complex than is suggested by the supposed dichotomy between service delivery and conscientisation, an issue which is explored further in this book's Conclusion.

As NGOs become more involved in large-scale service-delivery (or grow for other reasons), and/or become more reliant on official funding, one might expect some fall-off in their flexibility, speed of response and ability to innovate. Although organisational growth can be managed successfully, bureaucratisation poses problems for any agency, as do the complex appraisal and reporting requirements which accompany official aid (Edwards and Hulme 1992, 1994). When official agencies finance service-delivery they expect contracted outputs to be achieved and are less interested in a 'learning process' (Voorhies 1993; Perera 1995). Time and space for reflection may be reduced and the ability of NGOs to articulate approaches, ideas, language and values which run counter to official orthodoxies may also be compromised. These issues are discussed later in this chapter. A further concern is that the willingness of NGOs to speak out on issues which are unpopular with governments will be diluted by their growing dependence on official aid. There is evidence from Africa that NGOs which depend on external funding (though not just on official funding) are more likely to be ignored as 'illegitimate' by their own governments in policy debates (Bratton 1989); in the USA, the largest operational NGOs (which are all heavily dependent on USAID) tend to avoid a campaigning role, no doubt fearful of the consequences that would follow if they spoke out too sharply against government policy (Smith 1990; Salamon and Anheier 1993; Smith and Lipsky 1993); and a context in which NGOs compete with each other for government grants seems unlikely to foster the collaborative relationships on which effective policy alliances are built (Fowler 1992; Edwards 1993; Covey, this volume).

Finally, NGOs which depend on official funding often perform poorly in the crucial task of 'local institutional development' (Esman and Uphoff 1984), the gradual strengthening of capacities and capabilities among grassroots organisations to enable them to play a more effective and independent role in development. This is because many official agencies are unwilling to support the long-time horizons, slow careful nurturing and gradual qualitative results which characterise successful institutional development (Carroll 1992; Fowler 1992). Such work is difficult to 'sell' to the politicians and their constituents on which aid bureaucracies depend for their budgets (LaFond 1995).

The point of presenting this evidence is not to claim that NGOs perform *less effectively* than other organisations (public or private) in these various tasks; simply that they often perform *less well* than their popular image suggests. A comparative analysis of performance between NGOs, governments and commercial operators is beyond the scope of this book, although there is reason to believe that any differences which do emerge have less to do with inherent traits and more to do with factors which cut across the public-private divide (Tendler 1983). In any case, comparisons with other types of organisation which perform less well (something at which NGOs excel!) do not provide grounds for arguing that current NGO performance is satisfactory: NGOs should always be striving to serve others better.

NGO accountability

Accountability is generally interpreted as the means by which individuals and organisations report to a recognised authority, or authorities, and are held responsible for their actions (Edwards and Hulme 1994). Accountability is a complex and abstract concept, however, and relatively little research has been conducted on this topic with regard to NGOs and GROs (Brett 1993). Although accountability is viewed as a desirable organisational characteristic, empirical studies commonly indicate that both leaders and subordinates in public and private organisations[5] seek to avoid accountability (Fox 1992). The common perception that, somewhere else, there are organisations that are perfectly accountable must be dismissed. However, there is clearly a level at which the absence of accountability begins to make the likelihood of ineffective or illegitimate actions by an organisation much more probable.

Effective accountability requires a statement of goals (whether in adherence to certain rules or achievement of identified performance levels), transparency of decision-making and relationships, honest reporting of what resources have been used and what has been achieved, an appraisal process for the overseeing authority(ies) to judge whether results are satisfactory and concrete mechanisms for holding to account (ie, rewarding or penalising) those responsible for performance. GRO and NGO accountability may be formal (for example, an evaluation of whether agreed objectives in a programme have been met) or informal (for example, ongoing discussions between partners). It may emphasise the honesty and efficiency with which resources are used (commonly referred to as 'probity'), or the impact and effectiveness of the work (commonly called 'performance'). Avina (1993) usefully distinguishes between short-term *functional accountability* (accounting for resources, resource use and immediate impacts) and *strategic accountability* (accounting for the impacts that an NGO's actions have on the actions of other organisations and the wider environment).

Crucially, GROs and NGOs have *multiple* accountabilities – 'downwards' to their partners, beneficiaries, staff and supporters; and 'upwards' to their trustees, donors and host governments. Multiple accountability presents any organisation with problems, particularly the possibilities of having to 'over-account' (because of multiple demands), or being able to 'under-account', as each overseeing authority assumes that another authority is taking a close look at actions and results. Legally, most NGOs, as non-membership organisations, are accountable to their trustees, who often exercise only a very light hand in governance (Tandon, this volume). NGOs cannot be formally accountable to their beneficiaries, however much they may want to be (Uphoff, this volume). By contrast, GROs are accountable to their members. Both usually have an obligation to account to the governments of the countries in which they operate, although in practice this often means only brief annual reports and occasional audits. Morally (in accordance with values of participation and empowerment), and in terms of their wider claims to legitimacy, NGOs are accountable to other constituencies, most obviously beneficiaries and contributors. But of course equal accountability to all at all times is an impossibility. Many of the concerns expressed about the weak accountability of NGOs relate to the difficulties they face in prioritising and reconciling these multiple accountabilities (see Table 1.1).

Although the accountability of GROs (to their members) may seem more straightforward, there is surprisingly little evidence that they perform better than NGOs in this respect. Indeed, Carroll (1992, p 89) finds the opposite to be true in Latin America. These conclusions are confirmed by Bebbington and Thiele (1993, p 21), who state that 'we cannot say *a priori* that any one type of organisation is inherently more or less responsive to, or representative of, the needs of the rural poor'. In GROs, problems of accountability often arise due to social and political factors (such as interest-group manipulation), whereas among NGOs, economic factors, and particularly links to donors, are likely to be more influential (Pearce 1993). Indeed, it is NGOs, especially those based in the North, that come in for the most damning criticisms. Lehmann (1990, p 201)

Table 1.1   *The accountability matrix (for a hypothetical Southern NGO)*

Forms of accountability and quality of accountability at different stages in the accountability process

	Functional Accountability[1]			Strategic Accountability[2]		
	Capacity to demand reports and information	*Capacity to appraise reports and information*	*Capacity to operate sanctions*	*Capacity to demand reports and information*	*Capacity to appraise reports and information*	*Capacity to operate sanctions*
Beneficiaries/ members	Low[3]	Low	Low	Low	Nil	Nil
Trustees	Medium	Low	Medium	Low	Low	Low
Private contributors	Medium	Low	Low	Medium	Low	Low
NGO network	Low	Low	Low	Low	Low	Nil
National government	Medium	Low	High	Low	Low	Low
Official donors	High	Medium	High	Low	Low	Nil
NNGOs	High	Medium	Medium	Medium	Low	Low

[1] Functional accountability = accounting for resources, resource use and immediate impacts.

[2] Strategic accountability = accounting for impacts on other organisations and the wider environment on a medium- to long-term basis.

[3] Alternatively, the matrix could include short statements on the capacity of different authorities at different stages, rather than nil/low/medium/high.

calls their lack of accountability 'extraordinary', while Smillie (this volume) finds that 'Northern NGO survival has been almost completely delinked from performance', since they appear under little obligation to tell the truth to their supporters (Edwards 1994). While NGOs may contest these assertions, we can find no evidence that the contemporary accountability of NGOs is satisfactory.

Measuring impact and effectiveness in an uncertain world: 'interpretative' accountability   A great part of the dilemma faced by GROs and NGOs lies in the nature of the work they do and the messy and complex world in which they do it – measuring performance in relation to the kind of development subscribed to by most NGOs is an extraordinarily difficult task, particularly in relation to 'empowerment' and other qualitative changes. As Drucker (1990) points out, the ultimate objective of 'non-profit' agencies is 'changed human beings'. There are few agreed performance standards available to NGOs in this realm, beyond probity and some quantifiable impact indicators in certain types of NGO activity such as service-provision and economic development. Neither is there any obvious 'bottom line' against which progress can be measured. Unlike businesses (which must make a profit), and governments (which must face elections), the 'bottom line for NGOs shifts according to the situation at hand (Fowler, this volume). Organisational, as opposed to project, indicators are even more difficult to find, especially given the seeming obsession of many NGO managers with size and growth as indicators of 'success'. Indicators of the *quality* of organisational performance are very rare (with the exception of the 'social audit' described by Zadek and Gatward in this volume), and the general lack of satisfactory evaluative mechanisms is a serious drawback when it comes to GRO/NGO accountability. Because so few fixed, absolute standards exist, NGO evaluation (even more than evaluation in other organisations) is inevitably a matter of judgement and interpretation. This is the line of argument developed by Guba and Lincoln (1989) in their work on 'Fourth Generation Evaluation', and applied specifically to social development by Marsden et al (1994). The same line of reasoning is employed by Uphoff, Biggs and Neame, Fowler and others in this volume to emphasise the non-linear and 'open systems' nature of NGO work and the need to adapt concepts of performance-measurement and accountability accordingly.

In addition, NGOs and GROs are rarely able to control all (or even most) of the factors which influence the outcome of their work – macroeconomic performance, state policy and the actions of other agencies are obvious examples. Handy (1993, p 15) lists at least 60 variables which influence the effectiveness of any organisation, while Uphoff (in this volume) points to the 'second- and third-order effects' of NGO actions which are essential for sustainable development but are ignored in most evaluations. When positive long-term results are achieved, this is not because of one organisation or project acting in isolation, but because a whole series of forces and actors come together to produce, for example, a sustainable change in agricultural production or the development of a strong grassroots federation. This makes measuring 'strategic' accountability in its most fundamental sense almost impossible – no organisation can be held accountable for the impact of forces which are beyond its control, although, of course, NGOs can and should be able to account for the way in which they use their resources within the framework set by these forces. As Rondinelli (1993) puts it in the context of CIDA, the question becomes whether agencies use their resources 'effectively, efficiently and prudently to achieve reasonable progress toward worthwhile development objectives', including how well they learn from experience and judge the costs and benefits of putting resources to different purposes. This still leaves a great deal of room for interpretation, which is why, as laid out in the next section, accountability must be a process of negotiation among stakeholders rather than the imposition of one definition or interpretation of 'effectiveness' over another.

For some NGOs and GROs, however, there is also a political dilemma to accountability. If the organisation's overt or covert goal is 'empowerment' – ie, making those who have little power at present more powerful – then transparency on this issue will, at best, make it easier for vested interests to identify what is happening and thus more effectively oppose it or, at worst, lead to the deregistration and closure of the organisation for being subversive (and perhaps violence to staff).

Negotiating performance and impact among stakeholders: multiple accountability   Since there are few absolute performance measures in NGO evaluation and no single bottom line, negotiation among stakeholders is the essence of accountability in this area. All NGOs and most GROs have, as mentioned above, multiple accountabilities. Therefore, definitions of objectives, interpretations of results and decisions on what response may be appropriate, all have to be negotiated among a wide range of actors. For example, are higher NGO overheads an indicator of effective performance (since they are essential for improved research, learning, monitoring and dissemination), or a sign of inefficiency? Presumably the answer to this question varies according to circumstance and opinion. As the contributions to this book show, NGOs and GROs in the South are often more interested in the wider questions of where NGOs fit in relation to society and politics, rather than the narrower question of how inputs and outputs are related at the project level, which is of prime concern to donors. Biekart's analysis of NGO accountability in Central America and Bejar and Oakley's description of current evaluation trends in Latin America (in this volume) both show how understandings of performance vary greatly over time and between different partners. The questions posed by Karim in his chapter are very relevant here: *who* defines accountability, *for whom* and *why*?

The impact of the New Policy Agenda and official aid: distorting accountability   An already complex situation is made even more difficult by official aid to NGOs and the demands imposed by the New Policy Agenda. Given the financial and political muscle of official agencies, there is an obvious fear that donor funding may reorient accountability upwards, away from the grassroots, and bias performance-measurement toward criteria defined by donors (Edwards and Hulme 1994; Fisher 1994; Tandon 1994). Many of the chapters in this book provide evidence of this problem, although it is difficult to disentangle the influence of official funding from pre-existing weaknesses in 'downward' accountability (see Desai and Howes, Shah and Shah, Gariyo, and Hashemi, all in this volume). Fox and Hernandez (1989) and Fisher (1994) provide some evidence that GRO leaders can be further distanced from their members by foreign influence and assistance, although this can be mitigated by the deliberate encouragement of new generations of leaders from within the organisation. Given that GROs are membership organisations, the reorientation of accountability away from the grassroots is a particular threat to them as *de facto* it turns members into customers.

The type of appraisal, monitoring and evaluation procedures insisted on by donors, especially their heavy reliance on 'logical framework' approaches and bureaucratic reporting, may also distort accountability by overemphasising short-term quantitative targets, standardising indicators, focusing attention exclusively on individual projects or organisations, and favouring hierarchical management structures – a tendency to 'accountancy' rather than 'accountability'; audit rather than learning. This is perhaps an inevitable result of the pressure for short-term visible results in order to keep Parliament or Congress happy. Accountability may focus too much on control functions – 'Is the money being spent properly?' – rather than on learning and sharing, something criticised by Smillie (this volume) in relation to NGO evaluation procedures adopted by CIDA in Canada. Compressed project planning cycles often leave very little time to learn the lessons of experience, let alone *use them*. In this process there is a particular danger that women will be penalised as qualitative changes in gender relations are inadequately monitored and women are excluded from senior positions in large, growing, hierarchical institutions.[6] The competitive nature of contracting also fosters an orientation towards treating information as a public relations activity (ie, releasing the good and hiding the bad) and this compromises transparency. The contemporary management of their external image by international NGOs and large NGOs in South Asia provides evidence of this. As Chambers (this volume) states, the 'self-deceiving NGO' is already a reality. There is, however, some evidence that donor funding may strengthen some forms of accountability by increasing external pressures for accurate reporting and more sophisticated monitoring (Tendler 1989; Bebbington and Riddell 1996).

Secondly, the sheer volume of donor funds made available to GROs and NGOs may result in problems of probity, especially where internal management and financial systems are originally based on informality and trust. The example of Sarvodaya in Sri Lanka provides a good illustration of this (Perera 1995). The organisation's accounting and reporting systems were adequate for a small and later medium-sized organisation, with an energetic leader and a highly personalised management style. However, rapid growth led to the breakdown of these systems and confusion on the part of the organisation and donors as to whether functional accounting was simply weak or whether it was hiding improprieties.

Thirdly, closer links with donors (and the suspicion of foreign influence this creates in government) may result in a move away from self-regulation to regulation from above by the state. Self-regulation is not sufficient to ensure accountability, but the informal consultative processes and codes of ethics that characterise the voluntary sector in many countries (North and South) have maintained a balance between 'room for manoeuvre' and regulation (Carroll 1992; Constantino–David 1992; ICVA 1991; InterAction 1993). Formal accountability procedures may discourage innovation and speed of response, and promote politicisation and patronage (Brown and Tandon 1992; Farrington and Bebbington 1993; Rademacher and Tamang 1993). Government co-ordinating mechanisms may also provide avenues for the state to gain access to NGO funding and information on organisations they consider 'subversive'. Possible avenues for government influence over NGOs include legislation, taxation, public consultation, co-ordination and official support, with the balance between monitoring, co-optation and outright repression varying according to political context (Bratton 1989; Clark 1995; Farrington and Lewis 1993). Not surprisingly, 'government–NGO relations are likely to be most constructive where a confident and capable government with populist policies meets an NGO that works to pursue mainstream development programmes ... and most conflictual where a weak and defensive government with a limited power base meets an NGO that seeks to promote community mobilization' (Bratton 1989, p 585). Most examples lie somewhere in between these two extremes, and the overall conclusion to be drawn by Brown and Tandon (1992) is that government–NGO co-ordinating mechanisms would perform best if changed from a hierarchical link to a 'bridge' between the two which can balance necessary accountability with essential independence.

The message that must come out of this section is that little is known about the changing nature of GRO and NGO accountability. This is a serious matter, given that GRO/NGO claims to legitimacy are premised at least in part on the strength of their accountability, particularly to the 'poor'. Indeed, the New Policy Agenda thrusts the question of legitimacy into centre stage, for if NGOs are becoming more responsive to external concerns, what is happening to the links – to their values and mission, and to their supporters and others – through which they claim their right to intervene in development? NGOs do not have to be member-controlled to be legitimate, but they do have to be accountable for what they do if their claims to legitimacy are to be sustained. Recent doubts expressed by Southern NGOs about the advocacy role of NGOs in the North (speaking 'on behalf of the poor') provide one illustration of this difficult issue (Edwards 1993). Although poorly understood and often ignored, questions of legitimacy and identity are crucial to the future of NGOs, and we return to these questions in our Conclusions at the end of the book.

The structure of this book

Part I of this volume (including this introductory chapter) provides the conceptual background for the case studies that follow. In Chapter 2, Norman Uphoff clarifies the distinctions which exist in terms of accountability between public, private and 'third-sector' institutions, and goes on to question the value of formal evaluation, unless this is seen and used in 'open systems' terms. Similar themes are addressed by Stephen Biggs and Arthur Neame, who focus on the consequences of 'linear thinking' for NGO accountability and emphasise the need to move away from evaluating the performance of individual NGOs and NGO projects. Part I is completed by Rajesh Tandon's survey of 'Board Games' – the neglected territory of NGO governance and its relationship to accountability.

Part II contains a series of case studies from different regions which describe and analyse what happens to NGO and GRO performance and accountability under different conditions. There are two case studies from Africa, four from South Asia, and three from Central and Latin America.

The third part of the book contains seven chapters, all of which represent ways forward in the debate over performance and accountability. Alan Fowler's chapter is both a critique of current approaches to performance-assessment and a description of one possible solution to the dilemmas they present – engaging stakeholders in 'combined social judgement'. On the basis of experience in Canada, Ian Smillie dissects current attempts by official agencies to strengthen NGO evaluation, and makes a strong case that NGOs need to 'put their house in order' by investing in their own research and learning. Next comes a detailed analysis by Jane Covey of these issues in the context of international policy alliances, which demonstrates that effectiveness and accountability can be combined successfully when certain conditions are met. Parmesh and Meera Shah, and Simon Zadek and Murdoch Gatward concentrate on innovative techniques to strengthen multiple accountability (participatory monitoring and evaluation, and the 'social audit' respectively). Both chapters show that concrete progress is possible in NGO accountability given vision, imagination and openness to change. This leads into Robert Chambers' account of the personal dimension to accountability and the absolute necessity for conscious action by individuals if NGOs and GROs are to improve their record in this respect. By way of conclusion, the final chapter of the book reviews the experience of all the other contributions and relates the lessons learned about performance and accountability to the future of NGOs on the world stage.

Notes

1. Throughout this book a distinction is made between non-governmental organisations (NGOs), which are intermediary organisations engaged in funding or offering other forms of support to communities and other organisations; and grassroots organisations (GROs), which are membership organisations of various kinds. Other authors make the same distinction, but use different terms. For example, Carroll (1992) distinguishes between 'grassroots support organisations' (which are NGOs), and 'membership support organisations'; GROs are also sometimes called 'community-based organisations' (CBOs). The most important difference between the two groups lies in their accountability structures: GROs are formally accountable to their members, while NGOs are not. However, many other authors use the term 'NGOs' to cover all forms of non-profit organisation.

2. Official aid agencies are those which are funded by Northern governments either directly (bilateral agencies such as the British Overseas Development Administra-

tion, or Swedish SIDA) or indirectly (multilateral agencies such as the World Bank and the European Union).

3. The figures here vary considerably, as do methods of calculating aid transfers to and through NGOs, and NGO dependency on official agencies. For example, the proportion of SIDA funds channelled through NGOs increased from 9 per cent in 1990–1991 to 30 per cent in 1994: SIDA funds over 2,000 NGO projects, while the British ODA is already funding over 450 Indian NGOs directly, and a similar number in Bangladesh. All five of the largest NGOs in the UK show a significantly increasing level of financial dependence on ODA, while in other countries (such as Canada, the USA, Germany, the Netherlands and Norway) dependency ratios of between 50 per cent and 90 per cent are common. In the South, the large South Asian NGOs such as BRAC receive most of their funding from external sources, although it is difficult to specify whether more of this is coming from official agencies rather than from traditional Northern NGO sources. The availability of official aid under 'social compensation funds' in adjusting economies has, however, been an important source of support for NGOs in countries such as Bolivia and Uganda (Arellano-Lopez and Petras 1994). For details of these trends see Smillie and Helmich (1993), Good (1994), Bebbington and Riddell (1995), Edwards and Hulme (1994) and German and Randel (1994).

4. Early work on this subject was carried out by Judith Tendler (1982, 1983); more recent studies include Fowler (1991, 1993); Lehmann (1990); Carroll (1992); Riddell and Robinson (1992); Farrington and Lewis (1993); Bebbington and Thiele (1993); Wellard and Copestake (1993); Vivian (1994); and Hashemi and Schuler (1992).

5. See *The Economist*, 29 January 1994, 'A Survey of Corporate Governance' for a discussion of the weakness of accountability in private sector corporations.

6. Some participants at the workshop from which this book emerged criticised us for not paying explicit attention to gender issues in the discussion of NGO performance and accountability. This remains an important area for further research, as we can locate no specific analysis of the many ways in which the definition of performance and accountability may be male-biased.

2

Why NGOs are not a Third Sector: a Sectoral Analysis with Some Thoughts on Accountability, Sustainability and Evaluation

Norman Uphoff

Will the 'new world order' which is said to offer development NGOs 'access to ever greater resources and influence' (Edwards and Hulme 1994) last much longer, and be any more beneficial, than the one announced after the fall of the Berlin Wall? The 'new world order' that American President George Bush proclaimed was mostly a creation of optimism and rhetoric. The one which suggests a new role of NGOs could prove to be constructed of the same materials and not much longer lasting. New relationships between public and private sectors around the world are resulting from a range of political, economic and social transitions and forces (Uphoff 1993, 1994). Governmental bodies are experiencing both a decline in fiscal support and in public credibility. Market institutions are gaining greater latitude and confidence with both ideological support and resource advantages. In this situation, NGOs are being described as a 'third sector'.

But this characterisation, I will argue, is misleading. The real third sector, located somewhere *between* the public and the private sectors in institutional space, belongs not to NGOs but rather to people's associations and membership organisations. These differ from institutions in the public and private sectors in that they undertake voluntary collective action and self-help. Such a distinction assigns NGOs to the private sector rather than to the middle sector. Which sector NGOs are considered to belong to is important with regard to the focus in this book on accountability, an increasingly prominent concern in development circles.

My sectoral analysis grows out of an insightful discussion by Guy Hunter (1969) of administration, economics and politics as means for promoting rural development. His classification was elaborated analytically in Esman and Uphoff (1984) by contrasting three alternative approaches to rural development, as shown in Table 2.1.

These three models represent modes of decision-making and activity that are alternative but complementary. They are based on different role relations, contrasting objectives and divergent motivations. These three arenas for decision-making and action correspond to the public sector (1), the private sector (2), and a very different sector (3). This third sector, which can be referred to as

Table 2.1   *Alternative approaches to rural development*

	1. Administrative approach	*2. Economic approach*	*3. Political approach*
Key process	Exercise of authority	Market interaction	Voluntary association
Institutions	Bureaucratic structures	Private enterprises	Membership organisations
Decision-makers	Legislators, executives administrators, experts	Producers, consumers and investors	Leaders and members or constituents
Guides for behaviour	Laws, regulations	Price signals, profit and loss	Agreements and consensus
Criteria for decisions	Policy and the best means to implement it	Efficiency, best ways to maximise profit and/or utility	Interests of members, precedents, purposes
Sanctions	State authority	Financial loss	Social pressure, group sanctions
Mode of operation	Top-down	Individualistic	Bottom-up

Source: Adapted from Hunter (1969)

the membership sector, the voluntary sector or the collective action sector, as a 'middle' sector is best seen as operating *between* the public and private sectors.

By definition, any organisations in the second and third sectors in Table 2.2 are non-governmental. But an examination of the roles that people find themselves in *vis-à-vis* these different kinds of institutions – and of the mechanisms for accountability they operate – suggests that 'NGOs' are best considered as a sub-sector of the private sector. This is implied by the synonym used for NGOs – private voluntary organisations.[1]

Table 2.2   *Complementary local institutions, by sector*

Public sector		*Membership sector*		*Private sector*	
Local administration	Local government	Membership organisations	Co-operatives	Service organisations	Private enterprises
Orientations of local institutions					
Bureaucratic Agents look upward	*Political* Agents look downward	*Self-help* Common interests	Pooled resources	*Charitable* Non-profit	*Business* For-profit
Roles of individuals in relation to the different kinds of local institutions					
Citizens or subjects	Constituents or voters	Members	Members	Clients or beneficiaries	Customers and employees*

Source: Adapted from Uphoff (1986, p 5)

* *Note:* All six kinds of institutions can have employees, but a hired workforce is most obviously essential for the performance of private businesses. Service organisations usually have some number of employees, as do offices of local administration and local government bodies. Membership organisations and co-operatives are likely to have fewer employees compared to other kinds of local institutions.

Ten years ago at Cornell, we undertook a large-scale study of local institutions and their contributions to development (Uphoff 1986). Based on an extensive review of the literature, we concluded that there are at least *two* important sub-categories of local institutions for *each* of the three sectors delineated above. The most significant differentiating factor was the way in which the different kinds of local institutions relate (ie, are accountable) to the people they are supposed to serve or benefit.

While any institutions not in the public sector can be called 'non-governmental organisations',[2] such a classification lumps together very diverse sets of institutions. It is true that business enterprises, for example, differ from typical NGOs in that the former operate 'for profit' while the latter do not. But their relationships with the persons whom they serve – clients and customers – exhibit essential similarities that set them apart from the categories of institutions shown in the middle of the continuum depicted in Table 2.2.

Membership organisations and co-operatives have much in common, because both are oriented towards self-help and are responsible to members, a role which is not central or often even salient for NGOs and business enterprises. Service organisations, the category in which I think most NGOs belong, deal with clients or beneficiaries. Such persons did not create the organisation they are dealing with and cannot hold it accountable for its actions in the same direct way that members can. Clients and beneficiaries of NGOs are in a 'take it or leave it' relationship that is similar to that of customers and employees of private firms. The relationship is different from that of persons who belong to and are served by a membership organisation or co-operative.

These differences can be made concrete by considering the provision of services by hospitals, which can be operated in any of the following modes:

- In a public-sector hospital, run by local administration (Ministry of Health) or a local government body (Town Council), patients enter as citizens and constituents with whatever rights and opportunities for redress this gives them, through the courts or through elected representatives.
- A hospital that is privately owned and operated, while it will be regulated by public laws, is basically in business to earn a profit from its provision of services. Its patients are essentially customers or consumers. Their option, if dissatisfied, is to go to another hospital, as they would go to a different store if they were unhappy with products or services.
- A charitable hospital operated on a not-for-profit basis is not much different from a private hospital, except that its managers give free care or are less insistent on being paid for services. That managers make decisions on behalf of trustees instead of owners is not a big difference operationally.
- A co-operative hospital, on the other hand, was set up at least in part with members' capital, and it exists to serve them. As members they help to set the rules and the fees, and if they have any complaints about service, they are much more 'empowered' to initiate corrective action than with a public, private or charitable hospital. Organisations that serve members are in a different situation regarding operation and accountability than are those

which fit the more conventional private or public-sector models serving patients as citizens or customers.

Most organisations referred to as NGOs thus belong, analytically, to the private sector, albeit to the service (ie, not-for-profit) sub-sector thereof. True, some NGOs have been created by and operate on behalf of members. But for the most part, NGOs serve persons who are *not* members of their organisation, and this makes them essentially service organisations, with mostly employees producing and distributing benefits. Only if most of an NGO's beneficiaries or clients are also its members is it appropriately considered as belonging to the third sector – ie, to the middle sector shown in Table 2.2.

It is helpful to make a distinction between NGOs and 'grassroots organisations' (GROs), although the two are actually overlapping sets. The first category is defined according to sector while the second is specified in terms of level (Uphoff 1993).[3] This means that some NGOs are GROs, and vice versa, while some, indeed most, NGOs are not GROs. Unfortunately, much contemporary rhetoric tends to equate the two categories (NGOs and GROs) without much analytical or evaluative thought. An appropriate way to view the relation between them is to see NGOs as in a position to help to promote and sustain GROs.[4] This raises important questions of accountability: whether NGOs are in some way, or even can be held, accountable to GROs and to the members whom they serve? Fashioning such links of responsibility could represent a real 'new world order'. But this is not easy, and indeed may not be feasible or desirable.

Some sceptical and affirmative thoughts on accountability

As a student of political science, I have been surprised that so little attention has been paid by people concerned with NGOs and accountability issues to the writing of Robert Michels, a Swiss social scientist who received much more attention earlier in this century than now. His admonition, 'who says organisation says oligarchy', thundered off the pages of his book, *Political Parties* (1915), which predicted that it was the fate of organisations generally to become dominated by a self-perpetuating and self-serving leadership. This has become known as 'the iron law of oligarchy'.

Service organisations in the private sector are entitled to function as oligarchies. This is their legal right and privilege, as long as they operate within the law. This is best seen in the way that foundations and trusts can use their resources with few restrictions, because the resources they dispose of are 'private'. Nobody expects foundations or trusts to be internally democratic or to let the recipients of their generosity make the decisions about amounts or conditions of benefits. NGOs as service organisations operate much like private businesses.[5] There are structural and philosophical reasons why one should not expect NGOs which are private-sector service organisations to function as agencies responsible to their clientele. In particular, the staff and trustees of such organisations have the burden of mobilising and managing funds which will keep their operation solvent. If beneficiaries could decide how much they would receive and when, such organisations would likely be bankrupt within a year. There is a fiduciary relationship between NGO staff and trustees and those who provide NGOs with their funds which is greater than their obligation to recipients of NGO benefits. If trust and confidence are not maintained with an NGO's contributors, it will collapse.

Thus, proponents of 'making NGOs accountable to their beneficiaries' face a structural constraint that cannot easily be done away with, however commendable this might be according to certain democratic or normative theories. There are good reasons to be sceptical that the more profound form of 'new world order' for NGOs and GROs suggested above can be realised. But there is a further qualification which flows from Michels' analysis. He was not the crypto-Fascist or arch-conservative he is often said to be by political commentators who have read only Michels' conclusion, not his evidence or reasoning. Michels was an active participant in the democratic socialist and labour movements of Europe at the turn of the century. His conclusion that organisations tend to oligarchy (his more qualified statement is more scientifically tenable than the stern equation quoted above) was based on his observations of the Socialist parties and trade unions operating in Europe over half a century.

Michels became disillusioned with these organisations' prospects of introducing greater democracy in their respective countries because they had such difficulty maintaining internal democracy. Leaders became autocratic. They controlled the party or trade union press. They dominated meetings. They engrossed their organisations' treasuries. Most alarmingly, they manoeuvred to be succeeded by their sons or favourite supporters. Such behaviour by leaders led Michels to despair about the prospects for genuine democracy. Yet interestingly enough, the one exception which he cited to his rule was the internal democracy displayed by aristocratic parties in Scandinavia. These held leaders in check with internal competition and frequent rotation. This paradox – that organisations which did not seek to promote democracy were themselves more democratic – led Michels to observe that such organisations had members with uniformly higher status, more education and greater economic resources. Sadly, organisations that had members with low status, little education and pervasive poverty were more vulnerable to the domination and predation of their leaders.

One implication of this analysis was that greater organisational democracy could be expected as social conditions (education, health, security, and so on) improved. Perhaps progressive parties and unions could contribute to such advancement even if they were not paragons of the democratic virtues they advocated. Interestingly enough, Michels' view is supported by one of the classic studies of the American trade union movement.[6]

This digression on social history is relevant to our current concern, which is how to increase the accountability as well as to improve the performance of development NGOs. We are interested in having NGOs assist and benefit the poorer sectors in poor countries, a difficult task in any case if these persons, households and communities are to become more secure and productive on a sustainable and self-managing basis. Michels' 'iron law of oligarchy', taken in its subtler form, predicts that one is least likely to find internal democracy in grassroots organisations where members are the least well educated, the poorest

and of the lowest social status. Anyone who becomes a leader under such circumstances is, first, likely to rank higher on these characteristics. But, second,
anyone who becomes a leader is likely to enjoy the benefits of greater status,
knowledge and income and to be reluctant to give these up. The longer that
someone remains in a leadership position, the greater will be the 'gap' between
leaders and members (now transformed into 'followers') in terms of economic,
social and informational resources.

There is evidence for and against Michels' propositions from the literature on
NGOs and GROs (Fox 1992; Fisher 1994), but unless we can refute or invali-
date his 'iron law', the grassroots organisations which advocates of greater
accountability want NGOs to be responsible to are themselves least likely to be
internally accountable to their own members. The more power that outside
agencies give to such organisations, the more benefits may be skimmed off for
persons in leadership positions or for those whom they favour.

This is not to justify NGOs operating paternalistically or autonomously *vis-à-
vis* GROs, invoking Michels to justify their oligarchical mode of operation.
Rather it is intended to sound a note of caution for those who seek accountability in an absolute manner, not considering whether or to what extent the
representatives and spokespersons of intended beneficiaries are themselves
accountable and indeed truly representative.

I myself have seen a grassroots organisation take root under what were
considered very adverse conditions and establish internal mechanisms of
accountability. From 1981 to 1985, with colleagues at the Agrarian Research
and Training Institute in Sri Lanka, Cornell faculty and students helped to
establish farmer organisations to improve irrigation management in a participatory way in what was considered the most run-down and debilitated irrigation system in that country (Uphoff 1992). Farmers in the Gal Oya scheme had
been resettled there 20 to 30 years earlier under often less than voluntary circumstances. They had a reputation for being very difficult and quarrelsome,
being also poorer and less well educated than most of their countrymen. While
organisation members were not the very poorest of the poor, they were small-
holders or tenants averaging less than two acres apiece, and many had half an
acre or less.[7]

Within a few weeks, farmers were taking impressive initiatives to improve
their system's performance, its equity as well as its efficiency. They instituted the
rotation of officers at the district level to ensure that there would be a broad
pool of experienced leadership for dealing with officials. They trained
'understudies' so that responsibilities of leadership could be shared. Farmers
gladly accepted our suggestion that they have farmer-representatives rather
than farmer-leaders, the terminology that the Food and Agriculture Organisation (FAO) and the government were using at the time our programme
started, because they appreciated that 'representatives' could be held accountable more readily than 'leaders'.

The structure of the organisation started from the bottom, which helped to
ensure accountability. Field channel groups managed and shared the water they
received from the distributary (or 'D') canal, doing channel maintenance and
water sharing on an as-needed basis. These groups, usually with between 12 and

15 members, operated informally, with each group choosing a representative by consensus.[8] Field channel representatives constituted a formally recognised distributary canal committee for the area that was served by each D-canal. Field channel representatives met periodically in an area assembly to have direct two-way communication with officials, and these assemblies chose representatives to sit on system-level and district-level committees.

The project management system that eventually emerged in Gal Oya and became the model for a national system of participatory management for all major irrigation schemes in Sri Lanka had a majority of farmer-representatives on the Project Committee and usually a farmer chairperson. While it might be thought that this system of 'indirect representation' would be less democratic, and less accountable, than electing Project Committee representatives directly through elections involving all the members, in our experience the system minimised the number of rich farmers or non-farmers – for example, merchants and schoolteachers – who could become farmer-leaders. All of the representatives in the system had been initially chosen by fellow farmers at the base and remained responsible for the smooth running of their field channel, involving much face-to-face contact with peers and an effective service or problem-solving orientation.[9]

The system of organisation established in Gal Oya, which took four years to put in place, continues to operate well almost ten years since outside assistance was withdrawn.[10] As noted above, this system has become national in scope, although with less investment in the establishment of farmer organisations elsewhere and probably with somewhat less effective performance. The organisational effort in Gal Oya was 'catalysed' by a cadre of dedicated young organisers, and farmers insisted that they could not have established this new system of organisation by themselves. But with some encouragement and appropriate support, they made the new organisation their own and have maintained it with at least as much internal democracy as is found in most local governments in the US or UK. The role of 'institutional organiser' has been accepted by the government and most donors, although not necessarily with the social science foundations and normative orientations that underpinned the effort in Gal Oya.

I mention this case to support a counter-argument to Michels' proposition which suggests that poorer segments of society, with appropriate outside support, can create effective institutions to which outside agencies – governmental and non-governmental – can and should be accountable. The first requirement is that the local institutions be themselves accountable to their members or constituents. This was an essential feature of the organisations in Gal Oya, and it has been maintained with varying degrees of fidelity in the subsequent organisations that have been established under the sponsorship of the Irrigation Management Division in Sri Lanka. The Mahaweli Economic Agency is presently introducing farmer organisations with the same principles of operation and accountability.

The debate with and within Northern NGOs about accountability should, in my view, be especially concerned with issues of *intra*-organisational accountability for the GROs they work with. This is possible but not easily achieved or sustained, as Michels' trenchant analysis and language warn us. This prediction should not be seen as a reason to avoid creating processes of *inter-*organisational accountability between NGOs and GROs, however.[11] It would be inconsistent, and would send the wrong signals, if NGOs were to insist on GRO leadership accountability if they were unable or unwilling to set a good example themselves in this regard.

As with so many things, the relationships to be institutionalised need to be established iteratively and progressively, with NGOs nurturing accountability at local levels while they create internal mechanisms for resource allocation, planning and evaluation that give local communities and representatives an effective voice in these processes. But such a voice only creates a degree of accountability. Responsibility will remain something that is shared between NGOs and those persons and communities which are expected to benefit from NGO activity. The amount and balance of control over programmes may change over time, moving more in favour of people at local levels. But accountability will remain a different matter for NGO programmes than with those that are authorised and funded from public sources. Thus, accountability for NGOs will remain something broader than just *vis-à-vis* those who are involved in NGOs' programmes.[12] NGOs are accountable certainly to their contributors, and also to any donor agencies which provide them with funds, but also to some extent to public officials, and of course to their employees (although this is not often stated explicitly). If this sounds complicated, just imagine a business executive telling an NGO counterpart – 'Welcome to the private sector!'.

Evaluation as a possible deterrent to sustainability: the importance of externalities

A separate concern is the possibility that efforts to promote 'evaluation' as a means for ensuring accountability, whether to the sources of funding or to the persons served by programmes, can conflict with the objective of sustainability, which is a pre-eminent concern and criterion in many development programmes these days. Evaluation is recommended or required to see that scarce resources are put to their best use, often in the name of sustainability. Yet the way that evaluation tends to be conceived and carried out can be inimical to sustainable development. There are great difficulties in knowing what is or is not 'sustainable'. The 'proof of this pudding' cannot be known until well after we are no longer around to 'do the tasting'. But that does not prevent us from making sustainability our current 'holy grail'. There are good reasons for seeking to ensure that the benefits gained from development programmes entailing considerable expense will not be short-lived.

Readers will be relieved that I do not plan to offer yet another definition of sustainability. Sustainability is not a matter to be dealt with by definitions since our words by themselves will not change what 'sustainability' is or is not, or what is or is not 'sustainable'. Sustainability is probably not a single thing anyway. I have tried to consider some theoretically grounded criteria that could help us to know when we were heading in the direction of sustainable development, or at least what would head us away from it.

One of the dynamics which makes for sustainable development (and hence a criterion thereof) is the achievement of multiple benefits from any particular cost. This means not only that the benefit-cost ratio is likely to be more positive in the short run, but also that more stakeholders will be created for the perpetuation of the activity or relationship in the long run. This can be discussed in the language of game theory, comparing positive-sum outcomes (where everyone wins or there are clearly more winners than losers), with zero-sum outcomes (where anyone's gain comes at someone else's expense, and where winners' gains equal others' losses as in a game of cards or chess). The least desirable situation is negative-sum, where everyone loses, or aggregate losses outweigh total gains.

In a world of zero-sum transactions, there are only transfers, no gains of value or productivity. With negative-sum dynamics, the system runs down to disorder and dissolution over time because more is being extracted from it than is being put in. Only in a world of positive-sum relationships is there a continuous accretion of productivity and value, making system sustainability possible. Speaking generally, positive-sum dynamics and relationships (situations referred to as 'win-win') appear to be the essence or crux of sustainability. In situations that are 'win-lose' (where someone's gain is someone else's loss), the relationship between individuals, groups, communities, sectors, nations, or humans *vis-à-vis* their environment, is at best an equilibrium one, and in the long run it is likely not to persist because no net margin of value is created and the people committed to maintaining it are balanced (offset?) by those with no stake in its perpetuation.

What will succeed in the long run are relationships that produce multiple net benefits, broadly dispersed, not narrowly calculated and distributed. These can be described in technical terms as positive externalities, which are benefits (greater than costs) that extend beyond the project, community or enterprise at hand. Unfortunately these days, projects, communities and enterprises are treated as closed systems for the sake of analysis, so that costs and benefits can be identified and compared.

Narrow constructions or calculations of benefits, restricted in scope and distribution, tend toward zero-sum thinking and practice. If people take the view that their benefits or advantages should or must come at someone else's expense, this is a zero-sum way of looking at the world. This is a closed-system, static perspective, but it is the one which finds much favour among policy-makers and analysts because it is thought to be more rigorous.

When evaluating the amount and distribution of benefits deriving from any particular project, programme, technology, subsidy, training, infrastructure or investment, people will minimise and even exclude externalities (positive and negative) in order to make rigorous (replicable) comparisons of benefits and costs, reckoning that these benefits and/or costs lie beyond the boundaries of the project, programme or whatever else is being considered.

As suggested already, to be sustainable, development must go beyond zero-sum processes where gains and losses are essentially equal. Rather it must promote and support positive-sum dynamics that achieve multiple benefits which outweigh the costs. The problems that arise when trying to evaluate benefits and costs are (a) that many are remote in time and space, so they are hard to identify rigorously with any particular investment or initiative, and (b) that many of the things that add most to our quality of life are not readily quantifiable. Things which are not measurable get ignored just as those which fall outside the system under consideration get excluded.

The demand for evaluation has pushed NGOs as well as everyone else trying to quantify results to close up the systems under consideration; analytically and artificially to count some things as 'inside' and other things as 'outside', dealing only with the former and making excuses as to why the latter are left out. In particular, positive externalities – benefits that accrue to persons or sectors outside the scope of the immediate organisation or programme – will be over-looked. Yet these are essential for sustainable development, many people receiving benefits from the same investment or expenditure, and many things being accomplished that elude rigorous measurement and comparison.[13]

Sustainable development requires both the attainment of second- and third-order effects (what Robert Chambers calls 'wider effects') as well as many people having a 'stake' in some institution, technology, practice or legislation so that it retains support. While there is not a simple correspondence between the number of stakeholders and a programme's prospects for longevity, having more actors regarding something as valuable and desirable certainly enhances its life chances. But what we see so often these days is pressure to *restrict* the scope of objectives, to assess only tangible things, to count only direct and not indirect benefits and costs (although this does not mean that there is no fudging of results). The process of evaluation tends to isolate and insulate activities, giving incentives to programme managers to maximise 'internal' net benefits and not to invest in those that would be 'external'. This is an oxymoronic short-sighted strategy for sustainability.[14] We need to be careful about downplaying and even discouraging positive externalities for the sake of achieving greater accountability, because such externalities represent the essence of sustainable development.

Accountability is commonly taken to require much advance specification of objectives and means, so that evaluation can be done in terms of the achieve-ment of those objectives and the timely utilisation of predetermined means for those achieving those ends. Yet we know from 'learning process' theory as proposed by Korten (1980) that this is not what is most essential to develop-ment. What is needed is an adaptive, creative, flexible process of matching available and expanding means to emerging and evolving ends, of fitting technology and organisation together in beneficial and sustainable ways, of mobilising additional resources because people's most keenly felt needs are being met. This, however, is an 'open system' view of the universe, one at odds with the kinds of cramped, 'closed system' assumptions which are required and promoted by an effort to do rigorous evaluation.

It is ironic, and even tragic, that in today's world, which says that it desires sustainability, that so much effort goes into thinking in closed-system terms in order to be able to achieve 'efficiency', as in economic benefit-cost calculations. Externalities get neglected and even disparaged as distracting analysts from the optimisation of returns from investment of scarce resources. This view considers only fixed amounts of resources, regarding them as a stock more than as a flow.

This view itself is inconsistent with a concern for sustainability, where rates and balances of flows are more important than stocks. I do not want to disparage efficiency, because in a world where sustainability is an increasingly important concern, we need to consider how best to use our limited resources to achieve the greatest and most lasting benefits. But in the name of efficiency, we have set up mental barriers which prevent us from looking for, and at, second- and third-order effects; for, and at, unmeasurable but admittedly important consequences; for, and at, co-generated benefits that cannot be readily attributed to any one source.

It is surely provocative to suggest that the 'evaluation movement' which has gathered pace within the development community over the last fifteen years is a deterrent to efforts to promote sustainability. I do not want to speak against evaluation *per se*, since wishful thinking that is not tested by observation of results has led to much waste of scarce resources. I believe that we need to have more rather than less evaluation, and indeed we need what Trochim (1992) calls 'an evaluation culture'. But how we do evaluations, and how much we sacrifice inclusive and imaginative evaluation for the sake of narrow and rigorous measurement, should be of concern to anyone wanting to promote the sustainability of beneficial programmes and activities. To the extent that we stress a complete pre-specification of objectives and restrict our evaluations to quantified costs and benefits, we will exclude many important factors, especially externalities, from consideration. We will treat projects, programmes, communities and institutions as closed systems, and will isolate them in our thinking – and in our interventions – from the economic, social, cultural, physical and other contexts in which they function (one hopes productively and indefinitely).

The importance of concepts and ways of thinking

This conclusion suggests the need to be more self-conscious and self-critical of our ways of thinking about things, getting away from naive experimentalist or empiricist notions of a world 'out there' that exists entirely independently of our own thoughts and perceptions. I am concerned that our concepts and thinking in this present era, when we need to think and act more expansively, more generously, more interdependently, are still based too much on narrow, self-centred, autonomy-seeking thinking and motives. The latter orientations are very much at odds with the much emphasised themes of accountability, sustainability and evaluation.

My own involvement with participatory development has led me to question the patterns and premises of thought that underlay my own graduate education in the social sciences, which I suspect was not very different from the training most others received. Some analyses by Albert Hirschman helped me to appreciate how much our preoccupation with 'equilibrium' (zero-sum) concepts in the social sciences stems from 17th- and 18th-century models of the physical universe. The development of thermodynamic theory in the 19th century popularised an 'entropic' (negative-sum) view of possibilities both for the present and the future. Fortunately for the prospects of participatory and sustainable development, the physical sciences in the 20th century have found new conceptions of reality that are more positive-sum in substance, and more useful for dealing with a broad range of phenomena, from the macrocosmic to the subatomic. Relativity theory, quantum mechanics, chaos theory, and now complexity theory have opened up new vistas on the natural universe that I find useful for the social universe as well.[15]

While this paper opened with several classificatory schemes, which I think are useful for comprehending and acting within the social universe, ultimately we need to combine such an analytical approach with a more integrative, synthesising one, transcending and utilising 'either-or' constructions with a 'both-and' frame of mind (Uphoff 1992). This can draw on the productive possibilities of apparently contradictory phenomena. As it turns out, accountability, sustainability and evaluation, like many other important but complex concepts, are fraught with paradoxes and do not lend themselves easily to 'linear' or reductionist thinking. Elaborating on this assertion would require another chapter, and indeed a book or more. But I do not want to leave this subject without expressing my growing conviction that however limiting physical resources may be, our minds are more constricting and they are where we should look for solutions to our various resource scarcities and constraints.

Notes

1. The second adjective, voluntary, is quite ambiguous as a description for PVOs since most depend heavily on employees and rely at most only partially on voluntary contributions of time or money for their existence.

2. Here I am not making a systematic distinction between 'institutions' and 'organisations' for the sake of brevity. In fact, a clear and important distinction should be made, even though the two terms overlap, as seen in the discussion of institutions vs organisations in Uphoff (1986, pp 8–10).

3. In Uphoff (1986), an inclusive set of ten levels for decision-making and action was identified, ranging from the international level to the individual. In between are the national level, the provincial or regional level, the district level, the sub-district level, the locality level (a set of interacting communities having some market, marriage and/or other connections), the community level, the group level and the household level. The three levels that are commonly understood as being 'local', ie, the locality, the community and the group, are what is usually meant by the designation 'grassroots'. For elaboration on this, see Uphoff (1993).

4. Carroll (1992) analyses the relation between 'grassroots support organisations' (GSOs), which generally correspond to the category of NGOs, and what he calls 'primary grassroots organisations' – ie, local membership organisations and co-operatives as classified here. His category of 'membership support organisations' (MSOs) is a hybrid between non-governmental and grassroots organisations in that these are the second or third tier of organisations which are accountable to local memberships.

5. It is true that not all NGOs operate as service organisations. But those which function as advocacy organisations are no more accountable in a structural sense to those on whose behalf they speak unless they are membership organisations, composed of, by and for persons who created the organisation and contribute the needed resources for it to operate.

6. See Lipset's study of the International Typographical Union (1956). This documented lively internal democracy within the ITU over many decades, with regular changes of officers by election, a *de facto* two-party system, an open union newspaper, etc. Typographers, however, had a relatively high educational level among manual workers and one of the higher statuses because they worked with words. Also in terms of higher status and job security, printers contrasted greatly with, say, teamsters or coal-miners, whose unions in America have been notoriously undemocratic (at least until recently).

7. We were told by the Deputy Director of Irrigation for Water Management that if we could make progress in Gal Oya, we could make progress anywhere in Sri Lanka. The senior civil servant in the district told the young organisers that if they could get even 10–15 farmers to work together, this would be a great accomplishment. We and they were expected to organise 10–15 *thousand* farmers (nobody knew for certain how many there were in the Left Bank area).

8. Since the base-level groups operated informally, tenants could be included along with settlers who had formal rights to their land. That these field channel groups attempted to serve needs equitably is seen from the fact that most of the rotations they set up to share water when it was scarce started by supplying the tail-end first. On the process of selection, which was structured to get truly representative farmers into responsible positions, see Uphoff (1992, pp 334–336).

9. The Chhattis Mauja irrigation scheme in Nepal, established by water users some 150 years ago to irrigate about 3,000 hectares in the terai region adjoining India, has about 4,000 members who annually elect a chairman and secretary at a mass meeting. They have been able to keep leaders accountable through direct elections. But their executive committee is made up of nine representatives who come from below through an indirect selection process (Pradhan 1983).

10. The International Irrigation Management Institute started but did not complete, an evaluation of the Gal Oya programme in the autumn of 1993. While a thorough study remains to be done, the main test of success is that farmers there consider the operation of their irrigation system much improved and feel that they can handle problems satisfactorily through the established channels (personal communication, D H Murray-Rust, November 1993).

11. The reference to NGOs here refers to both Northern and Southern NGOs.

12. Note that I have successfully avoided using the term 'beneficiaries', even with its mollifying adjective 'intended' in this paper so far. This paternalistic term is less objectionable than 'target groups', but not much.

13. It could be argued that neglecting both positive and negative externalities is acceptable because they will more or less offset each other. But in practice, things that are negative are more acutely felt and more easily identified, so positive externalities are more likely to be minimised or discounted in rigorous evaluation, for the sake of not 'biasing' the conclusion.

14. When we talk about sustainable development, there is no necessary implication of 'sustainable growth', which Herman Daly and others have castigated as indeed oxymoronic. Sustainable development need not mean that gross amounts of outputs are always increasing, only that the total of satisfactions produced by any given level and distribution of outputs is greater. Redistribution of goods and services could increase the total volume of satisfactions where distribution is quite unequal, for example. The concept of sustainability suggested here, focusing on satisfactions rather than outputs and based on positive-sum outcomes and valuations, takes a different tack than that which has attracted the critiques of Daly et al.

15. This line of thinking is developed in Uphoff (1992). Books which I found useful for

trying to rethink the way we understand the social universe, presenting new ways of thinking about the natural universe, include: Bohm and Peat (1987), Briggs and Peat (1984), Gell-Mann (1994), Gleick (1987), Jantsch (1980), Lewin (1992), Penrose (1989), Prigogine and Stengers (1984), Waldrop (1992), Wolf (1981), and Zukav (1979).

3

Negotiating Room for Manoeuvre: Reflections Concerning NGO Autonomy and Accountability Within the New Policy Agenda

Stephen Biggs and Arthur Neame

This chapter argues that NGOs run the risk of being co-opted by the new orthodoxy which is being promoted within the agenda of the 'New World Order'. On the surface this appears to be the result of increased funding to NGOs from official donor agencies: 'He who pays the piper plays the tune.' While at one level this is true, we argue that the formal, linear, mainstream approach to development planning (which is part and parcel of donor funding) is more of a threat to the development aspirations of some NGOs and individuals within them, than a growing dependence on donor funds *per se*. Funding has been and always will be a problematic issue for NGOs and other agencies. It is the way these funds are negotiated, and who is accountable to whom, for what, at what time and by what process, that is important.

That process of negotiation, and particularly the terms in which it is conducted and the parameters by which it is defined, is itself a reflection of power relations in international development. We suggest that a key task in the debate over accountability must be how to open up the negotiation process to greater popular scrutiny in a way that challenges the perceptions of funders, governments, NGOs, people's organisations and the public at large.

Linear approaches to development and room for manoeuvre

By the linear or mainstream approach we mean an approach which treats development as a set of predictable outcomes to be achieved through the ordering of project inputs and outputs through the 'logical framework' or its derivatives (see Fowler, this volume; Porter et al 1991). Although some official aid agencies are attempting to modify and soften this approach (through, for example, the introduction of 'process projects' in the case of the British Overseas Development Administration), it remains characteristic of most bilateral and multilateral donors (ODA 1992). Underpinning the mainstream approach to development is the implicit assumption that we know what we mean by 'development' and what interventions are required to achieve it. The logic starts with the assertion that there is a need for development in a particular place. So we talk of specific villages, regions or countries as though they can be defined in isolation. The logic also assumes that development can be measured and that spatial, administrative, ecological or technical boundaries can be defined and are unambiguous for the task in hand. Plans, inputs and outputs are placed within a detailed time frame, the end result being a set of desired and predictable outcomes. The process involves identifying 'constraints' to development that need removing, or 'gaps' that need filling, between existing conditions and what is desirable. Filling these gaps forms a major part of the rationale for NGO activities. The apparent common sense of the management techniques that are used in the mainstream development dialogue has a tremendous ability to co-opt people into thinking that the world did, does or should behave like the models says it should. A socio-political perspective puts such management and research theories, frameworks and techniques back into the toolbox and treats them as tools (see Seneratne 1990; Clay and Schaffer 1984; Long and Van der Ploeg 1989).

In the mainstream approach, NGOs are viewed as cost-effective instruments for the delivery of inputs and the achievement of outputs. Little attention is paid to factors and influences outside the NGO and the project. We argue that by adopting this approach to development planning, NGOs run the risk of ignoring the wider social and political context of development intervention and funding. But no institution can be divorced from the wider context in which it operates, and from the links which develop over time between actors and organisations in the same area.[1] Indeed, as we show below, it is these linkages and networks that underlie the effectiveness of both NGOs and of development interventions. In such networks, it is important that NGOs retain and expand their room for manoeuvre so that they can adapt to changing circumstances, maintain their accountabilities to different constituencies, and if necessary subvert or manoeuvre around vested interests. It is precisely this room for manoeuvre that is curtailed by the adoption of linear approaches to planning (Clay and Schaffer 1984).

The case for a greater role for NGOs: questioning current orthodoxies

Underlying much of the current dialogue on NGOs is the idea that they form a 'third' sector distinct from the 'first' (government) sector and the 'second' (commercial private) sector. Like Uphoff (1993), we view this as misleading.[2] NGOs are often put forward as appropriate vehicles to increase participation, protect human rights, strengthen local-level planning, or as agents of democratisation. Such assertions are not always supported by the evidence, and diminish the importance of the historical and institutional context which affects the ability of coalitions of social groups to find room for manoeuvre in reaching their goals.

The experience of Samakhya described by Korten (1990, p 5) illustrates these points. Samakhya and its associated people's organisation, the Multico-ops' Association (MCA), fought against the government of Andhra Pradesh and its ruling political party to restore democracy and member control to co-operatives. The division between the NGO (Samakhya) and the grassroots co-operative organisation (MCA) was very blurred and the actors involved in promoting democracy switched from using one organisation to another, depending on strategic and tactical criteria. Importantly, we are told that:

> *Samakhya had its own independent board of trustees consisting of prestigious and well connected individuals from Andhra Pradesh who were known for their outspoken commitment to an independent cooperative movement. Some were former government officials ... These and other Samakhya trustees had excellent political and administrative connections, and could speak with a powerful voice in support of independent cooperatives with little fear of being accused of seeking personal advantage. Samakhya's secretary, M. Rama Reddy himself had become an established political figure in Andhra Pradesh long before MCA and Samakhya were formed. From his earliest career he knew many of the key politicians and administrators in AP*

(Korten 1990, pp 4–5)

This case is held up as a great success for NGOs. While not disputing the issue that the NGO was clearly a major actor in bringing about significant institutional change, the wider context must be noted. From Korten's detailed narrative it is clear that some government officials were highly involved in working with the NGO in an unofficial as well as official capacity. They brought to bear their past and contemporary knowledge of working at very senior levels of government in order to help the NGO achieve its goals.

A clear lesson to be drawn from this case is that while Samakhya was legally constituted as an NGO, the actors within and around it found room for manoeuvre by working in a far broader arena than that offered by the NGO itself. The individuals involved did not succeed by working within strictly defined and specific notions of NGO, 'civil society', 'autonomy' or 'accountability', but by using their deep understanding of the roles that they, as individuals working in alliance with each other, could play within a specific context. The work of another very effective NGO, the Grameen Bank in Bangladesh, is also characterised by 'continuous concern with mobilising support and legitimization from a broad range of interest groups' (Von Pischke 1991).

The experience of many other organisations confirms that NGO staff and trustees come from a broad range of public and private-sector interest groups (Edwards and Hulme 1992). What characterises these cases is a history of negotiation, coalition and change in NGO structure and behaviour, in response to the interaction between the agency and its changing social and political context. One of the most significant observations of studies concerning NGO effectiveness has been that networking and coalitions with other NGOs, and with other public and private actors, are often the key to results (Harding 1994; Long and Van der Ploeg 1989). If one views development as the articulation of a series of local struggles and processes, it is obviously vital to understand the means by which networking succeeds. If NGOs are to tap into local processes in diverse arenas more effectively, it is also important that they recognise the diversity that exists within professions and bureaucracies, and that they acknowledge and network with the relevant experience wherever they can find it. Despite these lessons, the 'independence' of *individual* NGOs is still frequently used in advocating a growing role for NGOs in development.

NGO comparative advantage

It is often claimed that NGOs have a comparative advantage over the government sector in doing certain types of work. As Fowler (1990) writes, 'NGOs and their supporters share the view that, in comparison with governments, they are better able to:...'. He then lists 16 such advantages.[3] Advocates of this position believe that these comparative advantages derive from features such as: the way NGOs design their organisations; a stronger moral commitment to helping the poor; greater professionalism; a closer and more participatory working relationship with poor people; and an ability to innovate.

There are at least three problems with this analysis. First, one cannot have a non-government organisation unless there is government. The nature of the government, and what it does with its power and resources, determines whether an NGO might 'do development better'. By the same token one has to look at specific NGOs in particular contexts to see whether they 'do better' in these circumstances. There is no *general* case to be made.

The second criticism comes from economic theory. Neo-classical welfare economics argues that to achieve 'pareto optimality' it is more efficient for society if each actor concentrates on what they are best able to do – the origins of the theory of 'comparative advantage'. Problems arise, however, when markets are imperfect. Under these (real world) conditions, not only is overall economic welfare not increased by a particular actor following the logic of comparative advantage, but to the contrary, both that actor and society at large might be worse off. Neo-classical theory has little to say about the distribution of wealth and income. Since equity and empowerment are often the declared objectives of NGOs, it is strange that the language and arguments of neo-classical theory appear so significant in making the NGO case.

Third, Fowler (1990) states that the roots of NGO comparative advantage lie first, in the quality of relationships that NGOs can foster with clients; and second, in the way they create and design their organisations. Government-citizen relationships are said to be based on control and authority while NGOs are able to form unambivalent relationships with their clients and 'design their organisations in ways which are optimal for the situations and development tasks they themselves select.' In contrast, 'demands on governments lead to hierarchical and bureaucratic structures which rely on uniformity, standardisation and rigidity'. Our experience suggests that this is a romanticised view of NGOs set against a 'straw-man' representation of governments. The notion that NGOs 'select' their development tasks hints at mythical autonomy, and it is highly questionable anyway if NGOs are supposed to be acting in response to local needs and as agents of empowerment.

The hour of the 'third generation' NGO

In 1987 David Korten wrote a paper that has been very important to the growth in official support for NGOs. The paper suggested that NGOs move through a linear evolution to a 'third-generation stage'. From a focus on relief and welfare (first generation) they move to address the structural context of local self-help action through organisation and the mobilisation of local resources (second generation). Now was the time to seek changes in the institutions and policies at national and sub-national levels that inhibit effective self-help action (third generation). While having no quarrel with some of the details reviewed by Korten, we are concerned about the stages he suggested and the linear progression they supposedly represent.

NGOs have sought to change institutions for at least a century. The suffragette movement for the emancipation of women and the Anti-Slavery Society in the UK, are cases in point. On the other hand, many NGOs in the Philippines with a long-standing commitment to fundamental change have moved from concentrating on political mobilisation to the provision of relief and welfare, as a response to militarisation in 1987. This was not a 'backward' move on their part (as Korten's typology suggests), simply a humane one that suited the needs of the context. By the same token, the creation of Samakhya in Andhra Pradesh in India in the 1980s represented a specific response by NGOs and other actors who joined a flexible coalition to achieve their goals.

NGOs and civil society

Currently, in the Philippines as elsewhere, there is much talk of a new role for NGOs as leading actors in a vibrant civil society. But within the evolving economic and political context there is little questioning of whether NGOs are appropriate vehicles for the process which is called 'democracy'. Furthermore, democracy tends to be seen as a smooth, linear, time-based progression from one pre-defined set of outcomes to another. The Forum for Philippine Alternatives describes civil society in the following terms:

> *Civil society is an arena of social and political life autonomous from state domination where progressive values and political practices can be articulated, counter-hegemonic institutions can be created, which can nurture and nourish the creation of autonomous political actors who are able to articulate and defend their interests, propose alternative projects for structuring the state and society, and transform the relations of state and society.*

(Gershman and Bello 1993)

Such a position views civil society and the state as entirely distinct entities, and while it acknowledges the influence of civil society on the state it does not appear to acknowledge the link between state and society. The state is represented as the instrument of one particular group in society rather than as an arena for negotiation. Simplistic definitions of civil society and democracy trivialise philosophy and political science; the danger lies in the possibility that NGOs and donors may think that NGOs alone can ensure the 'delivery' of democracy and civil society – that these are goals to be achieved rather than processes and arenas that continually evolve. Such views, reinforced by donors and NGOs alike, portray Southern governments as passive bystanders (see Fowler 1992) and set up NGOs and people's organisations as the victims and pawns of a triumphant world capitalism. They fail to acknowledge that resistance to all hegemonies takes place in many different forms on many different fronts, and that NGOs may be just one small front on which praxis evolves.

NGOs as innovators

Some authors argue that NGOs have particular skills in developing new methods and approaches for research and development planning that government agencies and other development actors can adopt subsequently (Chambers 1992). However, a critical historical account of the growth of farmer participatory research methods shows that many of the new developments came from highly trained professional staff in government research institutions, universities, international institutes (such as CIMMYT and IDS, Sussex), as well as from practitioners in the field with few (or no) government or NGO affiliations. As regards research capabilities – the ability to collect, analyse and reflect upon data – BRAC, the largest NGO in Bangladesh, would be the first to admit that the development of a high-quality reflective research capacity is a difficult process, which they have struggled with for a long time (Biggs and Senaratne 1986). OXFAM-UK has taken years to develop a capability to produce documents that provide research guidance for its staff and for others (Pratt and Loizos 1992, Marsden and Oakley 1990). While action research is used by NGOs such as Proshika (Wood and Palmer-Jones 1990) it is a very demanding research methodology that requires considerable professional resources on the part of the people and organisations involved. At the level of technology development, where NGOs are sometimes seen as performing more effectively than other actors, there is also a need for caution. In a worldwide review of research projects on animal-drawn agricultural equipment, Starkey (1987) illustrates how NGOs appear to have been no better or worse than other (private and public) organisations in trying to develop new technology for poorer farmers. One has to look at the particular context to see if NGOs are any better in the development of methodological or other innovations. Where successful developments do occur, they are often the result of combined efforts between a large number of government, NGO, private and 'beneficiary' actors.

A duty to scale-up?

By any measure the level of developed-country (donor) funding of NGO activities has increased over the last ten years (Fowler 1992; Edwards and Hulme 1994). Fuelled in part by the availability of donor funds, many NGOs see growth as a 'duty'. It appears that some NGOs view an increase in their activity as synonymous with greater impact. Evidence of this growth-oriented mentality is especially common with regard to NGO entry into Eastern Europe – this is not to say that there is no role for NGOs there, but the haste with which NGOs have entered that arena with, by many accounts (albeit often anecdotal), mixed results, does beg the question as to whether NGOs are the reflective organisations they claim to be or whether, like their commercial counterparts in the private sector, they are simply responding to market opportunities – the widespread availability of official aid for NGO activities in Eastern and Central Europe after the fall of the Berlin Wall. Of course, there are NGOs that are not fixated on growth and are keen to maintain their identities. The danger lies in a tendency to conflate growth with impact and effectiveness in all circumstances.

In summary, NGOs must always be seen in a broader social and political perspective. When this is done it is clear that NGOs have much in common with formal and informal coalitions which have been exploring and developing room for manoeuvre under difficult social and political circumstances for many years. Generalised rhetoric about NGOs and their effectiveness does not square with the reality of local contexts and variations. More serious for us is the fact that the growing role for NGOs which this rhetoric engenders may make NGOs willing adjuncts of the mainstream planning approach. Uncritical support for NGOs plays to the formalising tendencies sought after by the large donors. In the guise of protecting flexibility and diversity, the current discourse actually limits the room that NGOs have for manoeuvre and confines them to the role of service agents within a 'modernising' model of development.

Acceptance of this dominant discourse may be logical to those who subscribe to the New Policy Agenda. Use of the language of the New Policy Agenda may also be acceptable to those who do not accept its practical implications but wish to enter into tactical negotiations with donors and governments. However, there is a risk that the techniques and language become so embedded in the NGO that any sense of critical perspective is lost; reliance on the linear, mainstream model, with its emphasis on developmental input/output indicators, becomes the essence of the NGO's existence. Such a lack of critical perspective detaches NGOs from the real-world politics in which they are situated, limiting them to ready-made policy options that stifle creativity and fail to challenge the dominant economic and political forces at global and local levels. This is not to subscribe to a simple conspiracy theory, or to write off Northern donors or Southern governments as monoliths, but to make the point that all development discourses have a habit of becoming new hegemonies – be it 'participation', 'dependency theory', 'liberalisation', 'civil society', 'sustainability', 'process projects' or a host of others.

Ways forward

We have no recipe or set of instructions about a better way forward. However, there are some signposts that might be useful to those wanting to retain and further develop the room for manoeuvre that NGOs have frequently offered in the past.

Questioning the withdrawal of government

It is argued by some that the retrenchment of government under structural adjustment policies implies an even greater role for NGOs in development. To accept this argument uncritically is to accept one of the first premises of the New Policy Agenda, but in so doing allows the state to opt out of many of the difficult and complex dilemmas that should be discussed within the open, public arena. Rather than taking on some of the former roles of the state, there may be cases in which NGOs (if serious about their commitment to challenging poverty and injustice) should support and facilitate the empowerment of the state or progressive elements within it. Such an approach would mean strengthening the will, not just to find a common cause with individuals and institutions within all social and political arenas, but to work to build a common cause, based on an individual's own judgements of what is feasible, desirable and within their own capacities.

In a discussion of social security in developing countries, Ahmad, Dreze and Sen (1991, p 28) argue that 'public action includes not merely what is done *for* the public by the state, but also what is done *by* the public for itself'. In this context they see a particularly important political role for NGOs in pressurising governments to recognise deprivation and to take action to reduce poverty. Uphoff (in this volume) argues that more emphasis should be given to the support of membership organisations rather than intermediary NGOs. However, one is left with the basic political question of which types of people's associations and membership organisations the state is going to help, respond to, ignore or discourage. The role of NGOs in acting to influence public policy still remains. Clearly, there are major differences between a powerful membership organisation representing the interests of large commercial farmers and a membership organisation representing landless labourers. To suggest that all membership organisations will lobby for (or that the state might introduce) general legislation which is 'fair-handed', is naive. Thus, while we agree with Uphoff concerning the general modes of behaviour of NGOs and membership organisations, we see a clear need to be aware of the interests and contexts in which all such organisations are acting. NGOs, government agencies and the private sector are made up of a great variety of people. NGOs need to move away from rhetoric which suggests that their staff are more committed to reducing poverty than those in the public sector, to an understanding that some public sector staff are as committed and effective in poverty-alleviation as any self-proclaimed activist. If NGOs become more reflective they will see in their own behaviour some of the actions of those in governments and the private sector that they often condemn (self-promotion, a failure to learn, etc).

The intractable nature of autonomy and accountability

If the New Policy Agenda does drive some NGOs into the linear approach to development intervention, then clearly this raises issues of autonomy and accountability. A return to a mythical autonomy is neither possible nor desirable for NGOs; rather, the question is how to *broaden accountability*. It might seem that the more accountable NGOs are, the less autonomy they have. Pure autonomy and multiple accountability are clearly incompatible. However, by increasing the number and types of arenas in which NGOs are accountable, they may create greater room for manoeuvre as they gain in the number of spheres in which they negotiate.

If NGOs are to avoid entrapment by the agendas of others and are to pursue creative relationships with their proclaimed multiple constituencies, then both formal mechanisms of accountability (such as legal regulations) and informal mechanisms (such as affective ties and patronage) warrant more transparent and serious consideration. Many NGOs are willing to devote time and effort to developing broad critiques of the framework and context in which accountability is constructed, but are less willing to undertake a thorough examination of the concrete mechanisms which both affect and are influenced by those frameworks and contexts. In seeking room for manoeuvre, NGO personnel (just like other individuals) need to acknowledge and understand these mechanisms and their effects.

For example, the use of patronage is condemned by some in NGOs without reflection on the fact that NGOs are, or can be, purveyors of patronage themselves (White 1991, Neame 1993). Patronage is constructed over time through the acquisition and dispersal of resources, with decisions being taken at both conscious and unconscious levels. Little time is devoted to informal decision-making processes such as these within NGOs themselves, although all who work for NGOs are well aware of their existence. Informal decision-making is part of the control and dissemination of information, and occurs just as often in the 'listening NGO' as it does elsewhere. The choices NGOs make regarding the information they give to their public subscribers, 'beneficiaries' or even their trustees are clearly open to control and manipulation. Acceptance of this fact is of paramount importance if greater transparency and accountability are to be achieved. It is at this point that the responsibility of the individual, as a member of an institution, and as a person who is willing to question their ideas of what is important and why, comes to the fore (Schaffer 1984; Chambers, this volume).

Conclusion

This chapter has argued that the issues raised for NGOs by the New Policy Agenda are not new. What is new is the form that the discourse is taking. The effect of the New Policy Agenda is to formalise, label and use NGOs as 'service contractors', 'agents of democratisation' or 'sources of innovation'. NGOs become instruments for the delivery of services, democracy or innovation on the basis of clearly defined inputs, outputs and NGO interventions. Such a view, we argue, brings about a return to the 'project mentality' of old; it ignores the complex historical, political, economic and cultural processes and power structures at work in the real world. Similarly, it fails to acknowledge the heterogeneity that exists among individuals and interest groups in all institutions, including NGOs. By adopting such a formalised approach, NGOs are encouraged to look only at their individual performance. This contrasts with much evidence that major achievements of NGOs come through operating as partners in formal and informal networks and coalitions involving other NGOs, government agencies and the private sector.

A further concern to emerge from the New Policy Agenda is the predilection of bilateral and multilateral funders for seeing NGOs as a panacea for many of the intractable problems of development. NGO concerns, and those of other practitioners and academics, centre on the supposed loss of autonomy that this might entail. This chapter has argued that the real concern should not be with loss of autonomy as such but with the erosion, rather than the necessary strengthening, of multiple accountabilities. NGOs, like other actors in the development process, have never been wholly autonomous of other actors or the contexts in which they operate. Since autonomy is always relative and shifting, the major issue facing NGOs is how to increase their capacity to negotiate with their multiple constituencies and thus enhance their room for manoeuvre. Such negotiations are always at the centre of NGO activities. They cannot be avoided. In the final analysis, negotiation requires that individuals in and outside NGOs are aware of, and responsible for, the terms in which the current debate is being conducted.

Notes

1. In a revealing paper on the work of a very large NGO in Pakistan, David Marsden (1990), identifies the normative development imperative in the work of the Aga Khan Foundation. The size of the NGO involvement, the funds coming from such agencies as the World Bank, Ford Foundation and OXFAM, and the full support of the Government of Pakistan would make a non-political and asocial analysis of the development project naive, to say the least.
2. Uphoff (this volume) argues that more attention and support needs to be given to seeing people's associations and membership organisations as the important 'third' sector rather than seeing non-membership NGOs in this role. Uphoff prefers to view NGOs as service organisations set within the private sector. Our point is that all organisations exist within and function by virtue of the particular configuration of power relations in which they are set. These frequently defy any notions of strict or indeed meaningful categorisation.
3. The list Fowler (1990) gives is: (1) Reach the poor, ie, to target their assistance to chosen groups; (2) obtain true, meaningful participation of intended beneficiaries; (3) achieve the correct relationship between processes and outcomes; (4) choose the proper mix of assistance – educational, technical, material; (5) be flexible and responsive in their work; (6) strengthen local level institutions; (7) achieve outcomes at less cost; (8) tailor interventions to the needs of specific situations; (9) experiment with alternative ideas and practices; (10) employ long-term, strategic perspectives and time-scales; (11) undertake people-centred problem identification and research (12) utilise indigenous knowledge and other local resources; (13) learn from and (re)apply experience; (14) analyse and identify with the reality of the poor; (15) motivate and retain personnel; (16) promote development which is sustainable.

We would like to thank Davine Thaw and Jenni Wishart, co-editors of the Olive Information Service, Durban, South Africa, for editing and improving an earlier version of this paper which was brought out in their *Avocado Services* as report no 07/94. We also appreciate the support and helpful comments from David Hulme and Michael Edwards. The *Avocado* paper covers the same ground as the paper in this volume, but in much greater detail.

4
'Board Games':
Governance and Accountability in NGOs
Rajesh Tandon

There has been considerable recent debate among donors and NGOs on the issue of accountability (Edwards and Hulme 1994). However, there is as yet no agreed definition of NGO accountability. While all parties aspire to a comprehensive view of the subject, in most practical situations NGO accountability boils down to the domain of finance. This narrow operational definition is partly a consequence of the ease of establishing specific and quantifiable criteria for measuring financial accountability. It is also partly due to the fact that donors (and other resource-providers) have been the most vocal commentators on the issue. The regulatory dimension of accountability has also been emphasised in many contexts (including India), being narrowly defined in relation to finance (submitting regular financial reports which are externally certified to ensure legitimacy). The regulatory context in which an NGO operates defines the laws, rules and procedures that prescribe parameters and behaviours relevant to NGO accountability. For a detailed analysis of these regulatory aspects in India, see Tandon (1989).

Therefore it is not surprising to find elaborate mechanisms and regulations being proposed and imposed to improve NGO accountability. This has been a recent trend in India where several European NGO donors (most notably EZE of Germany) have started to create formal, local and professional mechanisms for close monitoring and reporting of the financial aspects of the NGOs they support. However, the need to examine this issue from a wider conceptual perspective continues. As actors within civil society, NGOs are autonomous institutions inspired by a particular vision of the society they wish to see develop, pursuing their defined mission in that regard (Tandon 1991). Thus NGOs find themselves in a web of complex interactions in a particular context. The concept of multiple 'stakeholders' helps to further our understanding of NGO accountability. The constituency which is the focus of NGO interventions could be seen as one such stakeholder. When this constituency comprises of a local community where NGO programmes are carried out, further differentiation arises, creating multiple interests or 'stakes' within the broad category of community stakeholders. Donors and other resource-providers have a stake in the outcomes of NGO performance too. There is often a chain of donors, each being accountable to the next level in their hierarchies, thereby further expanding this aspect of stakeholdership. In this complex web of stakeholders one aspect of NGO accountability that is often neglected is that which relates to the NGO's own governance. There has been considerable discussion, training and codification of practice with respect to NGO governance in many countries in the North (as can be seen from the vast literature that has been produced by institutions such as the National Centre for Non-Profit Boards in the USA). But this has been a neglected area of attention and debate in most countries of the South (and in particular, in South Asia). Therefore, this chapter elaborates the different forms of NGO governance which exist in South Asia, examines the linkages between them and NGO accountability, and raises a number of questions in relation to the need to strengthen NGO governance from the perspective of performance, accountability and institutional development.

NGO governance

The governance of NGOs implies the totality of functions that are required to be carried out in relation to the internal functioning and external relations of organisations. It is not the same as NGO management. The governance of NGOs focuses on issues of policy and identity, rather than the issues of day-to-day implementation of programmes. Thus, governance implies addressing the issue of NGO vision, mission and strategy; it focuses on future directions and long-term strategic considerations; it addresses the issues of policy in relation to internal programming, staffing and resources; it defines norms and values that are the basis of institutional functioning; it includes obligations entailed in fulfilling statutory requirements applicable to the NGO; and focuses on defining the external positions that are consistent with the overall thrust of the NGO as an institution in civil society. Most importantly, the governance of an NGO is concerned with its effective functioning and performance in society. This is both a legal and a moral obligation. Therefore, governance requires the creation of structures and processes which enable the NGO to monitor performance and remain accountable to its stakeholders. In the 'for-profit' sector, most criteria for performance are monetary. In the case of NGOs, however, they are based on vision, mission and values. To that extent, creating and sustaining appropriate structures and processes of governance in an NGO is a much more complex and challenging task.

Forms of governance

In the case of most voluntary development organisations and NGOs in South Asia, certain patterns of governance reoccur regularly. For those NGOs which are legally incorporated, statutory forms of governance provide the basic framework. The two most common statutory forms are the *Society* and the *Trust* (Tandon 1987), which prescribe mechanisms for the purposes of governance in legal terms. This mechanism is variously called the Executive Council or Committee, Governing Board, and so on. Also included are statutorily identified positions such as Chief Executive Officer (CEO), variously labelled as Secretary, President, Convener, Co-ordinator, Director or Executive Director. The legal basis of these structures dates back to the colonial period in the Indian sub-continent, and so much of the details of these statutes date back to the 19th century. The present reality of such forms of governance poses serious questions in relation to the efficacy and effectiveness of governing mechanisms. Current practice displays a range of behaviour of what could be called 'board games', described below and concretised, each with a case study from South Asian experience.

1. Family boards

One of the common characteristics of many NGO boards is their family character. In both composition and style of functioning, these boards operate like a family, with all the necessary informality, affection and trust that a family-held small business demonstrates. At the formative stage, such boards provide support (emotional, physical and material) for the launching and stabilisation of the NGO. However, they do have limitations in situations of growth and expansion; they also demonstrate the behaviour characteristic of a patriarch in a family-run business in the face of assertion by his offspring. When new staff or volunteers begin to feel a part of such an organisation, family boards are unable to provide a competent governing mechanism.

> *Grameen Vikas Samiti in North Bihar was set up as a voluntary organisation in 1978 by Sudhanshu Misra. Misra was very active in the student movement inspired by Jayaprakash Narayan. When the Janata government in Delhi failed to deliver, Misra (and many others like him) felt disillusioned by party politics. His commitment to organise and empower the landless rural poor led to the rapid acceptance and growth of Grameen Vikas Samiti. When the Samiti was incorporated, Misra asked some of his family (wife, brother, father) to be co-signatories. Later, his wife's brother and his brother's wife also joined the Managing Committee. When the Samiti undertook an adult education programme in 1979, it recruited a full-time staff of 35 and 300 part-time teachers. The Samiti grew rapidly, but due to a sudden change in government policy, all adult education projects had to be wound up. This created a difficult situation for Misra as he could no longer pay his staff. When he announced the decision that most staff had to leave the Samiti, Misra was abused and demonstrations were mounted against him.*

2. Invisible boards

Many NGOs have a largely invisible board comprising a small coterie of friends and family, assembled by the founder(s), merely for the purposes of meeting statutory requirements on paper. The actual functions of governance are carried out by the founder(s), with or without the help of other staff in the NGO, and the board merely acts as a 'rubber-stamp'. It is not uncommon to come across examples where the board does not meet for many years and the founder(s) merely obtains the thumb-print of board members on the minute book from time to time. Such a situation clearly provides the founder(s) with the ease of pursuing his or her vision with speed and energy, unencumbered by the usual hurdles related to paperwork and bureaucracy. However, in situations where the founder(s) needs advice or support, the invisible board remains both invisible and inaudible. In addition, the absence of a clear separation between governance and management in such organisations reduces the avenues available for internal accountability.

> *Abhay Singh was a student activist in Osmania University, Hyderabad, who decided to work with tribal groups, and particularly in strengthening tribal knowledge, culture and art. He set up the Institute for Socio-Cultural Development in Hyderabad to support this work. Since he spent most of his time in the villages, he requested three of his college friends (now teachers in Hyderabad) to join the Governing Council of the Institute. The positive impact of Singh's work resulted in a grant to develop a large three-year project focusing on tribal culture. This grant helped Singh to set up a small residence-cum-office in the tribal area, recruit 10 outside students, and train nearly 30 tribal youths as part-time animators. Nearly two years after the project began, Singh and two of his colleagues were abducted by a militant Naxalite group active in the area. The media coverage of the incident resulted in a number of enquiries from the government about the Institute. When the Commissioner of Police in Hyderabad asked the three teachers (on the Governing Council of the Institute) to bring the Institute's files, documents and minute books to help the police in their search for clues to assist in tracing Singh's abductors, they pleaded complete ignorance of any of the organisation's paperwork.*

3. Staff boards

It is quite common for NGOs in South Asia to have a board largely comprised of current staff. Where an NGO has been set up by a group of people in pursuit of a shared vision, they themselves decide to become the board. In other cases, senior staff members are brought on to the board subsequently, similar to the concept of board representation by trade union/worker representatives on the boards of 'for-profit' corporations. Such boards are very effective in ensuring a shared vision and a common perspective on the direction of the NGO; there is also a collective commitment by the board towards the well-being of the organisation. These boards also help in the process of building and strengthening the stake which staff feel they hold in the future of the NGO. However, one of the major problems which arises in such cases is the confusion over, and the blurring of, the distinctions between the requirements of governance and the needs of day-to-day management. It is not uncommon to find situations in which staff confuse programmatic accountability to the CEO with shared responsibility for governance. In many such cases, staff representation on the board gets bogged down in issues related to the interests of the staff, sometimes at the expense of larger institutional concerns (a situation not too different from those corporations where workers' representatives were nominated to the board). Also, in situations where serious ideological, programmatic or perceptual disagreements emerge among senior staff in the organisation (a situation that is widespread in the functioning of most NGOs), the governing mechanism is unable to deal with disagreements rationally, since the conflict is brought forward and replayed in the board itself.

Such boards are also unable to provide a fresh, objective and balanced perspective on the strategies, programmes and functioning of the organisation. The staff develop perceptual blocks and vested interests in pursuing particular strategies and programmes; and these remain unquestioned by such a board because it is comprised mostly of staff themselves.

Akriti Sanathan in Gujarat was set up by five social workers who had worked together previously in a large rural development agency. They decided to create a new organisation in another district where they worked with women agricultural labourers. The Executive Committee of the Sansthan was made up by the five founding members. After five years of intensive work, the state government offered the Sansthan a large grant for integrated rural development in 250 villages in the area. Within the agency, debates within this 'gang of five' over whether to accept this offer became polarised around two personalities. An embryonic leadership struggle surfaced and divided the entire staff. Over the next two months, the Sansthan's fieldwork came to a standstill while the debate and conflict intensified. One of the five founders was acting as Secretary of the Sansthan, and one day signed a contract with the government to accept their offer. A week later, two of the original founders and thirteen other staff left the Sansthan and created another voluntary organisation a few blocks away.

4. Professional boards

The composition of these boards is based largely on the shared vision of a set of like-minded people, but also includes consideration of the professional and strategic requirements of the institution. In such situations, the composition and functioning of the board exhibits a more formal character: board appointments are made with careful consideration of the requirements and future direction of the institution. The board has a formal system of meetings, discussions, decision-making and recording (agenda papers, minutes and so on); members take individual and collective responsibility for different aspects of governance (such as sub-committees, and the roles of Chair, Treasurer and Secretary); the performance audit and review of the institution as well as that of the CEO and other senior staff is undertaken by the board on a regular and formal basis; and the institution is represented in external fora by different members of the board.

Such boards tend to provide ongoing professional direction to the institution and to help shape its policies and strategies in a more rational and coherent manner. In situations of stability, they ensure the periodic assessment of mission and strategy, and its translation into programmes and internal mechanisms. In situations of crisis, such boards are able to take on the true function of governance, rising above day-to-day management. However, in many cases it has proven difficult to generate and sustain a shared vision in such a board, particularly when the board functions merely as a collection of well-meaning and concerned individuals (and not as a coherent, unified and effective group acting together). It is also difficult to generate and sustain the commitment of the board as a stakeholder, particularly when individual board members do not serve on the board for long periods of time. Other studies tend to confirm these observations for NGOs elsewhere in the world (Billis and Mackeith 1993).

Sita graduated with a Masters degree in social work from the Tata Institute of Social Studies in 1970. She worked in a voluntary organisation outside Bombay among rural women, helping to organise a dairy co-operative. Later, she moved back to Bombay to set up an NGO called 'Creative Development' to assist women's groups to undertake livelihood projects. Sita decided to seek the advice of a few colleagues and in the process insisted that they join the governing board of Creative Development. These board members were: a professor from the National Institute of Bank Management, a scientist from the Indian Council of Agricultural Research, a graduate from the Indian Institute of Management currently working with Lever Brothers in Bombay, the directors of two other rural development NGOs from Maharashtra, and her favourite professor from the Tata Institute. During the first year, the board met three times to elaborate a set of policies which enabled Sita to carry forward the programme.

Even from this brief typology, it is clear that the form and functioning of governance mechanisms in many South Asian NGOs is inadequate from the perspective of accountability. Where the board is 'sleeping' or invisible, the full spectrum of governance functions cannot be performed properly. In many other situations, the style of functioning of the board also results in the curtailment of governance. Weaknesses in governance limit the possibilities of continuous, objective and appropriate feedback to the implementation and management functions of the NGO, including to the CEO.

Other issues

A key issue in the arena of governance arises in situations where the founder is the leader of the NGO for a substantial period of time. By its very nature the NGO begins to reflect the vision and perspective of its founder; its culture and programmes imbibe the style and background of the founder too. Over a period of time, the NGO's identity becomes very closely linked to the person of the founder-leader. In such situations the board is initially assembled by the founder, and most board members are individually known to and associated with the founder-leader. This has the potential to limit the autonomous identity of the board (even in the case of a professional board) and creates a particular set of dynamics. On the one hand, the founder-leader provides the bulk of the energy and ideas for the NGO, thereby building up 'sweat-equity'; on the other hand, the long-term sustainability of the NGO requires the institutionalisation of energy and ideas beyond one person. The conduct of the totality of the functions of governance in such circumstances poses a range of interesting and practical challenges.

The second issue of relevance to this discussion is the fact that *priorities in governance in an NGO change over time.* In the early formative stages, defining the vision and mission, and building a programme, takes precedence; once established, the NGO turns its attention to issues of growth in size, coverage and resources. The life-cycle of an NGO determines the priority which issues take in its governance. Thus, the composition and functioning of the board tend to be more informal and spontaneous at the formative stage; this helps in providing support and space for the founder(s). During the phase of growth and consolidation, the board needs to acquire greater formality and professionalisation in its structure and processes. This *temporal* dimension of governance requires understanding and attention if effectiveness and accountability are to be maintained.

Another issue in NGO governance that is gaining increasing currency (particularly with donor agencies) is the active role of different stakeholders. It is being repeatedly argued by some donors that beneficiary-participation and representation on boards is crucial to ensure NGO accountability to their 'clientele'. Some donors even ask for evidence of this at the time of approving a grant. In response, some NGOs provide for a 'token' beneficiary representation on their boards. A similar argument is often made for including donor representatives on the governing structure. Even governmental funding and regulatory agencies sometimes ask for this as a matter of right. For example, some states in India have attempted to incorporate such a requirement in their modified Society Registration Acts. Rather than simply acceding to these demands from donors and regulators, some NGOs have experimented with creative solutions to these demands.

In the case of the (legitimate) need for beneficiary participation in the planning and implementation of NGO programmes, this can be, and is being, carried out through systematic consultation and participation mechanisms on the ground. In the case of (legitimate) donor concerns to make an input into the direction and programmes of the NGOs it supports, regular joint review and planning fora are common practice. However, the demands of regulatory agencies are clearly aimed at strengthening controls over NGOs and should not be seen as legitimate merely for the purposes of regulation.

It is important to distinguish here between the concept of stakeholders and the concept of governance. A stakeholder, by definition, is any party which has a stake in the outcomes of an NGO. In this sense, beneficiaries, donors and regulators are all stakeholders, as are other NGOs and NGO staff. However, their stakes relate to the performance of the institution, not to its governance directly. Hence, their demands for access to the institutional governance of the NGO lies through the requirement that the NGO performs effectively. This is where *critical and regular performance monitoring* by stakeholders is the key to ensuring the accountability of the NGO to them. This situation is somewhat akin to that in 'for-profit' corporations, where consumers of its products or services have a stake and therefore a right to corporate accountability, without needing to be part of the formal governance mechanism of the company. Donors to NGOs are supporters of desirable processes and outcomes, whose interests and concerns must be matched by the performance of the NGO in order for resources to continue to flow. A major cause of ambiguity at present, however, is that undue importance is given to the existence of a shared vision and perspective among NGO and donor, and less emphasis is placed on the performance and results obtained. Accountability to donors needs to be more clearly related to output indicators than is the case in current practice, and not to NGO governance. Innovative practices and ongoing documentation of the best practice are needed to promote better performance accountability. Social audits provide one such approach (Zadek and Gatward, this volume).

Linkages to accountability

In the light of this discussion, it is important to understand the linkages which exist between NGO governance and accountability. NGO accountability is related to three dimensions:

1. *Accountability vis-à-vis its mission*: as an institution oriented to social change within the framework of civil society, an NGO needs to define, refine and pursue a clear mission.
2. *Accountability vis-à-vis its performance in relation to that mission:* demonstrable performance, both in process and outcome terms, is essential to generate feedback to the programmes and approaches implemented in a given time-frame.
3. *Accountability vis-à-vis its role as an actor in the civil society*: norms, rules and styles of functioning that match standards of being a good civic institution.

In all three respects, the governance of an NGO is a critical element. An effective system of governance enables an NGO to formulate, review and reformulate its mission in a changing context. 'Good governance' ensures that programmes follow the requirements of the NGO's mission; promotes a performance orientation and accountability in the institution; and requires that the values (integrity, participation, professionalism, quality, commitment), statutes (reporting and legal standards and procedures) and norms of socially concerned civic institutions are articulated, practised and promoted. An effective structure and process of governance in an NGO is absolutely critical for ensuring accountability in this wider sense.

Even in its narrow sense, financial and statutory accountability requires an active, alert and functioning board which feels both a legal and a moral obligation in these regards. Such a board provides a set of measures needed in the organisation to ensure the necessary checks-and-balances for proper recording and reporting according to agreed targets and rules.

PRIA's governing board has been conscious of developing standards and procedures of good governance over the years. Programme monitoring and review is carried out at least annually by a group of partners and concerned professionals. The board conducts annual organisational and staff reviews. A separate annual performance review of the Executive Director is carried out by the board. Over the past 14 years, PRIA has had three external evaluations. The board co-ordinates and facilitates these evaluations. A system of monthly internal audits by an external professional is used to generate feedback on financial management. The treasurer also reviews these reports with the Executive Director. During the years, PRIA's governing board has established high-quality formal policies of human resource management. Many of these policies, systems and procedures have become models of good practice for other NGOs in the region. The norms and procedures for the functioning of the governing board are continuously evolved, upgraded and established.

In recent years, donors and regulators (such as government agencies) have demanded better performance with respect to NGO goals and programmes. In the post-Cold War world, there are going to be even greater demands for 'demonstrable' performance. This will require better documentation of existing performance, as well as the enhanced, transparent and critical functioning of mechanisms for NGO governance. In this sense, performance, accountability and governance are likely to become linked with each other more and more closely. Particular attention needs to be given to improving this linkage in operational terms so that NGOs can face the challenges which are emerging proactively.

Future challenges

Inadequate attention is being paid to the issue of effective governance in NGOs in many countries of South Asia today. It is of crucial importance that NGOs, their supporters and their donors begin to understand the meaning and significance of effective governance and its contribution to NGO accountability. There is also a need to document, analyse and promote good practice in relation to NGO governance and accountability. Such interventions need to be viewed as part of the fabric of institutional development efforts needed to strengthen an NGO. Strategic planning and capacity-building need to include interventions directed at making its structures and processes of governance more effective. A number of such efforts, studies and manuals developed and used in countries in the North can help to clarify and support this challenge in the South (Conrad and Glenn 1976).

While a basic understanding of NGO governance already exists in most countries, considerable ambiguity remains with respect to the situation of NGO networks and associations. The considerations discussed in this chapter become even more complex when applied to a body that brings together a set of independent and autonomous institutions. Much of the practical experience with governance in such associations has been unproductive and frustrating. There is much useful experience in other countries from which our current understanding and practices could benefit. There is also a need to develop educational programmes and learning materials on the theme of NGO governance so as to strengthen NGO practice. The growing emphasis on NGO performance and accountability *must* include the challenge of making NGO governance more effective.

Part II
Case Studies

5
Scaling-up, Mainstreaming and Accountability: the Challenge for NGOs
Frits Wils[1]

In many fields – including poverty alleviation, women's emancipation and sustainable development – NGOs are ascribed a range of virtues, based partly on presumed advantages such as efficiency, effectiveness, flexibility, participatory approach and proximity to vulnerable people. However, such virtues are rarely proven: they are brought out in an invidious comparison with the 'vices' of the state. Another motive for emphasising the role of NGOs is ideological: those of a social-democratic persuasion attach great importance to bottom-up participation, especially of less privileged groups; more recent neo-liberal values prefer a reduced role for the state and a strengthening of private initiative. On the basis of such arguments, expectations of NGOs run high, especially if NGOs can overcome weaknesses such as their localism and limited outreach, lack of technical or professional expertise, and constraints in working both at 'micro' and at 'macro' levels.

'Scaling-up' and 'mainstreaming' represent two separate but interrelated approaches to overcoming these weaknesses and improving NGO capacity to utilise more systematically their experience in developing models which are more effective and efficient than those of the state in dealing with the problems of poverty and powerlessness among the poor. 'Scaling-up' relates to the challenge NGOs face in applying small-scale solutions on a large scale; 'mainstreaming' involves the conversion of such solutions from alternative, NGO-implemented or parallel programmes into the generally and officially accepted policy framework. 'Access strategies' are defined as those which empower poor people to gain access to the resources and programmes of third parties; 'parallel strategies' are those in which NGOs develop their own programmes and institutions. This chapter explores how NGOs respond to these challenges on the basis of research into the growth and dynamics of three big NGOs (BINGOs) in South Asia and six in Latin America (Wils et al 1988, 1990, 1993).

The capacity of NGOs to respond to these challenges is also related to issues of accountability. NGOs want to benefit as many people as possible, effectively and efficiently. This is an essential part of their mission, and both beneficiaries and donors hold them accountable in this respect. However, as NGOs scale-up or mainstream, they face the question of how to preserve their accountability to beneficiaries and donors without losing autonomy and identity (Edwards and

Hulme 1994). Accountability to the grassroots *may* conflict with accountability to donors, including governments. Much depends on *what* NGOs provide and *how* they scale-up and mainstream: the cases reviewed below show considerable variation in this respect, ranging from the delivery of services without empowerment through parallel programmes, to the promotion of self-reliant and autonomous popular movements which demand the redistribution of resources and power. The five strategies used by NGOs in the study to scale-up their impact are reviewed in sequence, before turning to the linkages which exist between scaling-up and accountability.[2]

1. The BINGO option

The BINGO strategy (increasing the number of staff, size of budget and direct outreach) is particularly visible in South Asia, especially in Bangladesh, India and Sri Lanka. In this region our research defined a BINGO (in 1987) as: having at least 500 staff, an annual budget of at least US$1 million, and working directly in 1000 or more rural communities. In Latin America, by contrast, such large NGOs are rare. In Peru and Bolivia, for example, the criteria for BINGOs (1991) were as follows: a minimum of 125 staff, an annual budget of US$1.2 million and a direct outreach covering 25,000 families.

What factors induce such growth in an NGO? Our research found the following factors at work:

■ the extent of real and perceived poverty in a country, and the failure of government agencies to provide an effective response;
■ the original vision of the founder(s);
■ the occurrence of disasters which demanded a sudden, sharp increase in staff, funding and outreach;
■ overcoming the fear of and, problems related to, growth inside the NGO during its expansion.

In addition, it appears that sectoral programmes favoured large-scale activity,[3] especially when the emphasis was placed on standardised and easily-replicable packages to meet basic needs (in health, education, credit and nutrition), rather than on productive activities.[4] Finally, the willingness (and sometimes even the stimulus) of donor agencies to underwrite the cost of expansion is an important factor.[5] Social compensation funds intended to cushion the impact of structural adjustment policies on the most vulnerable groups nearly always rely on NGOs as the principal channel of assistance, yet we found that such funds promote the growth of NGOs only in cases where the NGO's overhead costs are covered, thus enabling the NGO to increase its staff and not just its operational expenditures (Wils et al 1993).

The BINGO option certainly produces complexities at the level of management and internal organisation. The transition from group to institution is not an easy one. The original founder or founders often have great difficulty in relinquishing centralised control; the need for an 'external shield' and separate identity (*vis-à-vis* the state, donors and other NGOs) is often used by NGO managers as an excuse for retaining power in their own hands. Such management problems are often associated with crises in the internal organisation of BINGOs: the gradual emergence of (and struggles over) a clear organisational structure (a division of labour along sectoral lines and geographical decentralisation in decision-making to lower-level units); the evolution of a bottom-up planning system combined with a process of consolidation at higher levels; the formalisation of management, labour relations and working conditions of staff; 'flattening' the hierarchy by reducing the number of layers between senior management and field teams to no more than two or three; the gradual development of an intervention cycle which permits the programmed shift of staff from one region to another, promoting the autonomy of beneficiaries and enabling the NGO to increase its outreach over time without having to continue growing; and the elaboration of a Programming, Monitoring and Evaluation System (PMES) to balance a high level of decentralisation with the maintenance of a sufficient degree of centralised control. The latter is especially important in relation to information, financing, and the provision of high-level but costly technical expertise to field teams and grassroots units. BRAC, for example, employed brick-making experts whose costs, though high, could be distributed over a large number of producers.

These problems and solutions are well known to all who are familiar with modern organisations, whether private or public. But in the case of NGOs, they are embedded in a structure which is systemically 'flatter' and more decentralised than private enterprises or government agencies. It is this kind of structure which permits a BINGO to remain an NGO and retain the 'virtues' thereof: flexibility, a participatory approach and bottom-up planning. Nevertheless, growth from a small NGO to a BINGO is rarely smooth. Some staff and donors fear and resist growth, adhering to the gospel that 'small is beautiful'. Others consider vocation as incompatible with professionalism or specialisation, and consider withdrawal from a region on completion of an intervention cycle as tantamount to 'abandoning' or 'betraying' the NGO's target groups. Such problems must be dealt with constructively if the process of growth is to continue effectively.[6] For example, CEDEP in Peru and INEDER in Bolivia decided not to expand further. INEDER also opted to strengthen the autonomy of regions so that they could graduate from the programme, although in this case disputes over financing and authority reduced the effectiveness of this strategy. Hence, BINGOs differ significantly from one another despite having organisational similarities. Such differences reflect not just variations in context, but also the outcomes of ongoing debates and choices in decision-making. AWARE (in India) had the most 'political' approach of the NGOs in our research, supporting tribal people and Harijans to articulate a stronger identity, claim their rightful share of public resources, and organise themselves into a movement. In contrast, the Sarvodaya movement in Sri Lanka applied traditional community-development and service-delivery approaches. BRAC in Bangladesh was somewhere between the two (in 1987): it focused on very large-scale parallel service-delivery and development, while adopting a more careful approach to empowerment and organisation among beneficiaries. Our study accounted for these differences in terms of national policies with regard to the poor; the political space available to NGOs for engaging in 'political' activities (including non-party politics); the identity of poor people in socio-economic and ethnic terms; the extent to which a parallel or access strategy was viable; the religious background of the countries; and the BINGO's philosophy (Wils et al 1988).

2. Multipliers

Multiplying the scale of an NGO's outreach by working with and through other organisations is obviously easier in countries like the Philippines and India, and in Latin America, where the political space for popular movements is greater. Our research found that opportunities for working with existing popular organisations were most evident in Bolivia (including trade unions) and Brazil, making it possible for bigger NGOs in these countries (though still of only middle range from an South Asian perspective) to reach tens of thousands of families effectively. In Brazil, NGOs have also had success in supporting the establishment and rapid expansion of new grassroots organisations. In extreme cases, small NGOs can reach tens of thousands and sometimes hundreds of thousands of beneficiaries. For example, CESE in Salvador (Brazil), finances a small group of economists and accountants to work with federations of unions of sugar-cane workers; their work helps the unions to formulate an annual package of claims when bargaining with the plantation-owners, directly affecting hundreds of thousands of families. In such cases, powerful multipliers are at work.

Another example is AWARE, which seeks to empower newly established organisations of tribal people and Harijans to make and defend their claims *vis-à-vis* the state programmes which are targetted at them. Sooner or later these new apex organisations begin to act as multipliers of alternative models (such as different types of farming), a more assertive identity and new gender relations. Popular organisations may demand direct access to the NGO's donors and raise doubts regarding the NGO's role (as happened, for example, in Bolivia). Moreover, where such organisations exist,[7] they are often linked to political parties; this may or may not be an obstacle (depending on the NGO's own political ties) and may lead to clientalistic connections. But such connections may also evolve when the organisation owes its emergence, and many of the benefits it receives, to an NGO. There are few NGOs which know how to handle such risks by promoting the autonomy of grassroots organisations from the very start.

Opting for other kinds of organisations as multipliers (universities, church-related organisations, associations of professionals) only works well if they possess their own implementation capacity and have their own linkages with vulnerable groups. Such conditions rarely exist, although they are more common in the field of human rights work. For example, in repressive military regimes the churches often set up their own programmes to support the victims of human rights abuses, and NGOs have attempted to increase their outreach by working with and through such church-related programmes. An interesting example is AGRARIA in Chile which, while only consisting of four or five professional staff, had a considerable impact in the 1980s by working with and through diocesan programmes targetted at small farmers, and via their influence over academics and students in the universities in Santiago.

As vehicles for scaling-up, NGO networks do not emerge strongly from our research: the mere aggregation of the capacities and corresponding outreach of NGOs affiliated to a network produces no incremental net effect. Only when the network decides to *add* resources and activities to those already undertaken are net gains achieved, but such additional outlays are often not supported by donors.[8] Gains in outreach may also be made when NGOs succeed in increasing their efficiency and productivity as a result of an exchange of experiences in the network, and the adoption of similar methods of programming, monitoring and evaluation. As a result, the existing programme can be implemented in less time and resources are freed up for new tasks; the NGOs can take on more work with the same staff or provide a more diversified package of services to the same target group.

3. Planned diffusion of NGO alternatives

By means of seminars and publications, NGOs design an explicit strategy to influence key targets on the basis of alternative models (policies, projects, methods) which they have tried out in pilot projects and whose adoption and diffusion they seek to promote within and outside government. For example, NGOs like DESCO in Lima and BRAC in Dhaka organise seminars on policy issues, inviting politicians, policy-makers and professional associations to discuss subjects which have included alternative industrialisation strategies, the development of peasant agriculture and rural education.

4. Multi-actor programming: widening the horizon

When NGOs begin to think and act 'bigger', they can move to approaches which cover a whole city, province, department or state instead of a small number of communities. Even medium-sized NGOs can apply this strategy, relying both on their own staff and links with carefully identified multiplier organisations. Such strategies exist in Bolivia where bigger NGOs are beginning to consider a whole province as their working area, and in Peru where they covered a large part of metropolitan Lima-Callao or (in the case of IDESI) practically all departments in Peru (Wils et al 1993). Opportunities to follow such strategies increase under structural adjustment and the associated reduction in the role of the state, decentralisation and strengthening of civil society. In these cases NGOs dropped most of their traditional antagonism towards the state, although they still sought to maintain their autonomy and identity when applying models on a larger scale. What they *do* reject is *total substitution* for the state. In some examples, the NGO, together with committees related to a popular organisation, implements large-scale health programmes under contract to the Health Ministry in areas where such programmes never existed; elsewhere, NGOs (again with grassroots committees) undertake basic health and other activities complementary to those of the state. Such collaborative efforts entail official recognition and state subsidies for the cheaper and more effective models of the NGO, so long as they meet certain basic standards. NGOs may also start to work with regional planning corporations, chambers of commerce, parishes, colleges and professional associations in the development of a regional plan, carving out their own (sub-regional and/or thematic) niche.

Through such a multi-actor approach, and by bringing popular organisations into wider platforms or councils, NGOs can help to defend and articulate the interests of poor people at a macro-level and as an integral part of a broader plan. Thus, NGOs can help to secure multiple entries for themselves and for organisations of the poor into the process of designing and carrying out plans and projects for the region. This demands from the NGO a shift and flexibility in thinking so that they are more prepared to work with government and the private business sector, accept funding from them, and enter into the sort of commitments which entail accountability to local actors other than grassroots organisations. The NGO loses its isolated and very private position, becomes a 'public' actor and enters into a more open and transparent world of action.

5. Mainstreaming

Mainstreaming means the incorporation of NGO models into the official policy framework, involving the recognition of the model (new institution, a method of work, a special programme, a diploma for its training programme) and in many cases a (partial) subsidy for its implementation. Such models can be found in housing, primary health care, education, agricultural extension and technology transfer, associative enterprises, credit programmes, technical assistance for informal producers and support programmes for women. Even more than multi-actor planning, mainstreaming requires the NGO to widen its universe of thinking and action. Especially for NGOs born under authoritarian regimes, such a shift is a major step, and takes courage. It also raises difficult questions concerning the NGO's mandate and accountability: on what basis and with what mandate do they advocate alternative models – to the poor, to members or to donors? What criteria should such alternatives meet in order to qualify for public recognition and support?[9]

These questions thrust the role and identity of NGOs into centre stage. The public recognition which they enjoy from multi- and bilateral agencies, followed (with notable reservations) by their own national governments, pushes NGOs into the foreground as important actors in the field of poverty alleviation (and gender, human rights, ethnic minorities and ecology). But such public recognition rarely extends to the popular organisations with whom the NGOs are working. Should NGOs therefore speak on behalf of these organisations, or do so only via and/or together with them? NGOs respond to this question in different ways: some act as professionals committed to the cause of the poor but speaking out with a voice of their own, while others attempt to keep popular organisations involved as much as possible. Some NGOs situate themselves between popular organisations and government agencies, and attempt to bring the two together and facilitate a consensus on particular proposals and policies. As the work of Bratton (1989) and Fowler (1991) on African NGOs suggests, the weight of an NGO's voice at the macro-level depends on the technical quality of its proposals, the level of perceived popular support for them, and the capacity of the NGO to maintain good and workable relations with government. A real or perceived connection with grassroots organisations is therefore an important asset. These observations are even more valid for Asia and Latin America.

NGO alternatives are characterised by small-scale, low-cost and participatory design; the use of people's own traditional technologies; by being paced in their application in accordance with the target groups' own possibilities in terms of time, savings and inputs; by some contribution of these groups to the costs of operation and maintenance; and by effective co-management. It is these features (and especially grassroots participation, control and contribution) which render such alternatives viable, sustainable and responsive to . grassroots needs and possibilities. Were such proposals to be accepted as mainstream methods of organising the provision of basic needs, adjustments would clearly be required in the public sector, and in the roles and responsibility of state and civil society. Community participation and shared management would be incompatible with vertical, standardised and centralised government control. Hence, mainstreaming NGO models requires sufficient political, economic, social and institutional space to make room for them.[10] Scaling-up does not necessarily imply major changes in the relationship between NGOs and the state, especially when NGOs continue to expand their own parallel programmes through foreign funding. Mainstreaming, on the other hand, implies an important qualitative shift in the relationship between civil society and the state – between organised groups of the poor and access to policy makers and resources. Mainstreaming the adoption and implementation of NGO alternatives often demands reforms in the relationship between society and the state. For example, in rethinking traditional, centralised policies and programmes; decentralising decision-making and resource allocation from central to local levels; increasing the claim-making and participatory capacities of organised groups of the poor; moving the state from a dominant to an enabling role; and introducing new, public-private funding for social programmes.

In this process, informal grassroots and NGO solutions can be linked to formal systems and be granted a more formal status, but without losing their roots in the community. Co-financing of the sort already visible in municipalities in Chile and Colombia supports such systems, although reforms in the state are very hard to achieve, even in the limited forms related to structural adjustment policies. Difficult questions are raised by mainstreaming in this way. For example, does it not lead to formalised systems targetted exclusively (as in a parallel strategy) to the poor? Would not such a 'parallel' system for poor communities be seen as discriminatory, smacking of 'dual citizenship'? How would universal requirements (say, in the field of primary and adult education) be combined with the special needs of groups such as poor women and ethnic minorities? How could economies of scale be preserved when buying medicine, teaching materials and inputs for micro-enterprises, while simultaneously maintaining effective local participation and control in the design and implementation of programmes? How would the costs of such programmes be divided between state, grassroots and NGO? These and other questions will inevitably emerge as different actors learn to steer a course which is viable and sustainable. In the 'politics of mainstreaming', obstacles and opportunities have to be confronted continually as popular organisations and NGOs come to play more dynamic and 'public' roles of their own.

6. Scaling-up, mainstreaming and accountability

From the narrow viewpoint of cost-effectiveness as well as the broader perspective of NGO responses to the endemic problems of poverty and powerlessness, NGOs simply cannot avoid the challenge of trying to scale-up the effective outreach of their work. NGOs are accountable for their performance in relation to this challenge, to their own mission and potential, and not simply to third parties such as donors and governments. Of course, scaling-up must not be achieved at the expense of quality and depth, and our research shows that there is no necessary trade-off between scale and effectiveness. This applies both to the social and political effects of large-scale programmes and organisations, especially big NGOs which combine a multiplier and access strategy with empowerment (as in AWARE and IPTK, Bolivia); and to the social and economic effects of BINGOs such as BRAC, IDESI and FOVIDA (in Peru), and AWARE's access strategy in rural Andhra Pradesh (Wils et al 1988, 1993). The three criteria related to scale identified in our research (number of staff, total yearly budget – institutional and operational costs – and the number of families or communities reached, directly or indirectly) are interrelated but not necessarily strongly correlated. In any analysis of scaling-up, attention should be paid to each one of the three criteria separately, and to the ways in which the NGO tries to find an optimal combination among them. Yet among NGOs and donor agencies (including most of those in the Netherlands) there is still a strong current of opinion which continues to argue that 'small is beautiful' and 'big is ugly'. From our perspective, any NGO should, in principle, consider using one or another of the strategies discussed above to scale-up its impact (see also Edwards and Hulme 1992).

Current levels of interest in results and impact (rather than in activism and good intentions) reflect a shift in the external basis of legitimacy of NGOs and the source of their funding, both in Northern and in Southern countries. Whether or not the current neo-liberal near-hegemony persists, strengthening civil society and the role and position of the poor in it, remains a basic mission of NGOs which is often laid down in their constitution. The fulfilment of this mission demands that poverty and powerlessness are tackled on a relevant scale. Whether NGOs do this alone or together with other NGOs, 'making a difference' is, to an important extent, a function of mass. Hence, I would argue that there is also an internal basis of legitimacy for NGOs to scale-up effectively. The NGO itself may remain small or medium-sized, yet it faces a real challenge to maximise the outreach of its work.

The problems of NGO accountability referred to by Edwards and Hulme in their Introduction especially affect those NGOs which possess considerable absorptive capacity (the big NGOs), which renders them attractive to domestic government as well as to multi- and bilateral donors. To assume that these NGOs passively accept the conditions applied by donors is erroneous; our research shows that bigger NGOs have a significant degree of bargaining power, precisely because of their absorptive capacity, and/or because they have succeeded in developing viable alternatives in service-provision or economic support to the poor. They took the initiative, sought and obtained public financing for their own programmes. As in India and Bolivia, even when big NGOs agree to help implement government programmes, they succeed in reformulating and improving such programmes to a significant extent. For example, while helping to implement the government's health programme in its region under contract, IPTK managed to include the work of grassroots health services and committees, and to link these informal systems to the formal system of the government.

Other variables which affect the relationship between scaling-up and the accountability of NGOs 'upwards' to the state, are the type of programme and the approach adopted for implementation. As Tendler (1987) has noted, and as our studies of big NGOs confirm, social-service programmes often generate less social conflict locally than economic programmes, and are more readily supported by public agencies. In addition, an 'empowerment approach' which promotes autonomous apex organisations and the claim-making power and assertiveness of the poor in competing for access and control of (especially public) resources, is prone to upset the *status quo*, and appears less palatable to local government agencies and groups closely linked to them. On the other hand, central governments and official donor agencies vary in the degree to which they accept and are willing actively to support such an approach. A more equitable redistribution of power and resources, as well as considerations of sustainability and grassroots participation and support, are not the sole prerogatives of NGO discourse; they figure in public agencies too.

Hence, problems of NGO accountability (especially of big NGOs) should not be over-simplified nor be seen only in connection with their growing dependency on public funding. Such public sources (both domestic and external) are far from monolithic and vary considerably in interests and ideology: NGOs are not powerless either, especially if they are large in size. Our research shows that accountability to domestic and external donors is mediated by the nature and strength of NGO connections with the grassroots; it is the scope and depth of this connection that helps NGOs to legitimise themselves *vis-à-vis* domestic and foreign donors. Any move to distance NGOs from their grassroots connections must be resisted. A central theme in this debate is how to strengthen *downward* accountability among NGOs. Our studies suggest that NGOs that use an empowerment approach with autonomous apex organisations of beneficiaries (or with popular movements), were more accountable 'downwards' than NGOs which focused primarily on the delivery of services (such as Sarvodaya in Sri Lanka, CIPCA in Bolivia and CEDEP in Peru). AWARE in India, IPTK in Bolivia and FOVIDA in Peru, provide good examples of the former.

Thus far, downward accountability is poorly instrumentalised in most NGOs. Participatory programming, monitoring and evaluation systems are one of the best and most promising of instruments, especially when linked to contractual agreements between NGOs and their target groups. Examples include AWARE and CYSD in India, SUNGI in Pakistan, ENLACE in Mexico, SERGUS in Guatemala, and TIN-TUA in Burkina Faso. These agreements need to specify the gradual and systematic transfer (where possible) of projects and resources to organised groups at grassroots level in the course of an intervention cycle. Participatory monitoring can maintain accountability in this way as the work evolves (Neggers and Wils 1987). Such agreements also help to prevent (or at least weaken) NGO paternalism, and help to make their links with the grassroots more transparent and balanced than is usually the case.

Current decentralisation policies may also help to improve the local (rather than the external) accountability of NGOs, both in relation to grassroots organisations and to other sectors and groups in local society, whether private or public. This is particularly important when their respective resources are being pooled, articulated and programmed in the context of joint (micro)-regional planning. These and other issues render the challenge of NGO accountability more serious, complex and important than it has ever been before.

Notes

1. I gratefully acknowledge the important contributions of Jan Neggers (NOVIB) with whom I share many of the ideas set out in this article. I also thank Jacques Remmerswaal of the Dutch Ministry of Development Cooperation who helped in the Latin American studies, and the participants who actively contributed to my course at the Institute of Social Studies on 'NGDOs and Development'.
2. These strategies are similar to those presented in Edwards and Hulme (1992), who distinguish between 'additive' strategies (implying organisational and programme growth); 'multiplicative' strategies (networking, policy and legal reform through advocacy, working with government and training); and 'diffusive' strategies (spontaneous and informal).
3. The importance of a clear sectoral focus confirms Tendler's (1987) conclusions. It should be recognised, however, that sectorialisation does not exclude and often facilitates the articulation of intersectoral connections at an operational level.
4. More specifically, we found that in productive programmes, larger-scale operations usually referred to inputs, marketing, outputs, and the provision of support in areas like credit and training, rather than to productive activities proper. The latter tend to remain small-scale, require the assembly in loco of various kinds of inputs, and are themselves rarely amenable to large-scale operations.
5. The donor consortia for BRAC and other BINGOs in South Asia are good examples, something which still seems hard to achieve in Latin America.
6. It is possible that large NGOs generate a 'critical mass' which helps to overcome personalised tensions and conflicts. It would also be interesting to examine in detail what happens to staff turnover in such NGOs; a high degree of staff commitment may not be the best basis for sustained action since staff may be more vulnerable to frustration. In addition, salary levels and working conditions, including opportunities for upward mobility and training, are also important. Such conditions are often better in large NGOs than in small ones.
7. Autonomous popular organisations are more frequent in Latin America than in Asia and Africa.
8. What is needed is more than human and material resources. What is necessary (and here donors often hesitate) is special organisational measures (reflected in additional overhead costs) to design, monitor and evaluate the extra programmes.
9. The accountability of NGOs to the poor is often more of a self-professed obligation than a real and effective practice, supported by participatory systems, consultative or participatory bodies for policy-making and review, and so on.
10. In a sense, this means going back to the historical sequence of Western patterns of development, in which what later became public and universal programmes and provisions were developed through a bottom-up process from local to higher levels, sharing methods, modules, training, and resources. Many southern countries have attempted to reverse this sequence by starting with the end-product: a state made responsible for welfare, but without the resource base to make this possible.

6

European NGOs and Democratisation in Central America: Assessing Performance in the Light of Changing Priorities

Kees Biekart

Reassessing and rethinking aid policies

After visiting twenty European NGOs in 1993 to survey their policies on Central America, I was left with the impression that Northern NGOs (NNGOs) are experiencing an (often productive) crisis of identity. Mission statements are being reviewed, policies and priorities redefined, management reorganised and legitimacy questioned. Although some NNGOs have been temporarily para-lysed by this internal reassessment, it is a positive sign that profound rethinking is going on, which may give a new impulse to the debate on reshaping (non-governmental) development co-operation at the dawn of a new millennium.[1]

This new sense of urgency has coincided with the ideological changes of the post-Cold War period, but has also been influenced by tighter requirements for management and organisation, and by increased dependence among NNGOs on official aid. One of the questions arising from this reassessment concerns the impact of development projects implemented by NNGO partners in the South. Although many individual development projects have been successful, their combined impact on macro-structures has been disappointing (Edwards and Hulme 1992). The performance of NGOs has been seriously questioned in recent years by journalists, academics and former NNGO-workers.[2] As private contributors have become more critical and conscious of development issues, these public doubts have had to be countered, for example, by commissioning independent impact studies.[3]

A common conclusion of these studies is the difficulty of assessing the impact of NGO development programmes as a result of poor data, diffuse objectives, rapidly changing circumstances and poor-quality evaluation; performance cannot be quantified and has to be judged by anecdotal and circumstantial evidence. Issues of efficiency, internal organisation and financial management are easier to assess and have led to changes in policies and a number of useful recommendations. At the same time, evidence from Central America shows that the policies of European NGOs toward their local partners have changed sig-nificantly over the last 15 years, with important implications for the ways in which performance and impact are measured. The central question of this chapter is: what lies behind these changes if performance *is* so difficult to assess? [4] Are Northern agendas more important than impact when defined in local terms?

The following analysis is based on the results of a research programme initiated by the Transnational Institute, in which Central American and European researchers carried out an assessment of the impact of European NGO-financed programmes on democratisation in El Salvador, Guatemala and Honduras (Biekart 1994). The findings show some inconsistencies between performance assessment and decisions over programming, which shed new light on the changing relationships between NGOs in the South and the North. In particular, the changing political context for aid since 1980 has led to important shifts in policy and performance-measurement which have not been discussed or negotiated openly between Northern donors and their Central American partners.

European NGOs and Central America

Two issues need to be examined in order to understand the special position of Central America in current NNGO policy debates: the priority given to the region by European and Canadian NGOs and official agencies during the 1980s, and their widespread disillusionment following the defeat of the Sandinistas in the 1990 Nicaraguan elections.

Political priority during the 1980s   Aside from two earthquakes in the 1970s that attracted international humanitarian assistance, Central America rarely appeared on the maps of Northern development agencies before 1980. However, in 1980 aid began to increase rapidly, tripling to US$1.7 billion per annum by 1987 (Visser and Wattel 1991). Some 15 per cent of this total was provided by European and Canadian NGOs, and solidarity groups, who started to operate programmes first in Nicaragua, and from the mid-1980s in other Central American countries. Over 30 per cent of the total aid budget of some NNGOs was dedicated to Central America during this period. [5]

These large amounts of non-governmental aid (in comparison to the small size of the region) were a reaction to the political crisis which followed the victory of the Sandinista revolutionaries in Nicaragua in 1979. Under the newly elected President Reagan, the US Administration made the rollback of revolution in Central America into one of the top priorities for US foreign policy. Starting in 1981, the US intervention marked the beginning of a region-wide eruption of civil war which transformed Central America into a major battleground of the Cold War in the 1980s. One reason why so much assistance was channelled to the region by some European agencies during this period was their explicit rejection of US foreign policy. NGOs in Europe also saw the Sandinista revolution as a genuine, alternative development path worthy of strong support. In a context of widespread war and repression in Central America, social organisations that had emerged in the 1970s suffered a serious set-back. New intermediary NGOs were established by the political opposition, and they became the partners of European and progressive North American NNGOs in counterbalancing the activities of US-financed NGOs acting under the umbrella of 'counterinsurgency'. As one observer put it: 'only two institutions have consistently flourished in the Central American crisis: the military and the NGOs' (Lewis 1990, p 1).

For this reason, all development aid to the region had a strong political dimension. NNGOs were used by European governments to channel aid to SNGOs and grassroots organisations (GROs) in Central America, thereby avoiding direct contact with US-backed authoritarian regimes. Local opposition groups constantly referred to European NGOs as agencies of 'international solidarity', although many tried to maintain a more neutral profile. While Nicaragua was converted into a 'playground' for experimental development strategies, aid to NGOs in El Salvador and Guatemala served mainly to give more room for manoeuvre to a clandestine opposition struggling to preserve their physical survival, protect human rights, provide relief for refugees and displaced people, and channel resources to urban and rural social movements. The development discourse in Europe prioritised empowerment and poverty-eradication, but this masked the reality of political survival for local partners. European NGO field representatives were aware that these realities affected the quality and sustainability of SNGO projects, especially in areas of conflict. As a Danish NGO manager put it: 'when local project staff were contracted, political criteria were more important than the technical or administrative experience of the candidates.'[6] It was a public secret that funds for development projects were often diverted to political and military struggles. Long-term planning and strategy were absent from the Central America desks of most European NGOs at this time. Only a quarter of the NNGOs in our survey produced written policy documents on Central America, leaving policy decisions to the political judgement of local representatives. This pattern was to change substantially in the 1990s.

After 1990: the post-revolutionary era   The end of the Cold War coincided with the end of the Sandinista government, and their loss of credibility in the aftermath of the Nicaraguan elections.[7] Combined with the desperate military offensive of November 1989 in El Salvador and the reopening of peace talks, this provoked profound reflection among NGOs in Europe on development policies toward Central America. With the gradual return to peace, the region lost its status as a top-priority area for emergency assistance and international attention, although official and private foreign aid to Central America was not reduced.[8] However, the sudden political changes in the region generated unrest among the SNGO community, along with fears that foreign aid would be cut. For example, the transition to peace in El Salvador caused NGOs to redefine their ties with political parties and grassroots organisations, and take up a more co-operative relationship with state institutions in charge of the National Reconstruction Plan. The NGOs of the 1980s found this transition exceptionally difficult, especially since many were also criticised by their former beneficiaries for being paternalistic and corrupt.[9] The breakdown of the revolutionary perspective obviously generated disillusionment, with NGOs having to rethink their work in relation to democracy, development and the role of the state.

On top of the confusion created by changing political conditions in the region in the late-1980s, Central American NGOs were faced with a new aid discourse emanating largely from bilateral and multilateral agencies in the North after the end of the Cold War. Market-oriented strategies and 'good governance', combined with a more prominent and professional role for NGOs, appear to be crucial elements in this new agenda. Calls from the Northern donor community for greater efficiency and more professionalism increased, and it became clear that the era of unconditional funding born of political solidarity, was at an end. The Central American NGO community is taking a defensive attitude toward the demands emerging from Northern agencies as a result of these changes.

Democratisation and the limits to performance assessment   One of the goals of the Transnational Institute's research is to find out whether European NGO assistance has contributed to higher levels of participation and to the strengthening of GROs. However, reviewing the experience of Central America in the 1980s from the new and still confusing perspective of the 1990s is a difficult task. As other chapters in this book show, NGO performance-assessment is always a complicated affair; in Central America, the changing context for aid and development brings further difficulties. For example, the application of performance criteria concerning internal democracy to NGOs in Central America is now considered essential by donors, but these criteria were not in use ten years ago. This makes retrospective evaluation of NGO impact on democratisation misleading.

Measuring the impact of NGO activities directed at enhancing participation and organisational capacities is a complex enterprise not only because of the wide range of influences at work, but also because crucial data are not available. Reliable data from the initial stages of projects, and information concerning the political context at project-level, are scarce. Initial objectives and success criteria are rarely documented. As noted above, even European NGOs did not have written policy documents dating back to the 1980s. Obviously, this makes performance assessment virtually impossible.

In the 1980s, European NGOs rarely included impact assessments in their project evaluations, and were therefore obliged to judge the results of their assistance from personal impressions. Their judgements are generally positive, especially in terms of grassroots-level empowerment and political survival. As Oxfam-UK commented: 'the final balance of our work in Central America is positive if we use the indicator that many people managed to survive thanks to foreign NNGO aid.' Some NNGO staff members complained about the weak impact of SNGOs on government policies, but macro-level change was not the goal of NGOs in Central America at this time because of the scale of political repression that existed and its impact on the political space available for GROs and NGOs. Again, NGOs in Europe were applying criteria retrospectively which had not been used at the time that grants were made.

Our research also included participatory evaluation to find out what the beneficiaries of SNGO work felt about the results of empowerment-oriented projects. From these evaluations it became clear that donors and beneficiaries were using different definitions of impact and performance. Donor NGOs tended to overemphasise financial management and short-term material outputs; beneficiaries tended to look for modest changes in organisations over a longer period of time. For example, the impact of a training centre for union leaders in Honduras was praised by trainees; for them it had clearly contributed to closer collaboration between unions that had not wanted to work together before.[10] Union leaders measured performance in terms of high and regular attendance at classes, and the fact that some had managed to secure more responsible positions in the union as a result of their training. In other words, they valued modest changes with a non-quantifiable impact in the long-run. However, the main NNGO donor to the project announced that they would cut their funding, arguing that the training centre was using 'old-fashioned' methodologies, and that the organisation was too closely related to a particular political faction.

The fear of exposing confidential linkages between local NGOs and clan-destine political parties makes research on NGOs in Central America highly sensitive. Even independent local researchers in the team confessed that they felt unable to touch on this topic, for reasons of security and because SNGOs feared that aid would be cut if (even previous) linkages with politico-military parties were exposed. Even in El Salvador, where connections between SNGOs and the five political tendencies within the FMLN[11] are today being discussed publicly, both SNGOs and researchers avoided an issue which is crucial to any under-standing of the political survival mechanisms of the 1980s in that country.

The 'New Policy Agenda' of European NGOs in Central America

TNI's research focused on European NGOs because they have been the most committed to supporting the political opposition in Central America during the 1980s. Current changes in European NGO priorities can be analysed in three areas: financial commitments, thematic priorities and organisational demands.

Funding levels   After the collapse of the Nicaraguan revolution and the signing of the peace agreement in El Salvador, NGOs in Central America feared that aid to them would be cut drastically, and that any new aid would be channelled directly to the newly elected governments. However, the evidence (up to 1993) does not confirm these fears.[12] On average, European NGOs allocated the same amount to Central America between 1990 and 1993, and in some cases even increased their allocations, although the figures vary from one country to another.[13]

NNGO assistance to the rest of Latin America has certainly declined. For example, Hivos (a Dutch NGO) allocated 65 per cent of its overseas budget to Latin America in 1987, but only 48 per cent in 1992; the figure will continue to fall in the years ahead, as NGO programmes in Chile, Brazil and other indus-trialising countries in Latin America are closed down in the face of social, economic and political improvements. Will the same trend also affect Central America? The evidence shows that *official* aid to Central America from the United States, Italy, Spain and France has already been reduced (Hansen 1994), and pressure on official aid budgets will have repercussions for those European NNGOs which are highly dependent on funding from their own governments.[14] It is therefore to be expected that funding levels from European NGOs to NGOs and GROs in Central America will eventually decline. Consequently, they will have to look for new sources of funds from multilateral agencies such as UNDP and the Inter-American Development Bank, which have introduced significant new programmes in Central America since 1990.

New priorities   Given the great variety of priority areas for European NGO investment in Central America, and the fact that many only recently produced policy documents for the region, care must be taken in generalising about trends. However, two new (post-1990) themes emerged from TNI's research: production-oriented projects and advocacy. It is not surprising that the emphasis at project level has moved from political to economic survival. For example, the number of 'political education' projects has fallen in favour of projects that aim to strengthen market capacities.[15] In addition, European NGOs are pressurising their partners to redefine their role in democratisation, and clarify their responsibilities in relation to other actors in civil society. One of the frequent criticisms made of NGOs in Central America is that they have been substituting for the role of social organisations and political parties, and should start to play a more technical or professional role in the new political climate.[16] These new roles could include advocacy and technical assistance to newly emerging networks of social organisations in the region, although some NNGOs doubt the legitimacy of these regional networks.[17] Performance in both these areas is more easily assessable in the short term than previous strategies devoted to empowerment or methodologies of political education. This is, perhaps, no accident.

New organisational requirements   The most fundamental policy changes revealed by the research are found in the way in which European NGOs feel development projects ought to be organised and managed.[18] Tighter requirements for efficiency, cost-effectiveness and professionalism are now applied to NGOs in Central America. Internal reorganisation and market-oriented strategies are supposed to lead to economically sustainable organisations, and partner agencies are being pressured to diversify their funding sources and develop a greater level of self-sufficiency. Other requirements deal with improving accountability via systematic monitoring and evaluation.

   None of these new requirements will appear unusual to anyone in the donor community, but they have had a major impact in Central America. Although SNGOs admit that they should operate more professionally and efficiently, this was impossible during the period of survival in the crisis years of the 1980s. Central American NGOs consider it unfair to impose new criteria in response to perceived poor performance during previous years when NGOs faced very different conditions.

Consulting or imposing?   This brings me to my central argument. Changes in the policies of European NGOs towards Central America do seem to have been generated by changes in values and criteria that were in turn the result of developments taking place outside the region. They have nothing to do with the transition from war to peace in Central America, and this makes them hard to accept for SNGOs locally. Although efforts were made by donors to consult their partners on these new policy priorities, TNI's research encountered a widespread feeling that changes had been imposed. This reflects a one-sided transparency in relations between donors and partners: many SNGOs and GROs complained that they do not understand the reasons for European NGO policy changes, nor the relationship between these policy changes and the origins of NNGO funding. These feelings are directly related to weaknesses in partnership between European and Central American NGOs, and the generally low level of accountability of NNGOs towards their partners.

Faced by the revision and restructuring of aid policies by Northern NGOs, NGOs and GROs in Central America have taken up a defensive position. Mutual competition for new aid resources (extremely intense in the cases of El Salvador and Nicaragua) is weakening efforts to improve co-ordination, and threatens to relegate issues of quality to the bottom of the list of priorities. This is alarming, but understandable. Many SNGOs are still in the middle of a transition from war (when autonomy *vis-à-vis* donors was higher) to a post-war period where they find themselves more vulnerable to external pressures. This transition becomes more difficult the longer they lag behind in debates which are taking place within the Northern aid community.

Conclusions

Are the claims of inconsistency in European NGO policies reasonable? First, old and new policies are certainly sometimes applied simultaneously, which causes a good deal of the confusion. An example is Guatemala, which since 1991 is a priority for European NGOs in Central America following the successful end of the war in El Salvador. Key priorities in Guatemala (where civil war continues) are the return of refugees from Mexico and the protection of human rights. These are implicit political issues, as they were also in El Salvador during the war. However, the new enthusiasm of NNGOs for improved management and performance makes Guatemalan NGOs feel that they are being treated differently from their Salvadoran counterparts during the latter's civil war in the 1980s. At the opposite extreme, Nicaraguan and Honduran NGOs argue that it is inconsistent of European NGOs to diminish their activities in these countries and to increase aid to Guatemala, when Guatemala has lower poverty figures than they do. Herein lies the dilemma of delinking policy from performance in a rapidly changing environment.

Secondly, it is inconsistent to apply criteria on performance developed in the 1990s to the much more difficult period of the 1980s, in which aid to SNGOs and GROs was not used for development (except in Nicaragua), but to ensure the survival of the political opposition. The impact of European NGOs on democratisation in the region is difficult to assess since the data do not exist, although (as in El Salvador) the political opposition did survive in many countries, in part thanks to foreign aid. Criticisms now being made by NNGOs about the poor performance of SNGOs in the 1980s are unfair, and cannot be used to justify policy changes in more recent years.

In the light of these dilemmas, what can be said about the capacity of Southern NGOs to pursue their mission of social transformation in spite of the constraints put forward by the new policy agendas of Northern donors? In the particular case of Central America, it is possible to foresee a combined role for Northern NGOs committed to supporting the process of social transformation, and the community of local NGOs and GROs, on the following conditions: European NGOs need to make an effort to increase mutual co-ordination of their projects and policies in Central America, to prevent unnecessary competition and to improve joint advocacy towards their home governments and publics. More transparency and accountability toward their partners on internal policy discussions is vital; active involvement of SNGOs in policy- and decision-making will pay off in the long run. Policy-making should be based much more consistently on mutually agreed performance standards in order to prevent confusion and indifference setting in. It might even be better to drop the term 'partnership' in favour of more systematic attempts to reduce the financial dependence of NGOs in the South.

Although Central American NGOs and GROs are not enthusiastic about the new requirements for better management and more professionalism that are an inescapable part of the New Policy Agenda, they accept that this will benefit performance in the long run. However, their reactions to this debate go much further than negotiations over performance criteria, highlighting at least three much more fundamental changes.

First, the need to increase SNGO capacity to undertake policy-oriented research, produce viable policy alternatives and develop mechanisms for co-ordination and joint advocacy at the national and international levels, together with Northern partners. This is especially important for networks of GROs such as ASOCODE (the network of peasant organisations in Central America).

Second, the importance of developing local (Southern) standards for performance assessment, although this presupposes a self-confidence within the Southern NGO community that is often lacking, and the absence of the feelings of insecurity that are caused by widespread fears of aid cuts.

Therefore, and third, the crucial need to move to longer-term self-sufficiency and the exploitation of local financial resources. Moves in this direction could strengthen the legitimacy of SNGOs and make them less vulnerable to the policy shifts of NNGOs and official donor agencies in the North. This will make the development of an indigenous cultural and political identity much more probable, and improve the likelihood that NGOs and GROs in Central America will be able to pursue a mission for social transformation both effectively and efficiently in the late-1990s and beyond.

Notes

1. A good example is Riddell, R (1993).
2. Many examples could be mentioned, especially from Northern Europe, such as public reaction to the Dutch NGO impact study and the controversy in Belgium surrounding the publication of *Het Orkest van de Titanic* (Leuven: VUBPRESS/StudentAid 1993) in which a former NGO worker heavily criticised the Belgian NGO-community.
3. See Danida (1989); Riddell (1990); the impact study of four Dutch NGOs: '*Bete-*

kenis van het medefinancieringsprogramma, een verkenning' (Oegstgeest, GOM 1991); and Finnida (1994).

4. Alan Fowler's chapter in this volume lists some of the difficulties involved in measuring the performance and impact of NGOs.

5. For example, the Swedish NGO Diakonia allocated 38 per cent of its overseas budget to Central America in 1987; Oxfam-Belgium increased its expenditure for Central America from 27 per cent of its total aid budget in 1987 to 38 per cent in 1992.

6. Central America Co-ordinator of IBIS, a Danish NGO, in a speech to the Third International Consultation on Development Co-operation, Managua, 1991.

7. After the elections it became known that Sandinista government officials had taken advantage of their positions to confiscate former state properties, which became known as the *piñata* (a traditional Nicaraguan birthday game for children).

8. Official aid from European governments grew between 1987 and 1993, but declined thereafter (Hansen 1994).

9. See *Pensamiento Propio* 87 (January–February 1992) and 91 (June 1992), in which the regional co-ordinator of ASOCODE (the network of peasant organisations) openly criticised the NGOs they were working with. This generated a public debate in Nicaragua and Costa Rica on the role of NGOs and their relations with GROs.

10. The case study looked at the Honduran NGO IDEPH and the Dutch NGO Hivos.

11. The Farabundo Marti National Liberation Front has been the principal political and military opposition force in El Salvador during the decade of civil war.

12. We calculated that combined European NNGO aid to Central America increased from US$120 million in 1987 to nearly US$200 million in 1992. The European NNGOs we surveyed in 1993 had already made their commitments for the coming years and did not foresee drastic cuts before 1995.

13. Nicaragua has been the highest priority throughout the 1980s in terms of aid allocations from European NGOs. In 1990 El Salvador became the main recipient, and since 1992 Guatemala has been given the highest priority. This variation explains why complaints about aid cuts are made, especially by the well-organised NGO communities in Nicaragua and El Salvador.

14. Three major Dutch NGOs (Cebemo, ICCO and Hivos) and three German NGOs (EZE, Friedrich Ebert Foundation and the Konrad Adenauer Foundation) are 100 per cent dependent on government funding. This makes them very vulnerable to official policy changes.

15. This change of emphasis from 'political relevance to economic relevance' (as it is called by many NNGOs), was in the case of the Honduran NGO, IDEPH, perceived as a rejection of popular education. However, the donor agency (Hivos) explained that popular education could never be an end in itself and had to be treated in the future as an integral element of development projects.

16. This was the central message of the Dutch NGO Cebemo to its key partners in the region when discussing new forms of co-operation (see Cebemo (1993)).

17. The Danish NGO Danchurchaid commented that it is not always clear who these regional networks of farmers' and workers' organisations represent, nor who controls them. The non-church-based NGOs in Europe (like Oxfam-UK, Ibis, Hivos and Novib) have been the most supportive of regional advocacy efforts.

18. All NNGOs surveyed mentioned the improvement of organisational capacities among partners as the major challenge in Central America, with variations in emphasis: the Swedish NGO Radda Barnen considered 'internal democratisation of partner organisations' as the major priority, whereas the Danish NGO IBIS mentioned management-training and institution-building of SNGOs as its main challenge in Central America.

7

From Accountability to Shared Responsibility: NGO Evaluation in Latin America

Hector Béjar and Peter Oakley

In Latin America today NGOs are the subject of much critical comment and debate, most of which is coming from European Governments and NGO financing partners in Europe and Canada. At the same time, multilateral organisations like the World Bank, the Inter-American Development Bank, UNDP and others are 'discovering' NGO virtues and skills. What are these qualities? In Latin America it could be argued that the close relationship NGOs have with grassroots organisations (GROs) is their greatest strength. NGOs show a real commitment to change in their societies and generally they work with lower overheads than governmental and multilateral organisations; the level of salaries, office space and facilities of most NGOs in Latin America are evidence that they function on very tight budgets. At the same time, the number of NGOs is proliferating in line with global trends (UNDP 1993). In several countries – Brazil, Colombia and Peru, for example – this growth has been spectacular: in Peru in 1980 there were an estimated 218 registered NGOs working on development issues, a number which had grown to 897 by 1993 (Noriega and Saravia 1994).[1]

But as expectations of NGOs have grown, the non-governmental community has become more concerned about 'impact', 'assessment', 'evaluation', 'cost-benefit analysis' and 'sustainability'. In this dialogue, Latin American NGOs are becoming the targets of more critical observation. In this debate it is important to recognise the influence that macro-level policies have had on NGO work in Latin America. Recent years have registered important changes which are reshaping the macro-context in which Latin American NGOs work. In post-structural adjustment economies, there is emerging evidence that some of the vitality of grassroots organisations has been swept away by the free market. For example, the major trade unions of state employers have either lost influence or even been dissolved as massive lay-offs have greatly reduced their membership. Similarly, many industrial workers' unions have been weakened through loss of membership due to the prolonged recession. In rural areas in Latin America, violence and the rolling back of enthusiasm for land reform in the 1970s have debilitated a range of social movements and organisations. In this situation the relationship between NGOs and GROs in Latin America has inevitably been weakened (El Taller 1993).

In this context new social actors have begun to emerge who are beginning to replace the more traditional forms of popular organisations. Some, like women's groups and organisations of small businesses, are already beginning to link up with existing NGOs through training and credit programmes. Other actors, such as the swelling ranks of the unemployed, working children and casual workers are visible and large in numbers, but as yet lack organisations or spokespersons to represent them. In this situation new issues and problems have arisen; for example, in countries affected by violence, human rights are an increasingly important area of work. New groups are becoming the target population for NGO work: microenterprises, children, women and victims of violence. In fact, there is a new agenda and with this new agenda comes the need for new methodologies of NGO work. NGOs are assuming a more direct dialogue with their societies and governments, and frequently they play a protagonistic role in defending human rights and the protection of environmental resources. At the same time, they continue to work in providing welfare services to those hardest-hit by economic and social change. NGOs are obliged to attend to a population in extreme poverty and, as a result, their expectations of structural change in society have had to be postponed.

In recent times, many of the resources of Northern NGOs have begun to be provided by Northern governments (Hulme and Edwards 1995). The amount of public funds managed by Northern NGOs has been increasing for some years. Increasing dependence on government funding strengthens the chain of influence which derives from government policies, continues through Northern donor agencies, follows on through Southern NGOs, and ends with GROs or directly with target groups in the South. In this process, the presence and weight of Northern governments are becoming more and more important. However, having compared the costs and benefits of this approach, some policy-makers in the North now think that this process is too expensive. They argue that it is necessary to diminish or even eliminate the role of one of these intermediaries – the Northern NGOs (Bebbington and Riddell 1995). If these recommendations become a reality, Southern NGOs will depend increasingly directly on the support of Northern governments and multilateral organisations. And if this trend were to continue, in the long term civil society's role would tend to decrease and accountability to governments would tend to increase. On the other hand, the impact of international co-operation and private development initiatives should not be exaggerated. They form only a small proportion of financial and trading links which operate in a world where barriers erected by the richest countries are maintained at the expense of the economically weak. Often, the benefits provided by international organisations are erased by the costs of commercial and other financial forces.

Therefore, it is very difficult to measure 'results' and to evaluate the work of NGOs in Latin America without taking a global approach to international co-operation. Of course, it is not our intention to say that actors in the South are not accountable at all in this difficult situation. Rather we suggest two key propositions: first, responsibilities must be shared by NGOs in the North and in the South; and secondly, NGOs must work together to secure changes in global macro-policies. In theory, the concept of shared responsibility also refers to governments, multinational enterprises, multilateral organisations and financial institutions. However, in the South, the reality is that policies are often dictated by or imposed on governments by the international financial institutions. Faced by this situation, the key task is to abandon unequal relationships between donors and recipients in favour of an effective South–North dialogue around common and practical tasks. This also means that it is necessary to have a common commitment toward (and understanding of) the strengthening of civil society throughout the developing world.

Evaluation and accountability

Like development agencies in other parts of the world, Latin American NGOs have in the past decade or so had to come to terms with the question, 'How effective are we?'. How far can we argue, in general terms, that NGOs are able to achieve what they state that they intend to achieve? This is not, of course, an exact science; nor is it possible to produce authoritative statements which represent an accurate description of the whole universe of NGOs in the region. The NGOs from whose work these conclusions are drawn are intermediary NGOs who concentrate on information work, strategies to multiply their impact, advocacy and institution-building (Carroll 1992). They are not service-providers. For such NGOs, accountability is currently seen largely in terms of satisfying the donors who support them; trends toward 'downward' account-ability (to the people they supposedly serve) are much less strong. These NGOs argue that they make a reality of the current 'popular' view of NGOs as development agencies: participatory, flexible and innovative. They also agonise; they agonise over the whole process of programme and project evaluation; they often question its relevance and they have at times widely conflicting views of how to go about doing it. 'Evaluation' is an emotive word to most Latin American NGOs and its mere introduction to a debate can frequently spark off an even more intense exchange of views.

In trying to make some general statements and suggest some conclusions concerning NGO evaluation and accountability in Latin America today, we have drawn heavily from the lessons of practice in which we have been involved over the past few years, particularly from the following:

- An evaluation of the work of ADAR, a Peruvian NGO working in health among rural communities along the banks of the Peruvian Amazon. The evaluation was undertaken by a joint team of ADAR staff and external consultants and focused both on assessing the impact of ADAR's work in the health field, and on the institutional development of the agency itself.
- An evaluation of the work of KAUSAY, a Peruvian NGO which runs an integrated rural development programme in the 'altiplano' region of southern Peru. The evaluation focused on assessing the changing role and impact of an NGO with limited resources in a very difficult environment.
- A one-week workshop in 1994 with 12 Peruvian NGOs, facilitated by one of the authors. The theme of the workshop was Project Monitoring and Evaluation and it focused heavily on NGO evaluation methodology.

■ A one-week seminar in Colombia organised by Misereor, which brought together NGOs from all over Latin America to focus on qualitative evaluation.

■ A substantial evaluation exercise undertaken by two external consultants of a 12-year integrated rural development programme in the district of Santa Barbara, Honduras. The programme had been run by Save the Children-UK during this whole period and a principal purpose of the evaluation was to try to assess what might have been achieved during that period.

■ A review undertaken internally by two Brazilian NGOs in the north-east of the country (Retome Su Vida and GAPA-Bahia). Both exercises took place about 18 months after the beginning of each project and concentrated on trying to assess whether, in broad terms, the projects were on the right lines. An important aspect of these exercises was the involvement of a *companhero critico* ('critical friend') – an outside resource person who has a key role in helping the project both to formulate its ideas and to evaluate its work.

■ An evaluation of the Integrated Rural Development Programme (PRO-NORTE) in Nicaragua, which was largely quantitative.

■ An evaluation of the Caranavi Health Programme in Bolivia, in which the emphasis was placed on community involvement.

From these experiences, the following general observations can be made about the current state of play of evaluation work among NGOs in Latin America:

1. The first question is: what aspects of NGO work in Latin America are being evaluated? In many instances, the evaluation process is concerned with small-scale, isolated projects without any linkages between them. Evaluation may also refer to the overall work of an NGO in a wider context, and its capacity to establish a synergistic force in a local or national space; that is, its ability to mobilise and energise other social actors and capitalise on this to broaden the impact of its activities. When an NGO manages to establish an institutional presence within society, the wider context is especially important. In the first case (the small project), evaluation is a relatively simple issue, a question of measuring the achievement of objectives and goals independent of the wider context. In the second case (the effects of NGO work on the living conditions of the population), impact is much more difficult to measure. The issue of impact is currently one of the most widely debated among Latin American NGOs, but we have not yet found a way to measure the impact of an NGO in the life of a local group or on the national context more generally. Discussions of impact are often confused by a failure to specify whether it is being measured in terms of the NGO as an actor in development issues at a national or international level, or in terms of the broader effect of the NGO's work on the livelihoods of the people with whom it works. Too often there is a feeling that it is the NGO itself which is being evaluated rather than the work it undertakes. If the donor is content that the NGO as an institution is on the right track, then the assumption is that its project work must be equally sound.

The responsibility of Latin American NGOs

The impact of community-based development programmes in Latin America will not be achieved only as a result of the professionalism of NGOs, their growth in numbers or the increasing coverage of their work; to achieve this impact will also require the collective effort of government, business and civil society. All sides share an element of responsibility for ensuring that this impact is achieved. How ready are Latin American NGOs to assume this responsibility? Are they to be resigned forever to be merely the executors of programmes whose success is always in doubt? Or are they ready to take on this responsibility and to take the lead in seeking fresh approaches [to the region's chronic problems] from their own Latin American perspective?

Source: El Taller (1993)

2. The harsh winds of cost-effectiveness, Logical Framework Analysis and 'strategic thinking' have clearly hit Latin American NGOs head on over the past five years. In evaluation terms, the 1970s and 1980s were years of relative indulgence; the 1990s have brought with them new demands from a changing world of development assistance. There is no doubt that in earlier decades the dominant approach of Latin American NGOs to evaluation was 'interpretative' – an emphasis on description, explaining change in a historical sense and generally seeing evaluation as a people-centred, qualitative exercise. Increasingly fashionable (nay, obligatory) these days is a more technocratic approach to evaluation based on clear objectives, measurement, targets, quantitative outcomes, and so on. The change in emphasis is perceptible, as are the agonies which it has caused. The meaning of the word 'results' has been renegotiated and Latin American NGOs are having to be more specific, tangible and measurable in what they say they are going to achieve. Northern NGOs have led the way in all of this and, in the current order of things, the Latin American NGOs have had to 'swim with the tide'. But one senses national NGO's discomfort with this change; it is not an easy transition and any reversal in thinking would probably be gladly embraced.

3. The current evaluation vocabulary of Latin American NGOs is dominated by two words; *diagnostico* (diagnosis) and *sistematización* (systematisation). It is almost impossible to avoid the substantial use of these two terms in any project evaluation process. The *diagnostico* (or 'situation analysis') is the bedrock of the whole exercise; the meticulous and detailed description and interpretation of the context in which the project is taking place. It is the key element in the evaluation litany, an exercise which must be undertaken before one can take a step forward. To suggest that there is no *diagnostico*, or at least an inadequate one, would stop an evaluation exercise dead in its tracks! Clearly, the *diagnostico* is a critical element in any evaluation exercise; the issue is how much do we need to know before we move forward? Latin American NGOs tend to lean towards exhaustive situation analysis and eschew attempts at a 'quick and dirty' approach.

Sistematización is undoubtedly the current favourite term of Latin

American NGOs and it is not easy to nail it down to any particular interpretation. *Sistematización* reflects an internal ordering and sequential
interpretation of actions and activities. Supposedly, *sistematización* produces an effortless flow of information and analysis in order to understand
what is happening at any moment in time. At present, *sistematización* in
evaluation among Latin American NGOs lacks a common language and has
a very broad remit. In terms of ordering and providing a focus, *sistematización* can give an evaluation exercise a clearer perspective and can help to
structure what can often be a diffuse process. On the other hand, *sistematización* can appear to have no apparent direction or outcome; it can lead to
continual invention and reinvention and it is almost always difficult for an
outsider to grasp its real character. But few evaluations in Latin America are
currently launched without a commitment to 'systematise' the whole activity.

Latin American NGOs' relationships with groups

An important issue is the relationship between NGOs (in Latin America) and
the base groups with which they work. In terms of the concept of participation,
too often this relationship is defined only in terms of the NGO's 'involvement'
in the running of base groups. There is little evidence that this involvement
works the other way round. Latin American NGOs have yet to really manage
this issue of participation; what it does not mean is either that the NGO 'takes
over' the base group or the other way round.

Source: Misereor (1993)

---

4. The development vocabulary of the 1960s and 1970s maintains an over-
    whelming presence in the theory and practice of Latin American inter-
    mediary NGOs. A conceptual veneer hangs over the way in which most
    NGOs see the world; it inevitably spills over into their work in evaluation
    and NGOs are still struggling to come to grips with it. 'Awareness creation',
    'human promotion', 'participation' and 'critical analysis', for example, are
    still fashionable concepts and form the bedrock of the conceptual per-
    spective of many NGOs. Yet after over 25 years of promoting such con-
    cepts, Latin American NGOs still struggle to explain what these concepts
    mean in practice and how it is possible to understand their effects. There
    have been major leaps forward in terms of wrestling with qualitative
    notions of evaluation but, to date, the conceptual still dominates and
    practical tools are lacking. There is little evidence, for example, of any
    substantial evaluation of the widespread use of *concientización*. Curiously,
    Howard Richards' seminal text 'The Evaluation of Cultural Action', based
    on such work in Chile, is perhaps more widely known and consulted outside
    of Latin America than within the region (Richards 1985). It is important to
    recognise the major contribution that Latin American NGOs have made to
    the work of organisations in the region; but the pressure is mounting on
    NGOs to break through a conceptual barrier and begin to develop the
    practical tools at project level which would explain advances made in this
    critically important work.

5. In terms of practical evaluation methodology, one tool which is common among Latin American NGOs is the 'evaluation package'. This package has no fixed content or single meaning; but it is a term which is used to describe a fairly common approach to project evaluation among NGOs in the region. The variable elements in this package are as follows: it is an internal exercise; it can last for up to four months; it is often 'accompanied' in the sense that an external agent plays a facilitating role (see below); it is based largely on the analysis of verbal descriptions of work to date; and it takes place through a series of internal meetings in which the whole exercise is played out. It is an exhaustive and detailed approach which, it must be said, can often become lost in a wealth of description and comment; it eschews the 'quick and dirty' and seeks to leave no stone unturned. Eventually, the process produces a report which is the base from which future actions move forward. The whole process reinforces the internal strengths of the project team and helps to develop a common vision of where things are going. On the downside, as a single approach to project evaluation, it allows for little variation and can often appear as an exaggerated response to a stage in project evaluation which demands a quicker and less complicated approach.

6. Who evaluates and who is evaluated? Some NGOs in Latin America and their European partners are developing an evaluation system whose objective is to support the institutional development of the NGO. This system is called in Spanish *evaluación acompañada* ('accompanied evaluation'). Within it, donor agencies analyse the institutional development of the NGO which is being evaluated, together with staff from the NGO itself. Equal importance is given to both sets of actors. Such a system requires a permanent dialogue and the examination of the common problems which arise between the partners, reinforced with specialised technical inputs when necessary. Rather than evaluating a project after it has finished, the 'accompaniment' approach puts the most important questions 'on the table' from the start. When the dialogue between donor and NGO, or between NGO and GRO, starts from an open discussion of their respective interests, the inevitable tensions which arise in the evaluation process can be managed more effectively.

Project monitoring and evaluation in Brazil

The close monitoring of the development of this project had two principal elements: (1) the regular following of the project, on the part of the funding NGO, through frequent visits and meetings and discussions on appropriate indicators to evaluate the project, and (2) the appointing of a 'critical friend' ('companhero critico') who would serve as a sensitive link between the NGO and RETOME. This concept of the 'critical friend', who is a neutral outsider whose fundamental role is to support the project team and to serve as an independent point of contact between the team and the NGO, is an interesting innovation in project monitoring and evaluation in Brazil.

Source: SCF (1994)

Conclusions

The issues raised and the comments made in this review do not come from an authoritative empirical study of NGOs in Latin America; they have been made after personal reflection on NGO evaluation activities in several countries over the past few years. It could be argued that most Latin American NGOs still find themselves in the conceptual circles of the 1960s and 1970s. As terms like accountability and evaluation become common currency, this circle is not renegotiated but strenuous efforts are made to incorporate new terms within it. For some Latin American NGOs, accountability is framed in terms of society as a whole, not to particular social organisations or sectors. Inevitably, however, the pressure is now mounting to improve accountability at the programme or project level. Furthermore, given the explosion in the number of NGOs in the region in the 1980s, and the apparently tenuous relationship they appear to have with their supposed constituents, it is necessary to raise the question of NGO 'legitimacy' (Pearce 1995). NGOs have concentrated on raising their profile, building and playing a greater role in civil society, and developing contacts at the international level. But in the process, the interests this 'movement' is supposed to represent, its accountability to those on whose behalf it claims to speak, and the real outcomes of its work, are all too often relegated to a secondary position on the NGO agenda.

In summary (and though the evidence is not conclusive), Latin American NGOs have not evolved very significantly as a 'species' since the 1960s and 1970s. The passion, the commitment, the macro-analysis and the broad involvement in society are all there; and these elements continue to maintain their primacy despite the harder-edged and more critical world of accountability which lurks on the horizon. Perhaps this is not such a bad state of affairs; as actors in the broader social movements of Latin America, NGOs can point to substantial impact, at times, in countries such as Chile, Brazil, Nicaragua and Bolivia (Lehmann 1990). They still suffer, however, from a genetic fault in terms of a propensity to exaggerate and a tendency to mount time-consuming and circular exercises when more discrete action would be more appropriate. Furthermore, the centres of power still tend to dominate: urban, middle-class and professional, speaking 'on behalf of' the less powerful in the region. But with all their faults, inconsistencies and contradictions, and in comparison with the supposedly democratic governments of the region, we are convinced that 'legitimacy' and 'accountability' are being raised more seriously on the agendas of Latin American NGOs today. The legitimacy of NGOs is being severely tested as their links with popular movements are weakened and have yet to be firmly established with new and emerging social groups. Furthermore, NGOs in Latin America, like their counterparts in other parts of the world, struggle in their own particular fashion to explain the effect and impact of their work. It is not difficult to pick holes in their practice and it is important not to be complacent, but for all their inadequacies, NGOs in Latin America are the only real and viable agents of the social changes which are necessary to provide a better livelihood for the increasing millions who live in poverty in the region.

Note

1. NGOs are defined in this paper as local intermediary organisations, not Northern NGOs or grassroots organisations. In most Latin American countries, the concept of an NGO refers to an institution formed by professional people (not always volunteers) who work on development, environmental or human rights issues, frequently in support of GROs.

8

Accountability and Participation: a Case Study from Bombay

Vandana Desai and Mick Howes

This chapter reviews the experience of Apnalaya – an organisation working in the slums of Bombay – as a means of testing a number of more general propositions about the nature and determinants of NGO accountability under the New Policy Agenda.[1] It is divided into four sections. The first summarises the broad themes to be explored. The second provides a brief overview of the organisation and its work. This is followed by a more detailed exploration of the activities undertaken, and the forms of accountability associated with each one. In a concluding section, we return to the propositions outlined at the beginning of the chapter to ask how relevant they are in the light of Apnalaya's experience, and what implications they might hold for the future. The main thrust of our argument is that the New Policy Agenda has begun to impinge upon what Apnalaya does, and that some of its implications are indeed negative. At the same time, we aim to show how pressure for greater accountability, if responded to in particular ways, can be converted into a force for positive change.

The problem of accountability

In their chapters, Edwards and Hulme, and Fowler, suggest that the ways in which NGOs presently account for what they do reveal a number of inadequacies. Reporting of performance tends to focus on the achievement of immediate outputs, and only rarely delves into the longer-term and more fundamental effects and impacts with which NGOs are supposed to be especially concerned.[2] Attention is restricted mainly to 'functional' accountability to the exclusion of the 'strategic', ie, to what is happening at the level of individual projects as opposed to the achievement of wider programmatic goals (Avina 1993). Accountability is generally interpreted as 'the means by which ... organisations report [upwards] to a recognised authority ... and are held responsible for their actions' (Edwards and Hulme, this volume), with insufficient attention directed 'downwards' to the views of intended beneficiaries.

These difficulties stem, at least in part, from the fact that, unlike governments (which must submit themselves for periodic re-election) or businesses (which must make profits in order to survive), NGOs have no readily acknowledged 'bottom line' against which performance can be measured. This is made worse by the tendency for the broad social goals which NGOs set themselves to be influenced by a wide range of factors beyond their control, making it hard to attribute causation or apportion credit or blame for any changes that may arise. Furthermore, unlike civil servants, who must report to government and be available for cross-examination in committee, NGOs generally have no one particular body to whom they are accountable, or single mechanism through which they may be brought to account.

An already difficult situation is complicated further by the increasing support NGOs are now receiving from governments and official aid agencies. The types of activities which these official bodies have conventionally supported, and the hierarchical structures which have arisen to administer them, embody a view of development as an essentially linear and predictable enterprise. This is at variance with the far more contingent and unpredictable 'open-system' world perceived and inhabited by NGOs. Imposed systems of accountability deriving from 'linear' world views, with targets and sanctions to be imposed in the event of non-achievement, reinforce other pressures for NGOs to transform themselves into routine service providers, reducing in the process their capacity to explore new ideas, or to tackle the more deep-seated and intractable problems of institutional development. It may therefore be that the economic dimension of the New Policy Agenda now being pursued by the major aid donors conflicts with, and may ultimately supersede, the political objective of promoting wider participation, stronger democratic institutions, and a more vibrant civil society.

Apnalaya: the organisation and its work

Apnalaya was founded in 1972 to provide day care to children in one small part of Bombay, and has grown into an organisation which works with slum dwellers in five different areas. Although building most of its activities around a core competence as an innovator in the development of health and educational services, it has adopted, from the outset, a 'non-directive' or 'participatory' community-development approach, based on the principle of working with local organisations to identify and act upon people's own priorities. Experience on the ground therefore reveals no one distinctive model, but rather a series of initiatives which reflect the expertise of the organisation and the distinctive needs of the people with whom it works. Drawing on its direct experience with communities, Apnalaya has sought to build a distinctive role as a provider of training to other NGOs and government organisations, and as a source of ideas which it disseminates through networks and other fora. It does not see itself as a provider of services *per se*, and only takes on operational involvements as a means of keeping in touch with realities 'on the ground'.

Apnalaya (which means 'sharing') was founded by an Australian diplomat, and has benefited from the active involvement and encouragement of an English social worker who is resident in the city. But from the outset, it has been an Indian-run organisation, which has only occasionally received foreign financial support, and which draws its primary inspiration from Indian rather than international sources. A number of formative influences have helped to make it what it is today. In the early years, Apnalaya sought out the experiences of innovative health and education programmes, and these were to prove highly significant in shaping subsequent developments. The work of the Foundation for Research in Community Health and the educational experiments of Anutai Wagh, were of particular importance in this regard. Academic contacts at the Urban and Rural Community Development Department at the Tata Institute of Social Sciences played an important part in identifying models and exploring how they could be adapted to urban conditions. The Department has also supplied several of Apnalaya's professional social workers. Apnalaya now employs 55 people, comprising a core of professional social workers, and a larger body of para-professionals, community-based workers, and other helpers recruited mainly from within the slums themselves. More than 75 per cent of the staff, including the Director, are women, but the organisation has not embraced an overtly feminist agenda.

Money is raised from a variety of sources. Individual donations and contributions from charitable trusts have proved particularly important, helping Apnalaya to build a substantial corpus, which has tided the organisation over its periodic financial crises. Some support is received from central and municipal government, a portion of which derives ultimately from international donors. Funds may also be channelled from official sources through specialist NGO funding bodies. The underlying trend has been for annual income and expenditure to rise steadily, although often with large annual variations: total expenditure for 1994 is estimated at 1.5 million rupees, or approximately £30,000.

The diverse influences which have shaped Apnalaya, the different ways in which it is funded, its non-directive approach, and the relative informality which remains possible in a small organisation, have all combined to produce a rather fluid structure. Of late, this has given rise to a certain amount of internal dissatisfaction, with staff sometimes becoming frustrated by a lack of clarity in their roles. The system which has now evolved approximates to a matrix structure. This is built around five geographically defined Community Development Projects and four cross-cutting activity-based programmes, covering Early Childhood Education, Drug Prevention and Rehabilitation, Training, and Aids Awareness and Prevention. The location and close association of some of the programmes with individual project offices means, however, that a clear distinction between the two is sometimes difficult to maintain.

As indicated earlier, Apnalaya now operates in a number of different locations, but its greatest challenge and largest input have been at Shivaji Nagar, where it first started work in 1976. Built on low-lying and poorly drained land in a peripheral area of Bombay, this is a sprawling slum which is home to approximately 300,000 people relocated from slums in other parts of the city over the past thirty years. The area suffers from a range of problems. Infrastructure is rudimentary. Health-care provision is poor, and infant mortality rates unusually high. With the exception of a small number of households with relatives in the Gulf, living standards are generally low, with most people depending for their livelihoods on a range of poorly paid casual or informal-sector jobs, including rickshaws, handcart operation and vegetable selling. Tensions exist between the Muslim majority, who comprise some two-thirds of the population, and the Hindu and other smaller minorities. Communal institutions are fragmented and generally weak, and there is a high level of criminal activity. Together with the sheer size of the slum, these factors combine to produce a challenge of a quite different magnitude to that which Apnalaya confronts elsewhere. Nothing approaching the comprehensive delivery of services to all households which can be contemplated at its other, much smaller sites, is feasible.

Activities and mechanisms for functional accountability

How, then, does Apnalaya account for what it does? In addressing this question we focus mainly on what happens at Shivaji Nagar, the project which encompasses the broadest range of activities, including all the cross-cutting programmes. As the location which poses the most severe challenge, Shivaji Nagar provides the most demanding test of Apnalaya's capacity to account for its activities. We look first at the system for accounting for individual activities, discussing them in the order in which they arose historically.[3]

Community development

Work began with broadly based community-development initiatives, designed to help young people to organise themselves into a youth group, and then to begin the process of identifying the form which projects should take. Using support provided by the Tata Institute for Social Sciences, initial emphasis was given to management and leadership training. A number of initiatives then followed in areas such as drug and alcohol abuse, which in turn lay the foundations for some of the developments which are described below. These and subsequent activities have centred around a building provided, at a nominal rent, by the Bombay Municipal Corporation (BMC). This has been maintained by community members, and was extended in the 1980s using community labour and the support of local contractors. Further building costs, the salaries of social workers and other staff and a range of other expenses over the years, have been covered, for the last three years, by a grant from the Housing Development Finance Corporation (HDFC), an independent body established to address housing needs in the city. BMC does not require Apnalaya to account for what it does in the building, but the organisation is dependent upon BMC's continuing goodwill and therefore occasionally sends in a written report of its activities, which is not usually acknowledged. HDFC requires light quarterly ex-post reporting and provides limited feedback, indicating whether it is satisfied or not. HDFC staff are also invited to attend events organised under the project, where they have the opportunity to meet beneficiaries and find out for themselves what has been going on.

Education   Following from the early community development work, the next major initiative to be undertaken involved the establishment of three pre-schools run by women teachers recruited from the community and provided with training. The schools cater for about 30 children each. They are also used as teacher-training and support centres under the Early Childhood Education Programme, which services other pre-schools in the area. Apnalaya's schools use the community development centre and are therefore not liable for rent. Teachers' salaries and materials were previously covered by fees, but parents' incomes have fallen behind general increases in wage inflation and are now only sufficient to meet the cost of materials. Salaries are covered under the HFDC grant, while an NGO funding agency known as Child Relief and You (CRY) funds the training programme.

Apnalaya provides a quarterly report covering enrolment and attendance rates on the schools which it runs itself, and organisations sending trainees supported by CRY to Apnalaya courses are also obliged to report on their progress. Over and above this, Apnalaya is planning an evaluation study to ascertain the degree of success achieved by its former trainees in other schools. This will go some way towards satisfying a perceived need within the organisation to move beyond the rather narrow and exclusively quantitative forms of assessment required by funders. In addition, parents of pre-school children are invited to a monthly meeting to hear about what has been going on in the school, to receive the results of any medical checks that may have been carried out, and to raise any matters that may concern them. These meetings are generally well attended, although parents feel constrained from offering much by way of substantive comment by their lack of knowledge of the education system.

Drugs   Most of the drugs work in Shivaji Nagar is preventive and the salary and other expenses which this entails are covered from Apnalaya's general funds.[4] Over and above this, counselling services for addicts and their families are provided in a room which is made available without charge by the Bombay Municipal Corporation in its nearby Urban Health Centre. As is the case with the main building, there is no formal reporting requirement, but Apnalaya sends a letter and report once a year. Apnalaya also runs a day-care centre at Malad to which addicts from Shivaji Nagar and other locations may be referred. In addition to the salaries of the four staff members, a number of other costs are incurred. For some time, all these costs, together with the counselling service, were covered by a central government grant. However, this was conditional on treating 30 people at any one time, a target set without visiting the premises, which only had the capacity to deal effectively with 15. Various other conditions were imposed which required Apnalaya to depart from well-tried procedures: when these were not complied with, the grant was withdrawn, obliging the organisation to draw on its corpus fund to keep the centre running. This is one of a small but potentially important number of instances where attempts to tighten accountability have failed. Its wider significance is discussed in the final section of this chapter.

Riot relief   The riots which engulfed Bombay in 1992 and 1993 confronted Apnalaya with a completely new situation, and one which was to exert a powerful influence over its future development.[5] Riots were at their most intense in Shivaji Nagar, where many lives were lost, large numbers of people suffered injury, housing was destroyed and livelihoods were seriously affected. Nearly all of the victims were Muslims. Apnalaya, supported by the Tata Institute and other voluntary organisations, was able to draw upon its contacts and local knowledge to make a critical contribution to the relief and rehabilitation work. In the immediate aftermath, hundreds of people were treated at emergency clinics. Cases of missing people were followed up, assistance was provided in identifying the dead, and counselling offered to their families and to others who had been traumatised. Food, fuel, blankets and other requirements were distributed. As a first step in the process of rehabilitation, Apnalaya coordinated the initial collection of data on loss of life, injury, damage to property and prospective police cases, which was then processed by the Tata Institute and submitted to the relevant authorities. In the absence of any official provision, a special loan scheme was set up in consultation with local representatives to restart small businesses. A similar channel was established for funds for the replacement of housing and for other forms of economic rehabilitation, and assistance provided in the preparation of a large number of claims for compensation. Efforts were made to restore relations with the police.

These activities involved Apnalaya in the receipt and channelling of funds from a diversity of government, NGO and other sources, for which it accounted collectively after the event. Two important effects followed for Apnalaya from the riots. The first was a reinvigoration of its community development work, with a number of new initiatives launched to strengthen local groups and promote harmony by bringing people together to work on common problems such as TB control, drug abuse and HIV/AIDS awareness.

Health   The second major effect of the riots was to bring the organisation into contact with residents of a particularly disadvantaged part of the slum for the first time. This provided the impetus for a new initiative, involving the establishment of a clinic offering immunisation, ante-natal and more general medical care, and the training of community-level health workers, who have now started to engage in a wider range of preventive activities. Salaries and training costs are covered under a grant administered by SOSVA (another NGO support agency) under a central government programme funded by USAID. Vitamins and vaccines are supplied mainly by the Bombay Municipal Corporation (BMC). The bulk of the medicines required are provided by CONCERN (an international NGO). Other trusts and pharmaceutical companies make smaller contributions. User charges cover the balance, which amounts to some 40 per cent of the total cost. The SOSVA grant is tightly regulated, with specific targets being imposed for different areas of work – for example, 10 children per 1000 population have to be immunised each year, and similar goals have been set for family planning work. These objectives have proved difficult to measure and the data time-consuming to compile. Performance has to be reported and discussed at quarterly meetings with SOSVA, where the difficulties encountered have been raised; thus far the government has offered no response.

In return for the support they provide, BMC expect regular indications of the numbers of people treated, which they then include in their own reports as if they had supplied the services directly themselves. Apnalaya points out that this is not a very meaningful indicator, since the success of a primary heath care programme should be measured by a reduction, not an increase, in the number of people presenting themselves for treatment. In the meantime, Apnalaya has been recording its own impressions of the benefits arising from its intervention, a form of monitoring which it feels is more meaningful than those required by official bodies. For example, people now come forward voluntarily for immunisation where previously they had to be rounded up; they now tend to complete the course rather than dropping out midway; and weaning practices have been improving in response to the advice that has been offered.

Strategic accountability

Three formal mechanisms are used by Apnalaya to satisfy accountability 'upwards'. The first is the annual report on expenditure which has to be made to the Indian Charity Commissioners. This is complied with, but no feedback is ever received. The second is the obligation to report every three years to the Income Tax Department in order to obtain the certificate which gives a 50 per cent tax exemption to anybody providing the organisation with financial support. These are largely regulatory procedures, designed to ensure that the organisation engages only in activities which are consistent with its charitable status; they do not require that a *strategic* view be taken of its work. The third mechanism is provided by Apnalaya's own Board of Trustees. This is a two-tiered body, comprising a group of appointed members, who in turn elect an Executive Committee. In the early years there were as many as 30 members, but the number has now been reduced to fewer than 10, nearly all of whom are active as volunteers in the day-to-day running of the organisation. The President, for example, is currently one of the doctors working on a health project.

Formally, the committee meets quarterly to review expenditure, funding, new activities and any problems which may have arisen. In practice, and in keeping with the 'non-directive' style of Apnalaya as a whole, most business is transacted at weekly meetings of senior staff which committee members also attend, or even more informally through the day-to-day contacts which take place. In Tandon's terms (this volume), this is not an 'invisible' board, but neither is it a 'professional' one. It is a hybrid of Tandon's 'family' and 'staff' types, with the typical combination of strengths and weaknesses they embody. The practical consequence is that the board does not really require the organisation to take a strategic view of its overall portfolio of activities and programmes either.

While there is no strong pressure for strategic accountability coming from above, Apnalaya argues that the merits of alternative initiatives and courses of action are actively reviewed 'from below'. It holds monthly meetings for parents, and keeps open a number of more informal channels with these and other groups it serves. The willingness of consumers of educational and health services to meet at least part of their cost introduces an element of market discipline. The fact that a high proportion of staff are recruited from the communities they serve keeps the organisation in touch with what people really want. Perhaps most importantly, Apnalaya's determination to strengthen local institutions which can articulate and participate in the satisfaction of needs, should in itself ensure that proper account is taken of local views.

All these arguments are valid, but a residual concern remains. Apnalaya's non-directive approach means that the organisation must be on its guard to avoid becoming a mirror image of the community it seeks to serve, with all the class, gender, ethnic and other inequalities this embodies. Apnalaya is alert to this danger, and works hard to circumvent existing power structures wherever it can. Inevitably, however, compromises have to be made, and to this extent, the ideal of full downward accountability cannot be attained. It is also true that accountability mechanisms only operate at the level of individual project locations and do not encompass the entire spread of the organisation's work.

An assessment of the accountability system in Apnalaya

Taken as a whole, what are the key features of Apnalaya's accountability system, and to what extent do they conform with the expectations reviewed in the introductory section of this chapter?

Principle and practice

It is obvious from discussions with staff that the organisation is strongly in favour of the principle of greater accountability, and its record appears strong compared to other NGOs. There are clearly identifiable mechanisms in place for the majority of the activities in which it engages. While some of these are externally imposed, there is a clear willingness to go beyond formal requirements and seek alternative indicators when those on offer fail to reflect the true significance of what is being attempted. A fairly high degree of accountability has been achieved under circumstances where no outside evaluations have ever been carried out and where the organisation has been under relatively little external pressure. However, this is not to suggest that all of the difficulties anticipated in the literature on accountability have been avoided.

Determining longer-term impact

Apnalaya does appear vulnerable to the criticism that it focuses too heavily on immediate outputs in its reporting, to the exclusion of longer-term effects and impacts. This may not matter very much in relation to certain aspects of health and education, where longer-term consequences can be difficult to trace, and where, for example, the numbers of children enrolled in schools or receiving immunisation may provide reasonable proxies for desired outcomes. But in other areas it would almost certainly be desirable to explore further down the chain of causes and effects than is presently the case. Apnalaya has itself recognised this in relation to its teacher-training programme. A similar course of action may well be appropriate with regard to the strengthening of institutions in Shivaji Nagar and elsewhere, where the demonstrable success of some groups in generating new activities needs to be set against the (currently unknown) number which have fallen by the wayside. Data on inputs to particular activities are also hard to come by and would greatly strengthen Apnalaya's capacity to analyse its work. Given the complexity of what Apnalaya is attempting, the presence of other agencies offering overlapping services, and the volatility of the environment in which it operates, it may be very difficult to prove success conclusively, but the easier task of demonstrating that it has not failed in key areas would in itself represent a considerable advance on the present state of affairs.

Taking a strategic view and accounting 'downwards'

The earlier discussion of Apnalaya's activities showed how the organisation does take on board the views of those with whom it works; the small size of the organisation and the ease with which senior staff can visit project locations, are also important contributory factors here. At the same time, strategic accountability at best operates only at the level of what is happening in individual project locations. Equally important is the capacity to define core operational competence or to determine what can be supported most cost-effectively; to decide whether to consolidate in existing locations or expand to new ones; and to determine the optimal balance between operational, training and wider opinion-forming work. In these areas, Apnalaya is weaker, although at root this may simply reflect the lack of a clear 'bottom line' or ultimate authority to whom they must account.

Negative implications of the New Policy Agenda

The implications of the New Policy Agenda are more difficult to evaluate since Apnalaya has been partially insulated by its unusual capacity to raise private funds locally. But to the extent that Apnalaya *has* been exposed to new trends, its experience clearly confirms the negative consequences anticipated in the literature. This is particularly apparent in some of its dealings with government, where demands for information are increasing rapidly, and which, given the relative shortage of reporting skills within the organisation, are now beginning to constitute a serious burden on managers. An already difficult situation is exacerbated by the imposition of unattainable targets without prior consultation, in a fashion which suggests the continuation of traditional bureaucratic high-handedness, with only the most superficial commitment to enhancing the performance of those receiving resources (see the example of the clinics described above). This impression is reinforced by the widespread tendency of officialdom not to offer any response to the information they receive. The likely longer-run result is that reporting will become a mechanical exercise devoid of real meaning or purpose. In the words of one member of the organisation: 'reporting is like throwing messages in bottles into the sea – you never know if anyone is reading them or not'. Put in slightly different terms, there is a danger that the political dimension of the New Policy Agenda will be subverted by the existing hierarchies and authority structures through which it is filtered, with the end result that energy drains away at the grassroots level, rather than being generated and focused in the fashion that was intended. Criticisms that NGOs are insufficiently accountable 'downwards' pale into insignificance by comparison with the performance of official bodies.

The sustainability problem

These difficulties are exacerbated by a desire among donors to achieve 'sustainability', which translates into an unwillingness to commit resources for anything more than a three- to five-year period. While Apnalaya also wishes to achieve self-sufficiency, circumstances conspire against this objective and the 'linear' view of development on which it rests. This has been apparent in attempts to recover costs in pre-school education and health activities, both of which ultimately foundered as a result of an unanticipated deterioration in the wider economic circumstances of intended 'customers'. The system adopted by CRY in its support for pre-school teacher training recognises these problems of targeting and linearity. Indicators are agreed, not imposed, and no rigid targets are enforced. This is far more sensible where so much uncertainty surrounds the outcome of any undertaking. The relatively light ex-post reporting of the type encouraged by the HDFC and used quite widely in other areas of Apnalaya's work seems similarly appropriate.

New directions

Our research suggests two broad conclusions. The first is to confirm that the effects of the New Policy Agenda are indeed potentially perverse. The second is that, even if such an agenda did not exist, it would still be in the interests of the organisation (and those whom it seeks to serve) to review and improve its accountability mechanisms. The need for repositioning which the New Policy Agenda imposes on NGOs can thus be turned, at least to some extent, into a positive opportunity. But for this to happen, innovations are required in accountability at both functional and strategic levels. At the functional level it is important to recognise that Apnalaya is engaged in a number of types of activity and that different forms of accountability may be required for each one: institutional development work should be distinguished from the development and delivery of services. The former, as embodied in Apnalaya's attempts to strengthen local groups and build effective leadership, can only partially be assessed in itself – to a large extent it rests on the level and types of other activity generated. Within service provision, it is also necessary to separate activities which address known and predictable problems from those provided under unstable conditions, such as riot relief, where only light and ex-post forms of reporting could reasonably be expected. A further distinction should be made between mature services, where it is legitimate to require that targets should be set in advance, and those, such as HIV/AIDS, which are experimental. In the latter, relevant criteria for assessment can only be developed as the process unfolds. Mature services should be further subdivided into those – like pre-schools, at least under earlier economic circumstances – where the capacity to recover costs from users itself provides an indication of relevance and success, and those – like primary health care – where a heavy element of subsidy is likely to be involved. Finally, over and above any attempt to assess what Apnalaya is doing 'on the ground', provision needs to be made to review its performance in influencing the behaviour of others through its training and opinion-forming work.

Strategic change

Developing a range of mechanisms tailored to the requirements of these different functions would help to create a genuine system of accountability in place of the patchy provision which currently exists. This could then pave the way for a second and more strategic set of initiatives which would serve to support the changes taking place at the functional level. Externally, this might entail the appointment of a more professional and active board for Apnalaya. Internally, it might be desirable to create clearer roles in research, policy and information. For an organisation which has been in existence for 24 years, and which regards itself as being in the business of disseminating ideas, Apnalaya has committed rather little to paper. The creation of a specialist position of this kind would make it possible to draw together, and make more accessible, the wealth of ideas presently stored in individual diaries and other forms throughout the organisation. While helping Apnalaya to improve its overall effectiveness, such changes would also enable the organisation to project an image more in keeping with present orthodoxies. A certain amount might have to be sacrificed in the process, but such an initiative would be likely to gain Apnalaya the space and support it requires to preserve its core values of innovation in response to the expressed needs of those it seeks to serve.

Notes

1. Apnalaya provides one of the case studies from Vandana Desai's research on urban NGO effectiveness, and from Mick Howes' project on NGOs and the development of grassroots institutions. Both are funded by the Economic and Social Committee on Research of the UK Overseas Development Administration, to whom thanks are due. We are also very grateful to the staff and associates of Apnalaya for their co-operation, their willingness to talk openly, and their comments on the draft of this paper. The views expressed and any errors, however, remain entirely our own responsibility.
2. The notion of a sequence leading from inputs through outputs, to effects and impacts (see Casley and Lury 1982, pp 2–30) provides a useful starting point for thinking about questions of accountability, but is, at the same time, subject to the criticism of 'linear' development models discussed a little later.
3. This part of the discussion draws heavily on Apnalaya (1994a, 1994b).
4. This part of the discussion draws upon Nadkarni (1992).
5. This account paraphrases Apnalaya (1993).

9

Strategies for Monitoring and Accountability: the Working Women's Forum Model

Janaki Ramesh

Empowering women and enabling them to succeed in their daily struggle for survival is a mammoth task way beyond the scope of individuals or organisations, even very large ones. Only through the concerted efforts of mass-based women's movements can the discrimination which women suffer, in spite of their hard work and invaluable contributions to national economies the world over, be challenged. Today, it is imperative that governmental efforts to promote the well-being of women and uplift their status are supplemented by NGOs. One such movement which has grown into one of the largest NGOs in the developing world is the Working Women's Forum of India (WWF). This chapter explores the monitoring and evaluation strategies adopted by the Forum to measure its performance and ensure its accountability to its members, donors, the government and to society as a whole.

Activities

The WWF was established in 1978 in Madras as a grassroots union of poor working women. The WWF was never a social service organisation providing welfare services to the poor. From its inception, its main strategy has been not to help, but to empower poor women and to enable them to challenge the existing exploitative and oppressive power structures in society. The first activities of the Forum centred on the provision of credit facilities to poor women in urban slums. In 1980, the scope of WWF's activities was broadened to include the provision of health and family welfare services and training and advocacy programmes. What started as a union of about 800 women has grown today into an organisation of over 200,000 members in the three southern states of Tamil Nadu, Andhra Pradesh and Karnataka.[1] Efforts are under way to extend its outreach to other states, including Orissa and Bihar.

The WWF is characterised by its grassroots orientation and by its feminist approach, by the promotion of leadership among poor working women, and by its large-scale outreach. As a movement, its purpose goes beyond material assistance to raising awareness and promoting collective action for social change. As a recent independent evaluation report concludes, 'it is a mature organisation with credibility and recognition at the community level' (UNFPA

1994). The activities of the Forum fall into three main categories: credit, family welfare services and training. While credit services are provided under the auspices of the Indian Co-operative Network for Women (a national co-operative), the other two components are implemented directly by the WWF. A dedicated band of health workers, drawn from the grassroots, are specially trained to cater to the health and family welfare needs of the community. The Research and Training Division of WWF, staffed by 'Target Group Research Investigators' (TGRIs) and headed by the Director, is engaged in continuous training of members and research to study the impact of the Forum's development work on the lives of members, and to devise new strategies and programmes for their benefit.

In the credit programme of the Indian Co-operative Society for Women, all beneficiaries become shareholders of the society. The disbursement of loans to groups of individuals rather than to each member individually brings an element of peer pressure to bear on repayment. The group is blacklisted even if a single member makes a default in their repayment schedule. Making beneficiaries into shareholders increases their interest in the performance of the credit society since they have a real stake in its survival.

The organisers employed by WWF have previously been beneficiaries of the credit programme, and they are entrusted with the task of identifying and evaluating the repayment capacity of potential beneficiaries. The organisers, who are allotted specific geographical areas, recommend deserving cases to the co-operative society's staff. The society's staff then conduct an inspection of the worksites of the potential loanees, formed into groups by area, to appraise themselves of the credit-worthiness of the applicants. Only after the staff have satisfied themselves are the loans disbursed. Each group elects one member to be the leader. The leader is entrusted with the responsibility of ensuring the prompt repayment of loan instalments and receives a larger loan as an incentive. This acts as an incentive within each group to monitor prompt repayment. This form of decentralised monitoring has ensured the continuous success of the credit programme, despite a phenomenal growth in size (see Table 9.1). Income from loans and deposits fully covers the programme's direct operating costs, and 69 per cent of its total operating and financial costs, a significant achievement in itself (UNFPA 1994, p 20).

The element of peer pressure in the group serves to ensure prompt repayment, while at the same time providing a very effective monitoring system. The repayment rate of 98 per cent achieved by the co-operative in 1994 is proof of the effectiveness of its monitoring methods. The organisers monitor not only credit repayments but also the use to which each loan is put – whether it is used for productive purposes, to further the business, or for other purposes. A WWF survey of 500 members in Kancheepuram indicated that many had increased their incomes by between 100 rupees and 200 rupees per month (the target is 300 rupees). Loans have enabled women to lessen their dependence on moneylenders and to gain more control over assets, such as houses in their own names. However, some are still unable to pay off their largest debts (such as freeing their children from bonded labour, which requires a lump sum of 2000–3000 rupees); the small size of loans poses a real problem in this respect (UNFPA 1994, p 15).

Table 9.1 *Working Women's Co-operative Society: progress of credit programme in three southern states of India – Tamil Nadu, Karnataka and Andhra Pradesh (1981–1994)*

Place	No of members in WWF	No of loans	Loan amount disbursed	Loan outstanding amount	Recoverable loan outstanding	%	Bad debts amount	%	Recovery percentage
Madras									
Central									
South	64,910	47,589	25,072,898	2,217,398	340,469	1.36	272,400	1.08	97.56
North									
Rural Tamil Nadu									
Adiramapattinam	27,842	27,582	10,644,800	1,951,560	118,050	1.11	148,200	1.39	97.50
Dindigul	25,150	25,048	9,894,200	3,286,195	80,700	0.81	44,300	0.75	98.44
Vellore	22,409	22,154	9,187,600	1,521,181	98,700	1.07	200,700	2.27	96.66
Kancheepuram	13,641	10,601	11,134,200	4,465,104	86,400	0.77	97,300	0.87	98.36
Dharmapuri	1,626	1,238	521,200	408,800	–	–	–	–	100.00
Karnataka									
Bangalore	30,074	22,636	8,945,800	2,385,600	270,700	3.02	115,300	1.29	95.69
Chennadaana	7,400	7,177	2,353,535	4,211,410	24,300	1.03	22,400	0.95	98.02
Bidar	15,520	15,043	4,761,000	488,022	108,200	2.27	28,600	0.60	97.13
Bellary	1,736	1,371	420,887	74,641	–	–	–	–	–
Andhra Pradesh									
West Godavari	44,649	44,144	15,351,400	1,201,600	19,400	0.13	9,400	0.06	99.81
East Godavari	14,176	14,366	4,924,600	844,320	4,200	0.08	4,300	0.08	99.84
Bhimavaram	11,761	11,619	4,146,100	803,600	2,500	0.06	1,100	0.03	99.91
Palakol	8,087	7,905	2,463,300	849,800	6,200	0.25	2,800	0.10	99.64
Totals	288,989	258,173	09,821,520	24,709,231	1,129,819	1.00	946,800	0.79	98.47

Source: WWF

Accountability

Using decentralised monitoring, grassroots involvement in planning and staff who come from the communities in which they live and work, the WWF has managed to preserve 'downward' accountability and retain its effectiveness despite rapid programme growth. Administrative costs have been kept below 15 per cent of the total budget of WWF throughout its history, and are covered increasingly by membership fees and interest on loans. The Forum made a decision early on to limit the number of its external funding sources and maximise income from its own members, thus reducing the time and energy required to meet the demands of multiple donors, and preventing WWF from being stretched in too many directions at the same time. It has never allowed foreign funds to compromise the ultimate objective of empowerment (UNFPA 1994).

The organisational structure of the Forum has itself contributed to the success of its monitoring strategies and the maintenance of accountability. The Forum adopts a 'bottom-up' approach wherein planning, implementation and monitoring emanate from the grassroots. Plans are not formulated at the top of the hierarchy and thrust onto the members. Rather, the members are involved at every stage of project formulation from inception onwards, so that all programmes reflect and fulfil their needs. Barring the President and a small number of others, the Forum's staff are all members of grassroots communities and are alive to people's needs and expectations. The President retains overall supervisory control only, leaving project implementation to the women members themselves.

The Research and Training Division of the Forum is engaged in conducting training programmes to increase members' awareness of their rights and responsibilities. On becoming members of the WWF, women undergo a one-day training programme where they learn about the goals and programmes of the Forum, the functioning of the credit society and a host of other related matters. Training is a precondition for access to credit. Effective accountability requires an honest statement of goals. The training helps to appraise members of the intended goals of the Forum, which can then be questioned, debated and monitored more closely. Such training is not a one-time effort but a continuous process. Leadership training is also organised for the group leaders. WWF staff undertake research to evaluate the impact of these training programmes and, where required, refresher training is provided.

The General Body of the WWF (containing all the members) meets periodically at the Forum headquarters both for review and to make policy decisions. Participatory decision-making processes ensure transparency and honest reporting about resource allocation and objective appraisal of achievements. This facilitates transparent judgement of whether the results achieved are satisfactory and provides a concrete mechanism for holding those responsible to account for their performance. Partnership, reciprocity, transparency and independence are hallmarks of the Forum. The General Body elects a Standing Committee from within its own ranks every three years, which is then responsible for planning and managing all WWF programmes. Credit groups have access to the Forum's overall agenda through their area organisers, who relay any concerns to staff at WWF or via the General Body. Any disputes are referred to the Standing Committee.

Accountability in the credit programme

The books of accounts that are maintained at the society office also help in effective monitoring of loan repayment and in highlighting any discrepancies that may arise. These books also serve to maintain the accountability of the Forum to the Indian government and to its donors. An independent evaluation team from UNFPA also visited WWF in 1992 and made its report public.

As stated above, all beneficiaries are made shareholders of the co-operative. They are required to hold shares to the extent of 10 per cent of the loan obtained. Thus, when a larger loan is secured, the shareholding also increases. Interest is charged on the loan at the rate of 18 per cent. Coupled with the money received as share capital, this provides a capital base for the society to function independently of the funds provided by donors. The members are more conscientious in repaying the loans because they desire more of their community to benefit from the society's credit programme. WWF organisers serve as a link between the Forum and the beneficiaries and help to maintain its accountability to members by virtue of belonging to the same community.

The functioning of the credit society is streamlined and its procedures simplified in order to facilitate the involvement of women who are largely illiterate. No forms have to be filled in (the society's staff do this instead), and no security is demanded but for the personal security of the loanee herself. The credit programme revolves around the economic empowerment of women so that they can help themselves. The government also conducts a periodic audit of the books of accounts of the co-operative, which furthers accountability to the authorities. The co-operative is supervised by a Board of Directors comprised of shareholders and elected by them once every three years. Women from grass-roots level are thereby represented at board level.

Accountability in the health programme

WWF health workers who implement the family welfare project are also drawn from the community, and receive special training from the Forum's training division and specialists in the field to enable them to function effectively. They are familiar with ground-level realities, and tend to be more accepted by the community since they are able to relate more effectively and to accept the advice of one of their own. Members know and relate to WWF staff *personally*. As role models, they gain the trust of other women who see them as 'sisters' (UNFPA 1994, p 12). Because they live in and come from the same community, WWF workers can be held accountable directly (though often informally) if anything goes wrong. The personal, rather than formal, relationships between members and workers have been a major factor in the success of the programme as a whole.

The health workers maintain registers containing details of all the families living in their allotted areas (family planning methods adopted, immunisation schedules, and so on). These records, combined with monthly review meetings

Table 9.2   *Working Women's Forum (India): progress report of comprehensive*
family welfare programme
(January 1991–March 1994)

	Madras	Kanchipuram	Vellore	Dindigul	Adiramapattinam
Total no of slums and villages	232	25	26	38	44
Total no of workers	180	30	30	30	30
Total no of families adopted for coverage of family planning methods	90,000	15,000	15,000	15,000	15,000
Total population	432,169	71,758	74,500	68,146	65,221
Total no of eligible couples	73,414	11,857	12,158	11,507	11,323
Total no of children under 5 years	56,964	8,737	9,406	7,630	7,333
Total no of permanent acceptors	41,779	6,641	6,072	6,316	4,871
Total no of temporary acceptors	25,390	3,412	3,629	3,782	4,125
Total no of family planning acceptors	67,169	10,053	9,701	10,098	8,996
Total family planning area coverage	91.49%	84.78%	79.79%	87.75%	79.44%

Source: WWF, 1995

at the Forum office, provide for effective monitoring of the project (see Table 9.2). Problems faced by the workers in their areas are discussed and collective solutions arrived at. Periodic Project Advisory Committee meetings also review project implementation.

Case studies

The value of WWF's activities to women, and the impact of grassroots-level monitoring and accountability in promoting effectiveness at a large scale, are illustrated in the following case studies:

1. Vijayarani, a health worker in Trustpuram, notes as follows:

> *When I first went and visited the slum households for a survey the people asked whether I had come to give them free gifts or ration cards. Men used to tease me and ask if I could do anything about the blocked drainage which was causing a lot of health hazards. To earn their goodwill, I engaged two persons as helpers and cleaned the drainage and asked the local municipal office to send corporation workers to remove the garbage. This incident evoked a great amount of support for my work in the neighbourhood.*

Likewise, Tulasi, a health worker in Vellore notes that:

Being a squatter settlement, all the occupants in my service area were asked to vacate the site. An order to this effect was passed by the Taluk office. I immediately gathered a few women and wrote a petition and sent it to the Collector through the President of Working Women's Forum. The Collector immediately issued a stay order and prevented the evacuation. This incident has increased the popularity of all the programmes of WWF in the community and the clientele respect my work.

2. Chandra is a micro-entrepreneur from Dindigul who had pledged her jewels, borrowed money at exorbitant rates of interest, and carried on her business with extreme difficulty. Talking about her life she says:

The interest charged by outside money-lenders is so high that I was not even able to meet the interest requirements from my profit. As a result, my jewels, vessels and other tangible items at home were all under mortgage. I joined the WWF after the WWF family planning area supervisor talked to me about the organisation. After the WWF training, I have become an active member of the local WWF group. We often sit down, talk about our problems and also come up with solutions. We understand our mistake of borrowing money at very high rates of interest. We have also decided not to go to money-lenders any more. In fact, when one money-lender approached me and asked me why I had not borrowed money from him this year, I told him about the WWF and its low-interest loan programme. Further, along with other women, I saw to it that he did not ever enter our area again. But for the Forum and its training, we would have neither realised that we were being exploited nor been able to overcome such exploitation.

3. Muniammal comes from Vellore. Her husband deserted her. She and her two children earn their livelihood by rolling *beedis* (cigarettes). Her one daughter is married. Discussing her life, she says:

My neighbours used to look down on me and my children because of the simple fact that my husband deserted us. Their constant talking behind my back prompted me to go to my husband. I requested him to come back to the family. However, he refused and also advised me to work and earn a living He further added that if I was not able to do this, I should commit suicide by jumping from the fort of the Vellore temple into the moat around it. This very nearly happened but for one person who saved my life. After this incident, I came to know about the WWF. I enlisted as a member, underwent training and also received a loan. Being a part of the WWF has helped me forget my troubles. I have now abandoned thoughts such as suicide. Through the training and other meetings at the Forum, I have been exposed to other women and their problems as well. I now understand that life is full of difficulties which need to be overcome. My life is now more meaningful despite my husband not being there. I certainly have the confidence and courage to face life as it comes.

4. In an area called Idayampatti (Vellore), the dwelling huts were to be destroyed. A notification to this effect had been issued by the local government authority (the Thasildar). The forum members decided to fight against this. They convened a set of training meetings to bring this issue to the notice of the women affected. After the meetings, it was decided to fight the demolition issue by giving a petition to the District Collector. This timely response from the forum prevented the destruction of the dwelling huts in the area. Apart from

dealing with the demolition issue, the training meetings also helped the women to become more aware of the other difficulties, such as lack of transport facilities, inadequate medical facilities, and the absence of labour legislation in the Beedi-Rolling Industry. These grievances were voiced to the President of India and to the then Prime Minister through a petition submitted to them in person. The women also staged a *dharna* (demonstration) outside the collector's office. It is to their credit that they now have special bus services for women, better working conditions and plans for converting waste lands into dwelling sites.

Conclusion

Students and researchers from India and elsewhere are given free access to visit the Forum and learn from its experiences. Sharing of experience worldwide takes place through Grassroots Organisations Operating Together in Sisterhood (GROOTS), a global network of like-minded NGOs. Future plans include establishing a training centre for NGO activists.

The Forum has lent credibility and strength to the struggles of poor women in India by providing them with organisational backing. These women are the Forum's greatest strength since they provide the mass base that lends credence to the Forum's existence. Today, WWF operates with the same efficiency and speed as in earlier times. Organisational growth has not impaired its functioning, largely because of its decentralised structure and mode of operation. Member involvement at all levels of the organisation provides the key to effective monitoring and strong accountability, both downwards to members and upwards to government and donors. The experience of the Working Women's Forum shows that donor funding and government regulation can be combined with accountability to the grassroots, and that credit-provision, welfare work and empowerment go together. The key to managing these multiple tasks and accountabilities lies in decentralisation and member involvement.

Note

1. 'Members' of the Working Women's Forum are defined as participants in credit-and-savings groups or as women who pay a membership fee.

10

NGO Accountability in Bangladesh: Beneficiaries, Donors and the State

Syed Hashemi

NGO activities began in Bangladesh in the aftermath of the war of independence in 1971 and the famine of 1974, and were initially restricted to relief and
rehabilitation. From the mid-1970s there was a shift in focus to integrated
community development programmes, heavily influenced by the Comilla
model. It was assumed that community development would benefit poor people
within communities, but structural constraints prevented the trickle-down of
benefits. Through their own field experience, NGOs realised that 'poverty (was)
not simply a problem of income differentials but also of the power relations
which constitute rural society' (White 1992). NGOs therefore began to target
specific groups left out of the development 'net'. The essential premise of the
target group approach was that special programmes were required to reach
groups excluded by prevailing inequalities in resource endowments, power
structures, kinship systems and gender relations. NGOs in Bangladesh therefore
shifted their attention from providing straightforward economic benefits, to
organising marginalised sections of the population into self-reliant groups
capable of resisting structural inequalities. Following the pedagogical approach
of Paulo Freire, 'consciousness-raising' was adopted as the underlying principle
for organising the poor.

The target group approach has successfully allowed NGOs in Bangladesh to
work with the rural poor and provide development inputs to a constituency
generally bypassed by government bureaucracies. Donor agencies, concerned
with the seemingly inescapable poverty of rural Bangladesh, have come to rely
more and more on NGOs as a better mechanism for grassroots contact and a
more effective safety-net for the poor. However, larger-scale NGO development
activity backed by increased donor funding has generated contradictions
between the state and NGOs, and has brought the issue of NGO accountability
into the political discourse. This chapter examines the origins of these contradictions in Bangladesh. It also explores prevailing relations between NGOs and
donors, and between NGOs and beneficiaries, to illustrate the need for, and
nature of, NGO accountability.

Government-NGO relations

Government-NGO relations in Bangladesh have moved through stages of indifference and ambivalence. However, in mid-1992 relations degenerated into all-out confrontation. Over previous years, government-NGO collaboration had increased in the spheres of relief distribution, family planning and health services, non-formal education and micro-credit. In fact, NGOs played an active role in the formation of a National Health policy and in the national committee for the distribution of 'khas' land for the poor. However, government had also developed an increasing suspicion of NGOs, which led ultimately to a decision to institutionalise a control mechanism through the establishment of the 'NGO Bureau'. The NGO Bureau was entrusted with authority to grant permission to NGO operations. While this represented an operational improvement over the previous system (in which the Cabinet Division bore responsibility for overseeing NGOs and granting clearance only after scrutiny by a large number of government departments), it also implied centralised control over NGOs.

The fall of President Ershad and the return to parliamentary democracy in Bangladesh (which was welcomed by most NGOs) could have been a signal to increase the freedom of grassroots organisations and NGOs to operate within civil society. However, the reassessment of NGOs by government which followed the return to democracy was guided by bureaucratic imperatives (ensuring control), as well as by a lingering suspicion that NGOs had been too close to the Ershad government. In late July 1992, the NGO Bureau sent a secret report to the Prime Minister accusing NGOs of 'irregularities and corruption' and charging that their activities were 'anti-state and dangerous'. A series of condemnatory articles followed in the media. Matters came to a head when on 20 August 1992, the NGO Bureau issued an order cancelling the licence to operate of ADAB, the co-ordinating body of NGOs, and one other NGO. Interestingly, however (for reasons explained later), the order was cancelled by the Prime Minister's secretariat within a couple of hours of its issue. While the immediate conflict was resolved, antagonism remained beneath the surface.

The NGO Bureau's report to the Prime Minister accused many of the leading Bangladeshi NGOs of resorting to illegal activities. It stated that about 50 NGOs had secured foreign funds worth about 1.4 billion takas without the permission of the government. It also claimed that many NGOs maintained illegal bank accounts and spent money on high salaries, air-conditioned cars and other luxuries, resulting in high administrative costs that amounted to 60 per cent or more of their total budgets. The NGO Bureau accused many NGOs of being donor-dependent and, at the behest of these donors, engaging in anti-state activities such as publishing magazines with a political content, participating in politics and local government elections, engaging in religious conversions and spreading fabricated anti-national propaganda abroad.

The NGOs immediately issued a rejoinder terming most of these accusations 'false and baseless'. Some of the larger Bangladeshi NGOs, with their fleets of air-conditioned four-wheel drive vehicles and plush offices, were easy targets for accusations of lavish lifestyles, particularly since such 'luxuries' are antithetical to the spirit of service that people in South Asia have historically associated with organisations working with the poor. The specifics of the NGO Bureau's criticisms suggested that NGO personnel received high incomes and fringe benefits that were out of line with salaries in other sectors of society. But in a comparative study of 'Benefit Packages Received by Functionaries of Government Organisation and NGOs', it was found that in terms of pay-scales, accommodation, transport, pensions and even foreign trips, high-level government functionaries were better-off than top-level NGO staff (Siddiqui 1987). Contrary to popular expectations, NGO personnel do not receive higher salaries or benefits than their counterparts in government. However, this is not to suggest that NGOs do not engage in a certain amount of lavishness. If one compares the major NGOs in Bangladesh with their counterparts in India, striking differences emerge in the level of resources that are available to them. Compared to their Bangladeshi counterparts, Indian NGOs seem more modest, down-to-earth and resource-scarce. This is symptomatic of the general abundance of foreign funds in Bangladesh. While it may be argued that four-wheel drive vehicles, motorbikes and computers are necessary for better performance, this has to be balanced by the search for low-cost alternatives so that some degree of self-reliance may be achieved, rather than constantly increasing dependence on donor-funding.

But such differences (real or imagined) were not the most important reason for the divergence in government-NGO interests; much more central was the issue of political participation. NGOs are explicit in foregoing the roles of political parties – ie, competing for political power at the level of state authority. However, when NGOs analyse poverty in terms of structural causes and define their objectives in terms of structural transformation, they intervene directly within the political space that defines the *status quo*. In so doing, development NGOs are clearly 'political'. This is usually acceptable to government if it involves providing inputs such as literacy, credit or employment, since these fall within the domain of traditional (charitable or welfare) efforts to assist the poor. However, when the poor are organised to articulate their demands, fight for their rights and struggle to change the structural basis of their subordination, a challenge to the *status quo* is definitely implied. Government agencies perceive their responsibility as maintaining law and order in the prevailing *status quo*, and therefore see NGO activity directed at 'empowerment' to be threatening. To a government that strives to preserve the present (no matter how inequitable the system may be), such activities are akin to a political challenge which seeks to undermine the system itself – hence the charges that NGOs are 'being political'. The case of Gono Shahajjo Sangstha (GSS), one of the most important NGOs in Bangladesh, illustrates this situation well.

Since its inception, GSS has been committed to conscientising the poor and assisting them to set up their own class-based organisation, with the eventual aim of contending for political power. GSS sees NGO credit-provision as an individualised attempt to promote economic welfare, which breaks down 'class solidarity' and hence leads to the maintenance of the *status quo*. In early 1992, GSS felt that their membership in the district of Nilphamari (in North Bengal) was strong enough to challenge the prevailing power groups in local-level elections. GSS put up slates of candidates in five unions in the district of Nil-phamari. Two features of this action were unique. First, GSS candidates (especially for the key post of chairman), were all from the poorest sections of the community. Other NGOs had at times supported candidates, but generally they belonged to the better-off sections of the peasantry – people who would be socially acceptable. Secondly, GSS candidates ran on their organisational 'ticket' and made a major statement of the fact that they were candidates of 'the organisation of the poor'. Local-level elections in Bangladesh are staggered over several days. In the first day of voting, in one union, GSS members won election to the office of chairman as well as the majority of the ordinary seats for members. The prevailing power groups, who up until then had taken little notice of the attempts of the poor to run for political office, saw this as a real threat to their long-standing domination. They could not accept having to report to a day-labourer as chairman. The dominant factions in all five unions (irrespective of their political affiliation) united together to unleash a reign of terror. GSS schools were burnt down, members (including women) were beaten up, and a house-to-house search was undertaken to confiscate all GSS books. In the elections in the other four constituencies, armed thugs ensured that GSS members could not reach the voting sites, and their candidates lost the elections. The government administration sided completely with local élites. The police refused to take action against the armed thugs and instead filed charges against GSS members. The Deputy Commissioner of Nilphamari had this to say: 'all of us want to help the poor and provide charity for them. But when the poor get uppity and want to sit on the head of the rich, when they want to dominate, that cannot be allowed.' He accused GSS of 'organising the poor', an action he felt was 'tantamount to fomenting a revolution'. He filed charges against GSS field-workers, saying they belonged to underground revolutionary parties. The police conducted raids and arrested some GSS staff. Other GSS members left their villages and stayed in hiding for months.

The GSS experience in Nilphamari indicates clearly that the reaction of the government administration stemmed from GSS' challenge to the *status quo*, a situation that government functionaries depend on for containing rural unrest and for maintaining day-to-day governance. They saw in GSS a threat to the social and political order which provides them with the authority to govern. They saw GSS as attempting to subvert the structure of power they were there to defend. GSS' functional literacy text (entitled 'The Book of Learning for the Poor') was banned and GSS was forced to move away from their strategy of confrontation. Their new strategy involves working with 'civil society' rather than helping poor people to organise on their own. A model of class harmony has replaced the previous model of class struggle. GSS' economic activities now substitute for their previous political activities.

The NGO Bureau's accusations against NGOs in the summer of 1992 were mostly predicated on the threat presented by such strategies. While on the surface the NGO Bureau backed off from its decision to revoke the operating licence of ADAB, it succeeded in sending a clear message which set the political boundaries for NGO action. In fact, just a few months prior to the govern-ment's report, a few of the more 'radical' NGO leaders had been called to the

Prime Minister's secretariat and 'scolded' for signing a statement demanding the death sentence for Golam Azam (the mastermind behind the murders of thousands of people during the war of independence). The NGO leaders were warned not to be 'political'.

Most NGOs in Bangladesh have given up strategies to organise the poor, sanitised their activities (if not their rhetoric), and chosen the path of delivering economic assistance. In fact, BRAC, which was using similar rhetoric to GSS in the late 1970s, has in the 1980s changed its emphasis to promoting credit-based economic improvements in the lives of the poor. While government attempts to seek greater accountability from NGOs continue, the decision by some NGOs to de-emphasise conscientisation signals that the government has already won the first round of the battle over accountability, since the conscientisation model must of necessity pit NGOs against government agencies, unless the government itself is committed to structural transformation.

Beneficiary-NGO relations

Although government-NGO conflict in Bangladesh arose from a determination by government to enforce greater upward accountability from NGOs, NGOs have never developed a countervailing system of downward accountability to the poor. It is interesting to note that while terms such as 'grassroots' and 'participation' permeate NGO rhetoric, the conscientisation approach is reminiscent of the 'vanguard party' of the 'old Left'. The underlying assumption is that 'declassed', urban-educated, middle-class NGO workers 'from the outside' must go to the villages to conscientise the poor so that they will organise to form their own class. This approach denies poor people their capacity to organise and struggle for themselves. Even a cursory look at the history of Bengal shows that the peasantry have organised themselves many times to fight against colonialism and feudal oppression. In NGO strategies there has never been a sustained faith in the ability of poor people to bring about their own transformations. It is this perspective that has disallowed any real participation of the poor in NGO activities or the development of systems of accountability to them.

This does not mean that NGOs are not effective institutions in working with the poor. NGOs in Bangladesh are better able to reach people at grassroots level because NGO workers are much more accessible. Generally, local government offices, with their 'peons' and curtains on the door, act as formidable (real as well as symbolic) barriers to entry for poor people. In contrast, NGO workers mix freely with poor people, visiting them in their villages and talking with them about their lives and problems. In spite of this, only limited efforts have been made to make NGO operations truly participatory. Beneficiaries are seldom allowed to make decisions on programmes or budgets, or even to participate in monitoring and evaluation. Their participation is limited to relatively inconsequential areas of decision-making. The solidarity and strength of groups of poor people is overshadowed by, and dependent on, the presence of the NGO. Members who want access to relief or who demand higher wages may do so less because of their own strength than because of the power of the NGO, which is more influential than the village landlord, the local contractor or the government functionary. NGO directors and high officials belong to the same social milieu as top government bureaucrats, military generals and ministers. New hierarchies and new lines of dependence are created (though less exploitative, certainly). A truly participatory development paradigm which integrates poor people effectively into the decision-making process remains largely unexplored in Bangladesh.

Donor-NGO relations

Most Bangladeshi NGOs are totally dependent on foreign funds. The volume of foreign funds to NGOs in Bangladesh has been increasing over the years and currently stands at just below 12 per cent of all foreign aid to the country (see Table 10.1). The high figure for 1989–90 is due to the volume of disaster relief aid disbursed through NGOs during the post-cyclone period.

Donors increased their funding from 162 NGO projects in 1988–89 to 986 in 1992–93, a five-fold increase in five years. The total amount disbursed increased from Tk280 crores in 1988–89 to Tk783 crores in 1992–93, a 180 per cent increase over the period. However, the disbursement of funds to NGOs is highly skewed. The top 15 NGOs accounted for 84 per cent of all NGO allocations in 1991–92, and 70 per cent in 1992–93.

High levels of donor funding have had two major consequences. First, NGOs have become donor-dependent, not merely in terms of the funding that is essential to their existence, but also in terms of seeking donor assistance to legitimise their activities. Second, upward accountability to donors has skewed NGO activities towards donor-driven agendas for development rather than at indigenous priorities.

These trends are exemplified by NGO responses during the period immediately after the attack on NGOs by the NGO Bureau in 1992. Rather than mobilising support from their own constituency (the rural poor), NGOs chose instead to seek the assistance of the donor community. In fact, it was strong intervention by donors that led to the immediate retraction of the suspension order by the Prime Minister's secretariat. When women from Nijera Kori (a Bangladeshi NGO which focuses on conscientisation) were involved in a violent conflict with shrimp cultivators in south Khulna, again it was the donors they

Table 10.1   *Flow of foreign funds to NGOs*

Year	Number of projects approved	Amount in crores* of takas	Total foreign aid disbursed in crores of takas	NGO funds as % of all aid to Bangladesh
1988–89	162	279.85	5339.13	5.70
1989–90	189	1088.26	6031.26	18.04
1990–91	865	639.20	6185.29	10.33
1991–92	695	576.12	6146.14	9.37
1992–93	986	782.82	6562.68	11.93

Source: compiled from NGO Bureau records.

* 1 crore = 10 million takas.

turned to. The Dutch ambassador himself visited the area to give weight to the NGO cause. Even now in the continuing struggle against religious fundamentalism, NGOs are actively seeking donor intervention. NGO dependence on support from donors is ironic, given the fact that the Bangladeshi government also attempts to legitimise itself through donor support. The World Bank's approval of the government's structural adjustment policies, a greater quantum of aid obtained from the Paris Club, and the US Government's praise for the administration's handling of the economy, are all publicised through the media to portray a government that is 'successful'.

Development agendas too are set in accordance with donor priorities. The emphasis on credit-based poverty-alleviation strategies in Bangladesh may have originated with the experience of the Grameen Bank, but moves among other NGOs to replicate this strategy stem from the easy availability of donor support. In fact, the emphasis on non-formal education, immunisation and diarrhoeal disease control, are all due to donor pressure. Conversely, the dropping of adult literacy from NGO agendas is due to the lack of donor interest in such programmes. Now that donor interest has turned to HIV/AIDS, it is only a matter of time before large numbers of NGOs begin to integrate HIV/AIDS into their activities. This does not mean that donors are funding programmes that are irrelevant or ineffective; simply that donor dependence creates a situation in which NGOs end up by reprioritising their own agendas. The shift in the focus of GSS from conscientising the poor to working to 'strengthen civil society' seems also, in part, to be the result of donor-driven rethinking. The term 'civil society' is a new 'buzz word' among donors. USAID is now gearing up to provide funding to strengthen civil society, perceiving this strategy as a logical element in its 'open market and open society programme'. Sanitised from its radical connotations, 'civil society' has come to mean systemic class harmony in which the situation of less privileged groups can be improved through gradual readjustments in the system. Donor funding is therefore provided to groups in society which pursue 'democratic' agendas. What is explicitly (and deliberately) missing from this definition of civil society are the political parties, trade unions and peasant organisations that have consistently fought against exploitation in Bangladesh.

Conclusion

Much of the debate concerning government-NGO relations centres on the regulatory powers of the state. The fundamental issue relates to the rights of NGOs to pursue their objectives unhindered by state coercion, and the state's authority to ensure the accountability of NGOs to specific laws. In Bangladesh the formation of the NGO Bureau and the drafting of the Foreign Donations Act specify a separate set of rules under which NGOs must operate. NGOs are regulated by the Bureau in the provision of licences to operate and permission to receive foreign funding. This is, of course, necessary to ensure legitimate sources of funding as well as legitimate (non-profit) avenues of expenditure. However, conflicts arise when the NGO Bureau extends its regulatory powers to determine what activities NGOs are allowed to pursue. Since there are specific laws that can deal with NGO activities which *do* pose a threat to the public good (increasing pollution, for example) or are fraudulent (running off with funds, for example), the real purpose of the additional measures adopted by the NGO Bureau is to provide coercive authority to deny any serious challenge to the prevailing system of power. NGOs cannot remain fully accountable to government while simultaneously launching a challenge to government power.

Most Bangladeshi NGOs depend on foreign donors for most of their funding requirements. This has created relations of dependence. While it is true that non-governmental development interventions in Bangladesh cannot be financed completely by beneficiaries (because of their levels of poverty) or by other domestic sources (at present), nevertheless there must be much greater efforts to mobilise local resources. No matter how strong an NGO might be, complete dependence on foreign funding will always pose a potential threat, either in the form of acquiescence to donor demands (however subtle) or the termination of funding sources.

In reality, the only way to counter the influence of government and donors is through increased reliance on beneficiaries – the rural poor. Only through the development of a system of accountability to the poor can NGOs truly transform themselves into organisations of the poor. Only by becoming organisations of the poor can NGOs truly prepare for a sustained struggle for empowerment. This implies that NGOs have to make a choice: between the four-wheel drive vehicle that comes with government licensing and donor funding, and the much harder conditions involved in living alongside poor people. Whatever decision NGOs make, they should remember that poor people in Bangladesh have shown that they have a great capacity to rise up and shake the foundations of the kingdom of oppression. The choices made by NGOs will determine which side of this struggle they are on.

11
NGOs in Bangladesh:
Issues of Legitimacy and Accountability
Mahbubul Karim

Non-governmental organisations (NGOs)[1] in Bangladesh embrace many fields but are largely geared to alleviating poverty and promoting sustainable development. Presently, they operate in more than 50 per cent of all villages in the country, involving over 3.5 million families as beneficiaries of their work (ADAB 1994). To the credit of NGOs in Bangladesh are a range of effective development approaches, models and innovations, especially in the fields of micro-finance and non-formal primary education, which have been recognised widely and in some cases adopted by official as well as private development agencies at home and abroad. Over the last two decades, the NGO sector in Bangladesh, as in many other places in the world, has also performed a major role in facilitating the process of institution-building among the poor at the grassroots (Clark 1991). This is crucial if the 80 per cent plus of the population currently living below the poverty line are to be empowered to participate meaningfully in national development and in the process of democratisation. There are, of course, many critics of NGOs in Bangladesh. They have expressed serious doubts about NGO performance, questioned their legitimacy and accountability, and argued strongly against their mode of operation (Muhammad 1988; Umar 1994). This chapter attempts to identify and assess some of these criticisms, especially those concerning legitimacy and accountability.

Genesis and evolution of NGOs in Bangladesh

NGOs in Bangladesh have their roots in the liberation struggle for independence. During the liberation war of 1971, efforts were made by many concerned young people to render medical and other humanitarian services in the refugee camps across the border in India, as well as 'underground' within the country, to alleviate the suffering of war victims (Wood 1994). In the post-war reconstruction period, several relief and rehabilitation programmes were launched both with and without international assistance by freedom fighters in different parts of the country. These were the pioneers in setting an alternative development process in motion in Bangladesh. Interactions with poor people in the villages soon revealed to these pioneers the dynamics of poverty in rural areas,

which led gradually to the transformation of their charity and welfare programmes into participatory development actions for poverty-alleviation (Task
Force 1991).

If seen in the terms of the four-generation model developed by Korten (1990),
NGOs in Bangladesh are now in the third stage of their evolution. In the late
1970s, there occurred a gradual shift from first-generation strategies (relief and
welfare services) to second-generation strategies characterised by small-scale,
self-reliant, local development initiatives for building people's capacity.
Throughout the 1980s, this thrust continued. Pursuing third-generation
strategies that focus on achieving policy changes at different levels is a recent
phenomenon, visible in Bangladesh since the early 1990s. This appears to be the
first indication of Korten's fourth generation of NGO strategy, one which is
characterised by a shift in emphasis from reform to transformational activity.

In terms of their origins, roles and geographical locations, NGOs in Bangladesh are grouped into three major categories: local, national and international. Both local and national NGOs are indigenous, and are engaged
mainly in organising, mobilising and empowering the poor, simultaneously
providing various services at the grassroots level. It is the scale of their operation that largely determines their status as 'local' or 'national'. In most cases
international NGOs provide support (financial, technical or both) to local and
national NGOs. The number of NGOs registered by the NGO Affairs Bureau
(NAB) has risen rapidly in recent years, from 669 in 1992 to over 800 in 1994
(NAB 1993).

Government control

The NGO Affairs Bureau, which functions under the Prime Minister's office, is
the government agency charged with controlling the activities of those NGOs in
Bangladesh that operate with foreign funds (which in reality means most NGOs
in the country). An NGO may be registered with the Ministry of Social Welfare
under the Voluntary Social Welfare Agencies (Registration and Control)
Ordinance of 1961, or as a Joint Stock Company, by the Ministry of Commerce.
This may be under the Societies Registration Act of 1860 or the Companies Act
of 1913. If the NGO receives any foreign funding in cash or in any other form, it
must be registered with the NAB first. To do this, it must operate under the
Foreign Donations (Voluntary Activities) Regulation Ordinance of 1978 and
The Foreign Contributions (Regulation) Ordinance of 1982, along with the
rules which have been framed to carry out the purpose of these two laws (NAB
1993). According to these laws and rules, no NGO is allowed to undertake or
implement any activity with foreign funds without prior approval of the project
and budget by the NAB. Furthermore, clearance from the NAB for the actual
amount to be received from the donor is required. NGOs have to submit a
variety of reports and returns to the NAB in connection with their work.

Self-regulation

The Association of Development Agencies in Bangladesh (ADAB), an apex
body of NGOs in the country, has recently adopted a Code of Ethics (ADAB

1993) as a step forward towards self-regulation for its nearly 700 members. However, this has yet to be fully enforced, as mechanisms for monitoring compliance are still to be finalised.

The code, entitled 'Declaration Regarding Definition, Statement of Purpose and Code of Ethics', defines NGOs as non-profit organisations committed to the development of the underprivileged and underserved. To sharpen their identity within the 'private sector', they have been renamed in the code as 'Private Voluntary Development Organisations' (PVDOs). The code specifies that the purpose of NGOs is to ensure sustainable development of the poor in Bangladesh through poverty-alleviation, building capacity and institutions among poor people, and increasing their participation in productive activities. The objectives of NGOs, as laid down in the code, are to raise the standard of living of the poor and to help them become worthy citizens of Bangladesh – more conscious, self-reliant and able to build and sustain the democratic process at the grassroots. The code posits that NGOs, besides generating their own funds, can accept resources and services from the public, business community, the Government of Bangladesh and external development partners. But these resources are to be exclusively used for the development of the poor, not for any personal profit.

The code intends to establish self-regulatory practices and norms for the member NGOs of ADAB in relation to the people for whom they work, the Government of Bangladesh, other NGOs, development partners and their own staff. Members of ADAB, for whom this code of ethics is obligatory, commit themselves to work for solidarity among the poor, democratic leadership and self-reliance, irrespective of caste, creed, religion and gender. Signatories must also be accountable and transparent to the government with regard to their activities and use of funds. The code also commits NGOs to enhancing solidarity with other NGOs by avoiding factionalism, divisiveness and overlapping. They must also promote competence, professionalism and the highest standards of transparency and honesty. The code makes explicit reference to the need to encourage democratic leadership, participatory management and transparency, including 'to the people'.

Proshika: a case study

Proshika (a centre for human development) was formed in 1976 with the aims of reducing poverty, protecting and regenerating the environment, improving women's status, increasing people's participation in public institutions, and enhancing people's capacity to gain and exercise their democratic and human rights. Proshika implements a wide range of activities that are geared to facilitating people's access to public resources, services and institutions, to enable them gradually to become self-reliant. Its programmes include: building people's organisations; development education through training and theatre; universal education; women's development; employment, income-generation and the provision of credit; environmental protection and regeneration; and health education and infrastructure. Proshika now operates in 6,006 villages and 108 slums in 35 districts, through a network of its own (72) Area

Development Centres (ADCs). Facilitating people's organisations is the core of Proshika's activities. Poor people are encouraged to form primary groups (with an average membership of 18) in villages and then to federate into broader organisations at the village, 'union'[2] and 'thana' level, called 'Co-ordination Committees'. To date, 41,205 primary groups covering 698,000 members have been formed, federating upwards into 3,809 committees at village level, 348 at union level, and 48 at thana level. So far, around 1.58 million people have participated in Proshika's development education programmes.

Proshika regards employment and income-generation as crucial ingredients for empowerment. It assists groups to engage in agriculture, irrigation, livestock development, fisheries, sericulture, apiculture, small and cottage industry and social forestry. These activities are facilitated by building-up savings, the provision of credit, and training, extension and technical support. Thus far, Proshika has extended 1,010 million takas[3] in loans from its Revolving Loan Fund to 49,492 projects undertaken by groups of poor people, matching their own contributions of 234 million takas. These projects have generated over 373,000 employment/self-employment opportunities to date. In the health field, Proshika has assisted groups to install 10,590 hand tubewells for safe drinking-water and 78,349 low-cost latrines to date. With the aim of expanding the literacy base in the country, Proshika's Universal Education Programme has set up 10,031 adult literacy centres and 301 non-formal primary schools from which 191,233 adult learners and 9,030 children have already graduated. Gender equity is a major focus of Proshika's approach to development. Therefore, it ensures active and equal participation of women in every sphere of its activities. Women's groups constitute over 53 per cent of all groups in the programme.

Proshika is a society registered under the Societies Registration Act and with the NGO Affairs Bureau (NAB) of the Government. The highest decision-making body of the organisation is the General Body, presently made up of 30 members from different groups and professions. In the Annual General Meeting, the General Body approves the annual report, the audit report and budget, appoints auditors and elects a nine-member governing body for a period of one year. The Governing Body makes major policy decisions within Proshika and sits at least four times a year to review the performance of the organisation. It also has the authority to appoint the executive director. Proshika practises a participatory planning process that begins at the grassroots level. Every year the process starts in April with each primary group making its plan in terms of social, economic and cultural programmes, on the basis of performance in the previous year, and assisted by Proshika staff. Each group's plan is taken to the Village Committee where it is reviewed and approved, and a village plan is developed. A similar process operates at all levels, with plans at one level integrated into plans at the next level up. Experience shows that each Area Development Centre gets to keep around 95 per cent of its original plan at the end of this process. All levels of Proshika's management are assisted by a Management Information System (MIS) developed over a period of time by its Impact Monitoring and Evaluation Cell (IMEC). The MIS has been developed to fulfil two purposes: the first is to monitor programme targets and achievements in line with Proshika's core objectives; the second monitors day-to-day management (personnel, finance, etc).

An impact assessment study conducted recently by Proshika in collaboration with Horizon Pacific International (Canada) shows that savings of group members have increased substantially over time. Women were found to be better savers and investors. The study also revealed that members are gaining increasing control over local-level arbitration systems and greater access to local government and public institutions. Over 90 per cent of the women interviewed in the study reported a marked decrease in abuse and oppression (IMEC and HPI 1993). The report of a seven-member mission appointed by the Proshika Donor Consortium to appraise Phase V of Proshika's work (July 1994–June 1999) observes: 'progress in Phase IV has been satisfactory. Targets have in most cases been met, improvements have been made in programme operations, and there is emerging hard evidence of socio-economic impacts. The transition to starting programmes in the urban slums of Dhaka has been successful.'

Proshika has built an organisation that is open, self-confident and practises collective decision-making. Proshika's management style will likely enable it to adjust to change without losing its basic vision or reducing its effectiveness (Mitchell 1994). As laid out above, Proshika is accountable 'downwards' via the participatory planning system at group, village, union and thana levels; and 'upwards' to its General Body, external donors and the Government of Bangladesh. It has to provide donors with half-yearly performance reports, annual activity reports and an audit report, and has to have its projects and budgets approved by the NAB. Proshika has worked out a strategy to reduce its dependence on donors. By operating its Revolving Loan Fund in an effective and sustainable manner, Proshika should be able to cover 65 per cent of its administrative and operational expenditures by 1999.

Criticisms of NGOs

NGOs in Bangladesh are viewed negatively by some, including individual members of the bureaucracy, the intelligentsia and political parties, and a number of organisations. Some of these criticisms, such as duplication and overlapping of roles, and lack of co-ordination, have some basis in reality, but others are far too generalised and not substantiated in practice. One of the most common criticisms made about NGOs in Bangladesh is that their administrative costs are too high to be acceptable. From its inception in 1990 up to November 1992, the NAB had approved as many as 816 NGO projects. Only 14 per cent of these projects had higher administrative costs than the generally accepted rate of 20 per cent, while the administrative costs of 76 per cent of the projects were below 15 per cent (NAB 1992). Similarly, questions have been raised about the cost of NGO programme delivery, contrary to general assumptions about NGO cost-effectiveness (Edwards and Hulme 1994). However, the evidence shows that NGOs in Bangladesh perform well in terms of costs. For example, the non-formal primary education programme of the Bangladesh Rural Advancement Committee (BRAC) has a running cost 25–50 per cent lower than that of the formal system (Smillie 1992).

Until recently, there existed a substantial gap between NGOs and other groups and institutions in Bangladeshi civil society, with many NGOs preferring to remain aloof. Perhaps they were under the impression that these groups and institutions had nothing to do with development. In retrospect, this was a great mistake on the part of the NGOs, and has helped to create confusion and suspicion about their activities. For example, the media in general became extremely critical and sceptical about the role and functions of the NGOs. But NGOs did not take account of the implications of this widening gap. It has also given rise to a great many stories (often invented) which have been damaging to their image. For example, one of the allegations brought against NGOs is that they are involved in financing political parties. This is totally baseless (Task Force 1991). These negative experiences clearly indicate a serious problem of information and communication. Fortunately, the popular democratic movement of 1990 helped to bridge this gap considerably.

Legitimacy and accountability

The criticism that has been most uncomfortable for NGOs in Bangladesh is the question of their legitimacy and accountability. NGOs are feeling uneasy about these questions, not because of the criticism itself, but due to the fact that historical weaknesses in the NGO sector are often distorted to create confusion about their basic role. The most important of these weaknesses is their dependence on external funds, and it is this which makes NGOs vulnerable to such sensitive criticisms. High levels of financial dependency exist in most Southern NGOs, and the same is true of Bangladesh. It has proven extremely difficult for NGOs to secure an alternative source base inside the country (although some progress has been made, for example, by BRAC, which now generates over one-third of its budget from internal resources (Edwards and Hulme 1994)).

The point that needs to be emphasised is that when such dependence continues to characterise every sphere of South–North relations, how can NGOs be expected to escape it? In Bangladesh particularly, where both the public and the private for-profit sectors rely heavily on foreign aid, is it realistic to ask or expect that only the non-profit development sector should be able to operate on its own resources? Are NGOs illegitimate just because they rely on external funding? Legitimacy and accountability cannot be judged only in terms of the funding context; the commitment of NGOs and the services they provide to people are equally important. In a truly democratic society, the people are the supreme authority in deciding who is legitimate and who is not. Therefore, why not leave this question to them? The beneficiaries of NGO work were never consulted by those who criticise NGOs in Bangladesh; they have not been asked to express their views about NGOs, despite the widely accepted fact that no development can take place without people's participation. The Bangladesh Constitution affords its citizens the right to form associations and organisations. Legally, any organisation operating in accordance with the provisions of the law is legitimate. But, of course, legitimacy is not simply a matter of legality; it also rests on the role and contribution of NGOs, and their relevance and effectiveness in the local socio-economic context.

In terms of accountability, Bangladeshi NGOs are regularly answerable to at least four different authorities. First, to their Board of Governors or executive committee and through them to the general members, since they are registered legal entities; secondly, to the government who approves their projects and budgets; thirdly, to the people (both the recipients and non-recipients of the benefits and services they provide); and fourthly, to the donors who provide the resources.

It is important to note that in a country like Bangladesh, where democratic norms, values and institutions are yet to be firmly established, the term 'accountability' has different meanings and connotations to different groups of people. In Bangladesh even the accountability of civil servants and elected representatives at all levels is in a 'diluted, diffused and fuzzy state' (Ahsan and Muslim 1994). In the name of greater accountability and transparency, attempts may therefore be made to impose unlimited control over NGOs. For example, NGOs in Bangladesh at the moment are making painstaking efforts to mobilise public opinion against a move by the Ministry of Social Welfare to enact what is according to them a 'retrogressive law' because some of its provisions contravene rights guaranteed by the constitution (ADAB 1994).

Before the end of the Cold War it was the leftist political forces in Bangladesh who opposed NGOs, identifying them as 'agents of imperialism' (Umar 1989). In the post-Cold War period it is the growing forces of fundamentalism who publicly demand a ban on the operation of NGOs, claiming that their activities are 'anti-Islamic' (Rahman, undated; Ahmed 1994). Criticisms of NGOs are invariably value-laden and ideologically based. Therefore, *who* defines accountability, *for whom* and *why*, are questions which need to be analysed very carefully.

Conclusion

This chapter is not intended to create the impression that NGOs in Bangladesh should continue to depend on foreign funding without making efforts to attain self-reliance, difficult as this may be within the existing world economic order; nor that current systems for accountability are satisfactory. The present arrangement cannot be preferred by NGOs simply because they are not sustainable (Holloway 1994). But what is the alternative? NGOs alone cannot find the answers. This is something that NGOs and donors must search for together, and this requires much greater interest and participation from the donors.

What NGOs should begin to do immediately is to build further the capacity of People's Organisations (POs) to enable them to take greater charge of their own development, so that POs who 'graduate' can provide support to NGOs by paying for the various forms of assistance they need. This is not the only option to be pursued. There are several other possibilities and mechanisms of self and local financing that should be explored. For example, the general public, businesses, banks and even the national government could be potential sources of local finance (Holloway 1994). Supporting appropriate and viable revenue-generating activities may be a meaningful option for certain types of NGOs.

Donors could also provide endowment funds. The key point is that it is only by reducing their dependence on foreign funds that NGOs will be able gradually to overcome the questions of legitimacy and accountability thrown at them by their critics.

As an active group in civil society (Tandon 1994), NGOs must develop linkages, common understandings and strategies for working together to strengthen the process of democratisation and the development of society as a whole. This is essential if NGOs are to create greater acceptance and a more positive image for themselves. Like all organisations and institutions, NGOs in Bangladesh must be judged by their results, not on the basis of ideology.

Notes

1. In this chapter the term 'NGO' refers to intermediary development NGOs, or 'Private Voluntary Development Organisations' in the definition used by the ADAB Code of Ethics.
2. The lowest level of local administration and government respectively.
3. In April 1995 £1 = 63 taka.

12

'Return to the Roots': Processes of Legitimacy in Sudanese Migrant Associations[1]

David Pratten and Suliman Ali Baldo

In the current climate of state retrenchment and disengagement in Africa, attention has shifted to the development roles of alternative, non-governmental forms of social organisation. Indigenous or externally inspired institutions which aggregate demands and build capacities at the community level operate as empowerers and potential partners at a significant interface in the development process. Community-based organisations (CBOs) are mediators between state and society, and between donors and households. The relationships created by this intermediary position highlight two areas of analysis within the wider debate on the legitimacy of development intervention. The first concerns the relationship between the organisation and its community, which we call 'internal' or 'downward' legitimacy; the need here is to examine the claim that CBOs represent their constituency effectively and provide appropriate and accountable services. The second, 'external' or 'upward' legitimacy, assesses the relationship between local organisations, the state and other donors. The issue here is whether stronger linkages between state and civil society, or donor and community, will make governments and funders more responsive and thereby enhance their legitimacy. This chapter explores the processes through which CBOs operate as legitimate local development agents for the communities they represent, in the context of migrant associations in Sudan. In particular it examines the assumption that CBO legitimacy rests on two key features – closeness to the poor and popular support. It also analyses the relationships between CBOs and the state (the principal external donor for these groups in Sudan), and questions the frequently proposed conflictual image of state and civil society. The case studies used came from riverain groups in the north of Sudan (Ed Debba in Northern State and Shendi in River Nile State), and communities in the west (Northern and Southern Kordofan States).

As migration increases and becomes more permanent, the connections between rural and urban communities in the Sahel have become institutionalised. Associations formed by migrants in national and international urban centres and based on a shared community of origin are common forms of social organisation. Set against a background of international isolation and the internal dismantling of civil society (Hamad 1993), migrant associations represent one of the most dynamic examples of community action in contemporary Sudan. Often referred to as 'ethnic welfare unions' or '*association d'originaires*', migrant associations can be defined as voluntary groups established by migrants to meet social needs in urban areas and to participate in the development of their home (rural) community.

In the urban environment these associations perform two essential functions for their members, providing both social security and social differentiation. They maintain rural identities but also assist the migrant in adapting to an urban system. Migrant associations therefore represent the reconstruction of rural institutions to reinforce traditional identities in the urban milieu – for example in lineage, burial and dispute-settlement. Yet while these cultural forms are persistent, they assume new meanings and functions in reorienting rural identities to urban life. In this way migrant associations play an important role in familiarising newly arrived migrants with urban status systems, not least in endorsing achievements and achieving social recognition in the host society according to 'modern' values. Migrant associations therefore represent intermediaries between rural and urban, and community and government, and are in this respect 'creative cultural combinations of old and new' (Jules-Rosette 1979, p 20).

Although Sudanese migrant associations were generally established to provide for urban social needs, their orientation to rural development does not appear to have been inspired by the interests of an urban educated élite, as Little (1965, p 29–30) suggests. Rather, in many cases, this is a reaction to rural needs. In this respect, CBOs can be seen as a cultural response to a rural agenda.[2] In the rural environment, Sudanese migrant associations are key actors in providing resources for local development projects, particularly infrastructure. Schools, clinics, mosques and water supply networks have all been planned, funded, built, run and monitored through urban-rural resource flows co-ordinated by the migrant community.

Legitimacy and identity

Local organisations are representations of community; community and organisation are not one and the same, but are linked through shared identity and interest. An evaluation of the processes linking organisation to community is central to understanding the representativeness and hence the legitimacy of CBOs. Concepts such as 'closeness to the poor' and 'extensions of base groups' (Carroll 1992, p 12) are not wholly adequate in explaining the relationship between a community (however constituted) and the CBOs which represent them. As Uphoff (1986, p 11) states: 'many mistakes in development assistance derive from too gross an understanding of an apparently simple term – local'. Yet the literature on local institutional development is occupied by typologies and definitions which by their very nature are decontextualising. However complex, these typologies provide no real substitute for ethnographic analysis in assessing the influence of the dynamic construction of identity on local organisational processes. Sharing a community of birth and retaining familial and economic links give migrants authority in local decision-making and in representing rural interests. Our analysis indicates, however, that the historical foundations and contemporary reconstructions of community identity are paramount in determining the internal legitimacy and performance of Sudanese migrant associations.

In Sudan, organisations formed on the basis of a shared community of origin represent the formalisation of mutual support strategies among poor migrants. Associations from northern Sudan have developed from club-houses built as social centres in neighbourhoods (*zawia*) which are dominated by migrants from a particular rural area and which often assume their name. Many of these club-houses were founded during the initial period of high rural-urban migration – for example, the Khartoum Club, which was established in 1952 for migrants from Gilas. The clubs provide accommodation for newly arrived migrants, although it is common for them to stay for only a week before moving into an *Azaba*, a hostel for five to ten migrants from the same community who share the costs of food and rent. Club-houses and associations also serve as a focus for maintaining rural ties and community identity. In addition to providing accommodation, the club-houses are used by migrant families to celebrate religious festivals, cultural evenings and fund-raising events, and in one case, as the bus-stop for a service to their home community in the north of the country.

For all Sudanese associations, the maintenance of rural attachment and identity is an important function, but for some it is absolutely crucial. One such group is the Shilluk from Upper Nile state who are represented in Khartoum by the Fashoda Benevolent, Cultural and Social Association (FBCSA). The current war in southern Sudan has affected the livelihoods and social cohesion of the Shilluk, 300,000 of whom were estimated to be displaced in 1993. This upheaval has led to fears that the history and practices of the group will be lost. In 1986 the FBCSA was formed, as one member put it, 'to preserve aspects of our cultural heritage which are still thriving, revive what is lost and develop the culture so that it may survive in a changing world'. In addition to the distribution of relief supplies and petitions to international agencies for small-scale rehabilitation projects, the FBCSA received a video camera from its members working in the Gulf with which it was able to film the 1993 coronation of the 'Ruth' (traditional leader) of Shilluk. The association now has a research and documentation unit which attempts to record burial, marriage, child upbringing and other customary practices of the Shilluk clans.

The case of the Kanar Union from northern Sudan demonstrates both the shifting nature of community identity and the importance of self-identification in legitimising local development activities. Northern Sudan is the seat of Arabism, Islam and nationalism in the country. Few migrant associations from the River Nile and Northern States are therefore based on ethnic loyalties, as is common in other regions of the country. Instead, associations are based on units of local administration – the village or a collection of villages called an *omodiya*.[3] Two such *omodiya*, Kuri and Gilas, are located to the east of the urban centre of Ed Debba in Northern State and are represented by clubs in Khartoum and other major towns in Sudan. The Kuri *omodiya* serves seven villages, but its association represents only three. Attempts to unite all seven in an *omodiya* club in Khartoum collapsed and a new association (the Kanar Union) was formed in 1991 by the remaining four villages, with the intention of representing the whole region, including the *omodiyas* of Kuri and Gilas. The union recognised that its central activity (the introduction of a large-scale irrigated co-operative project) required the co-operation and participation of neighbouring villages. Significant conflict around Kanar's identity has been generated in the process.

Kanar is not a place-name and does not refer to an existing *omodiya*. Rival theories claim that the name 'Kanar' is derived either from letters of the names of the villages which founded the association, or that it is the name of an ancient sheikhdom. While debates continue to rage as to Kanar's true identity, the majority of the neighbouring villages have refused to join the union or the project, and object to Kanar's regional pretensions. Fears that the Kuri and Gilas associations would lose their individual names on joining the union and be subsumed within a wider Kanar association have further heightened inter-village rivalry. There are, however, interesting exceptions to those communities who refused to join Kanar. One branch of the Kuri union is dominated by members from a village who, through inter-marriage, retain strong links with a 'Kanar' village, and who therefore support the union's project. The new proposals have also revealed rivalries within villages. In Kuri the decision not to join the Kanar project was taken by the democratically elected village committee (the rural branch of the urban association) in which an influential local family supported the motion in opposition to the family of the *Omda*, the traditional village leader.

A significant consequence of these power struggles is the proposal by the Kuri Union to codify the unwritten co-operation between its urban branches and to form a 'General People's Union', constituted on the same basis as the Kanar Union. Perceiving a threat to its identity, Kuri sought to reconstruct its community boundaries symbolically. Within the context of contested identity, it is also significant that of the 35 associations we encountered in Sudan, only the Kanar Union has engaged in community 'awareness raising' (in the form of a newsletter). Until September 1994, the Kanar Union spent all its income (from membership dues) on travel and accommodation arrangements for annual meetings held at the village level. These meetings provided an ideal stage both to bolster support and to foster a new identity.

Based on residentially-dispersed communities, migrant associations illustrate the fact that the legitimacy of local institutions rests, not simply on proximity to rural constituencies, but on shifting connections with the community they represent. The case studies show that CBOs are engaged in a reciprocal relationship with their constituencies. They are based on and maintain a range of cultural and economic linkages with their community of origin, and are at the same time instrumental in (re-)defining the symbolic and geographical boundaries of that community.[4] Within Sudanese migrant associations and CBOs more generally, *legitimacy through community identification* precedes *legitimacy through participation*.

Legitimacy and organisational processes

While the internal legitimacy of a Sudanese migrant association rests in the first instance on a secure, though shifting, understanding of a community's identity, 'popular support' through processes of participation is a key legitimising factor. Despite their community attachments, migrant associations elsewhere (notably in Nigeria) have been accused of using kinship and ethnicity as a cloak for the interests of their educated élite leadership. In this light, Nigerian 'home-town unions' have been criticised for their orientation towards the 'comparatively strong' rather than newly arrived migrants (Barnes 1975, p 87), and are seen as platforms for rival urban businessmen (Trager 1994). Although Nigerian associations maintain their popularity, participation has been significantly curtailed. In contrast, the legitimacy of Sudanese migrant associations as participatory development organisations is enhanced by a series of checks and balances; an inclusive, broad-based membership; and equitable, cross-community participation in fund-raising, implementation, decision-making and monitoring.

Migrant association membership procedures are open, flexible and familiar. Although membership levels are high, the proportion of members who actually pay their membership fees is small. In the Kuri People's Union in Khartoum, only 23 per cent contribute regularly. Elsewhere, different rates are applied to the employed, the unemployed and students, to encourage their participation. Members of the Al Maghawir association in Khartoum, for example, are divided into high-, middle- and low-income brackets and are expected to contribute up to 20 per cent of their monthly income to the union. The collection of dues and donations among urban associations in Sudan reflects rural processes of hospitality such as *kashif* and *mujib* in which neighbours and families contribute to the expenses of burial ceremonies.[5] The characteristic equity of these membership arrangements is also apparent in the terms for shareholding in irrigation co-operatives initiated by associations in their home villages. Restrictions are placed on the number of shares allocated per person, a policy deliberately introduced to prevent control by élites.

Participation through self-financing is also a key factor in legitimising CBO interventions, and while urban participation in fund-raising is culturally organised through customary practices, rural processes are also informal. In both northern and western Sudan, rural finances are raised through self-imposed taxes on sugar quotas. Ration cards were introduced in Sudan in 1990 to control the prices of wheat-flour, oil, tea, sugar, rice, lentils and soap. With most government subsidies now lifted, sugar remains a rationed commodity. In 1993 in El Duakhil (a village in Northern Kordofan State) villagers sold their sugar allocation to merchants and contributed cash and food to pay the 120,000 Sudanese pounds[6] required to hire a government bulldozer in order to dig a reservoir (*hafir*) as part of a plan to tackle the area's acute water shortage. The *hafir* was completed before the dry season and each family is entitled to 34 jerrycans of water per month, for which they pay five Sudanese pounds. A village water committee guards the *hafir* and is saving the fees to extend its capacity.

Although their financial inputs are generally limited, rural communities are instrumental in providing labour for construction projects. In Mali, rural communities claim that their participation in migrant association projects is 'not with our financial contributions but with our sweat' (Daum 1992, p 81).

The Sudanese context, by contrast, demonstrates that significant urban-rural labour movements are important in relieving or releasing villagers from additional burdens and dependence. Project implementation in Sudan is generally organised on the basis of *nafir* or *fa'za*,[7] a collective village work group. For instance, in Gilas village the rehabilitation of an irrigation pump and drainage network inundated with silt by the floods of 1988 was initiated by the migrant association in Khartoum and the village co-operative, but carried out by 18 successive *nafir*. It is common, however, for members of the migrant community to return to assist in projects and in *nafir*. In preparation for the flood of the River Nile in 1994, for example, the Kaboushia association called on unemployed members to travel to the town to participate in building *durab* (sand embankments) to prevent severe river-bank erosion. Other examples of collaboration include the building of a new mosque in Kuri village (Northern State), participation in brick-making (often for the repair of damaged school buildings) and educational trips home during vacations by students.

Urban-rural links are also key features in the accountability of decision-making in migrant associations. General assemblies for riverain groups are extensions of, and coincide with, the annual return home in September by migrants to monitor their harvest and settle their accounts with casual labourers. General assemblies analyse local problems, set priorities, agree on an annual project agenda, and solicit official support from invited dignitaries; they also provide an opportunity for the rural community to voice their opinions and, if necessary, to reverse inappropriate 'urban' planning. Extensive rural-urban dialogue generally ensures consensus in decision-making, but the experience of the Kanar Union also illustrates the harder edge to accountability which general assemblies – the migrant associations 'shareholder meetings' – can offer. For two years the Khartoum-based leadership of the Kanar Union lobbied government for a large-scale agricultural rehabilitation and irrigation project to grow wheat on village *gusad* land.[8] The 1993 annual assembly was the scene of considerable conflict and a shift in priorities. Represented by a 'Kanar' faction based in Port Sudan, villagers were frustrated by ongoing delays to the proposed 70,000 *feddan*[9] project, and the Port Sudan branch threatened to boycott the assembly if immediate action was not taken. An alternative irrigation scheme was therefore proposed which involved a more modest project using large pumps to improve the irrigation of the *jerif* land where villagers grow date-palms. This proposal was agreed, a new pump was received with state funding for the original project, and the leaders of the Port Sudan branch stayed in the 'Kanar' area to oversee preliminary work after the meeting. Importantly, the shift in priorities from wheat to date cultivation represents a manipulation of state funding. More significant, however, is the way in which the rural community (through the mediation of the Port Sudan branch) was able to postpone the large-scale irrigation scheme in favour of a project which met its immediate needs more directly.

General assemblies also provide an occasion to bring together the range of local structures and processes through which migrant associations plan projects, advocate policies and mobilise participation. Migrant associations therefore act as a node or 'apex' (Barkan, McNulty and Ayeni 1991, p 462) for intra-community support groups which represent a range of local constituencies. Significantly, these linkages also reveal degrees of overlap between governmental and non-governmental organisations. Through their branches, urban migrant associations link the migrant community with other affiliated organisations such as students groups, co-operatives and womens associations.[10]

Rural branches also oversee a network of organisations, including benevolent societies, sub-committees which monitor village projects, and a range of parastatal and religious groups such as *Shabab al Wattan* (the national youth organisation), the Holy Koran Society, the Working Women's Association and the Farmers' Union. The relative weighting attached to urban and rural branches is an important factor in the planning and decision-making process. Where the rural branch is considered to be the headquarters, contact with the migrant community may involve funding requests only.

A range of checks and balances combine to encourage participation and enhance the legitimacy of migrant associations. The key features here are the absence of financial restrictions on joining, traditional mechanisms of self-funding, cross-community participation, project accountability through seasonal migrant returns and general assemblies, and interlinked urban and rural organisational processes. Crucially in this context, these mechanisms are effective in counteracting the tendency for prestige projects or other 'urban' agendas to dominate.

Legitimacy and the development discourse in Sudan

Although on occasion the urban migrant community may act as an external donor in funding village requests, and while certain projects are entirely self-funded, migrant associations are also intermediaries between the community and other development actors. This forms the second, 'upward' axis of the legitimacy debate for CBOs: their relationship with external donors, including non-governmental agencies and the various wings of the state. Northern Non-Governmental Organisations (NNGOs) have worked with Sudanese migrant associations only on a sporadic basis. Several, including ACORD, Band Aid and Community Aid Abroad, have provided assistance to the Nuba Mountains Association in Port Sudan. Save the Children Fund (USA) and SOS Sahel have also responded to migrant associations' requests in western and northern Sudan respectively, but generally these groups are not involved in long-term NGO programmes. Rather, migrant associations are linked personally, institutionally, and through policy and ideology to the Sudanese state, which forms their principal source of external resources.

It is the nature of these linkages and their potential role in holding the state accountable to local demands that are significant in this discussion. It is often argued that a strong civil society with access to state machinery can make governments more responsive to their citizens and indeed foster a notion of 'citizenship' (Fowler 1993, pp 335–336). While religious organisations, trade unions, the Bar Association and independent student bodies have been subject, since 1989, to various strategies of state control (including monitoring, co-ordination, co-optation and dissolution – Bratton 1989), migrant associations have maintained their integrity. Their immunity may be attributed to a low profile (particularly among groups from Northern Kordofan), institutional and personal connections with the state (most pronounced in associations from Northern Sudan), and most importantly to their invaluable role as public service providers.

Clientelistic contacts and state approval further enhance migrant associations' own authority and effectiveness in representing their rural communities, but their role in holding the state accountable to local interests is debatable. Geographically dispersed, without a federated superstructure and with differential access to state offices and officers, Sudanese migrant associations' demands are irregular, isolated and unco-ordinated. Migrant associations do not challenge or influence government on a policy level, but rather respond to opportunities afforded by the state agenda. They are key participants in a bargaining process for services and amenities which would not otherwise be implemented, and in this sense effect a degree of state accountability. But this role should not be exaggerated; overall, Sudanese migrant associations are important actors in providing both appropriate project solutions to state programmes and in attaching local meaning to government policy.

The following examples illustrate this point. Responses to rural emergencies are particularly notable in relief efforts by migrant associations during the floods of 1988 and 1994 in Northern Sudan. The *El Siyasa* newspaper reported that, 'during the rains and flood disaster of 1988, the state apparatus stood like a mud-house in the middle of a sea of water and inertia'. Meanwhile, migrant associations were instrumental in providing relief supplies. For example, the Nubian organisations from Wadi Halfa, Sakout and Mahas established an operations room in their shared club-house. In Northern State generally, migrant associations lobbied government ministries for supplies, rented trucks or planes, and transported medical personnel, drugs, food and shelter to their rural communities where committees were established to target and monitor distribution. Preparations for the 1994 floods were substantially better. The government provided early warning of flood levels and the associations organised work groups of returning migrants to build flood defences. Nevertheless, relief supplies were still required, and it is significant that on this occasion associations in the Northern State attempted to co-ordinate their actions. Speakers from different migrant associations at planning meetings held in Khartoum echoed the sentiment of the Al Barkal Union, whose representative said 'we need solidarity to mobilise government support'. As a result, a joint committee was established to collect damage- and needs-assessment reports which were presented to the relevant ministers.

Projects in the health sector sponsored by migrant associations provide further evidence that, although access to the state and its limited resources is problematic, CBOs are able to provide effective and sustainable services according to local capacities and practices. Plans for upgrading the clinic in Al Maghawir, a village in River Nile State, were established at the local association's General Assembly held in 1992. The design for the clinic was drawn up by an architect-member of the association, and temporary accommodation provided by another. Personal connections with the Ministry of Health proved important for the association in identifying and recruiting a doctor, especially at a time when the exodus of trained medical staff from Sudan to the Gulf States is so acute that legislation has been passed to prevent it. In order to retain the doctor, the association has offered to supplement his state salary with 50 per cent of the profits from the clinic's private evening surgeries. The clinic's operation is monitored by a sub-committee of the rural branch of the migrant association.

In education too, migrant associations have lobbied for resources to maintain local capacities in line with national standards. Financial support for *khalwas* (Koranic schools) in the 1930s and early 1940s was followed in the 1970s by support to upgrade primary schools following government attempts to increase the number of years spent in primary education. Further reforms in 1992 increased the time spent in primary school still further and called for the construction of more classrooms. Parents and communities were called upon again to provide these facilities, and in response the Kuri association in Khartoum, for example, co-ordinated a fund-raising campaign and 'general return' to the village, in which 40 migrants travelled to participate in workshops to construct the classrooms. Clearly, migrant associations provide services which the government is unable to offer, and the view expressed by a member of the Al Maghawir students' association, who run literacy classes in the village during their vacations, is not uncommon: 'education is the responsibility of the state but it is lagging behind, so we had to do something'.

The patterns and themes discussed above are crystallised in the way in which migrant associations and the state appear to be engaged in a common discourse on national self-sufficiency called 'Return to the Roots'. While infrastructural projects demonstrate the role of migrant associations and CBOs in public service-delivery, 'Return to the Roots' sees a shift towards a closer partnership between these associations and the state. In official discourse, 'Return to the Roots' implies a search for the roots of Arabism and Islam, and a quest for self-reliance. The policy manifests itself in a number of ways which draw on traditional processes and self-help organisations. For example, state-level funding campaigns advertised as *nafirs* (work groups) have sought to encourage private and commercial investment in infrastructural development, such as the administrative headquarters for El Metemma Province in River Nile State, and the road from Omdurman to Dongola – *Tarid El Tahida* (the 'Challenge Road').

Since 1990, national self-sufficiency in food supply has been a key feature of this campaign and has focused on increasing agricultural production (particularly of wheat) in the northern region. The underlying message from the government is illustrated in comments made by the Vice-President, Major General Al Zubeir Mohamed Salih, during a visit to agricultural schemes in River Nile State in August 1994:

> the Salvation Revolution is keen to prepare all lands in the state for wheat cultivation with a view to reaching self-sufficiency in this strategic food crop which is being used as a weapon against the Sudan by the forces of arrogance in the world.

Source: SUNA Daily Bulletin, 23 August 1994

The lifting of subsidies on basic commodities and the extension of credit and investment funds through co-operative societies and the Agricultural Bank of Sudan have all been instigated to further this policy.[11]

For the migrant associations themselves, however, the policy of 'Return to the Roots' has a different set of connotations. It is seen as an opportunity to take advantage of state funding, as expressed in the following statement by the president of the Kanar Union:

> *The government is advocating agricultural development and there are schemes in the government's agenda targeting the Northern State. We thought that we should step in and join hands with the government and implement these plans: to be the implementors and beneficiaries.*

As a result of this policy, the Kanar Union, in common with at least ten other associations from the northern region, are planning a large-scale land rehabilitation and irrigation project. A significant implication of the way in which this proposal ties in so closely with the state agenda is that the project monitoring committee is composed of national and provincial ministers as well as officials from the union. A further indication of the dynamism of associations in responding to funding possibilities is the growth of agricultural investment companies, such as the 'Wifaqq Company for Investment and Development' in Northern State, in which the Gilas association intends to participate.

At the same time, regional interpretations of 'Return to the Roots' have added a fuller dimension to its meaning. Faced with ever more marginal urban employment opportunities and a chronic shortage of agricultural land and rural labour, the Kanar Union sees the national self-sufficiency campaign as an opportunity to encourage urban-rural return migration. The definition of 'Return to the Roots' offered by the Union's president also highlights the significance of urban-rural linkages in maintaining community identity:

> *The slogan 'Return to the Roots' we are advocating is literally meant to incite people to physically go back and develop the area and preserve rural values and heritage; it is a matter of preserving identity in a changing world.*

Government policies and migrant association strategies therefore represent a 'meshing' of national and local interests (Barkan et al 1991, p 463). Yet rather than defining priorities, migrant associations are engaged in a discourse with the state in which both the associations and the government are able to attribute their own meanings to the same process. Indeed, these examples indicate that 'development' itself is an idiom which provides 'an opportunity to perform joint acts in which each party can pursue its own initiatives' (Lithman 1984, p 263). Furthermore, the case studies outlined in this chapter suggest that a dichotomous view of state and civil society is untenable and that, analytically, space should be left for engagement and disengagement, congruence and conflict (Bratton 1988, p 418).

Conclusion

The two axes of legitimacy outlined in this chapter – internal and external – are central concerns in the wider debate on the performance and accountability of intervention by the non-governmental sector. As potential partners for NGOs, which are increasingly concerned with institutional capacity-building in the south, CBOs are assuming greater importance as representative, participatory and accountable intermediaries. In the wider political debate surrounding democratisation, 'good governance' and the potential for a strong African civil society to hold states accountable to their citizens, the brokerage role of CBOs is also significant.

As we have attempted to illustrate, however, the internal legitimacy of CBOs, which is often assumed or glossed over in terms of membership control, self-funding and popular support, rests on culturally organised processes. Foremost among these processes are the construction and negotiation of community attachment and identity, and the network of social checks and balances which enhance CBO participation and accountability. In terms of voicing local priorities in national or international agendas, the experience of migrant association-state relations in Sudan is cautionary. While Sudanese associations exert some accountability in the bargaining process for social facilities, their current impact on state policy is limited. Sudanese CBOs do not act as bulwarks against the state, but as intermediaries in negotiating and interpreting development in local terms.

Notes

1. This paper draws on a study entitled 'Rural-Urban Linkages: the Role of Migrant Associations in Sudanese Development' conducted jointly by SOS Sahel and Al Fanar Centre for Development Services. SOS Sahel is a UK-based NGO specialising in natural resource management working in Sudan, Ethiopia, Mali, Niger and Eritrea. Al Fanar is a research and consultancy group based in Khartoum. The research in Sudan is funded by the Ford Foundation. The study in Sudan forms part of a pan-Sahelian study also assessing local institutional dynamics in Mali and Ethiopia.
2. This is evident most dramatically in the formation of the Halfa National Committee when, in 1959, the governments of Sudan and Egypt signed the agreement for the construction of the High Aswan Dam with significant consequences for local resettlement and rehabilitation.
3. The system of native administration, abandoned by Nimeiri in the 1970s and recently revived, is based on a positional hierarchy of sheikh, *omda* and *nazir*, each representing corresponding areas – village, *omodiya* and *nazara*.
4. These cases provide further evidence of contemporary settlement theories which indicate that local communities (the village or village group) are constructed as much by shared institutions (meeting places, markets, projects and associations) as by physical features, and that in this respect community should be seen as 'a locus for discussing and implementing' (see Massaro 1994).
5. *Kashif* literally means 'list'. In rural areas a record is taken of names and donations

by a person sitting in the *furash*, the male section of the compound. *Mujib* is the equivalent process for women. In urban areas it is common for a *kashif* list to circulate among fellow office-workers.

6. At the time of writing, £1 sterling is equal to Ls 611 (Sudanese pounds).

7. *Fa'za* literally means 'emergency call' and is the term most commonly used in northern regions of Sudan. Customarily, *nafir* are called for agricultural production on the fields of villagers unable to weed or harvest due to household labour shortages.

8. Located on the banks of the River Nile, villages in northern Sudan cultivate land both in front of the settlements (*jerif*) and land stretching behind the village itself (*gusad*).

9. A *feddan* is equal to 0.42 of a hectare.

10. Migrant associations are male-dominated, a reflection of a conservative Sudanese culture. In urban centres, women (a migrant minority) form mutual support groups, participate in students' associations and in a few cases are represented on migrant association executive committees. In rural areas women participate in the religious and women's branches of national parastatals and in *nafir* where they prepare food for the labour groups.

11. Branches of the Agricultural Bank of Sudan have grown significantly from 34 in 1989 to 118 in 1994 (23 are located in Northern State).

13
NGOs and Development in East Africa: a View from Below[1]

Zie Gariyo

This chapter summarises some of the experiences of different types of NGOs in their attempts to improve the livelihoods of poor rural and urban communities in Africa. Based on evidence from fieldwork in Kenya, Tanzania and Uganda, the discussion highlights the perceptions of NGOs and grassroots organisations (GROs) towards development issues; discusses how support from Northern NGOs (NNGOs) influences the activities of Southern NGOs (SNGOs); and analyses the extent to which state action and policies affect development programmes and strategies in the region. During fieldwork in 1993, a total of 95 non-governmental organisations were surveyed.[2] A number of methods of data collection were used, including questionnaires, face-to-face interviews, and visits to project sites to ascertain the views and activities of NGOs in East Africa, and their perspective on development and welfare issues. Among the organisations surveyed, there were 21 apex NGOs, 25 intermediary NGOs, 36 grassroots organisations (GROs), and 13 Northern NGOs (NNGOs). Their activities ranged from service-delivery (credit, health, etc) to action-oriented research and lobbying (human rights, environment, etc).[3]

Table 13.1 shows that only a small number of GROs were surveyed in Tanzania and Kenya. This was because of the limited time (five weeks in Tanzania and three weeks in Kenya) available for fieldwork. However, more GROs were surveyed in rural Uganda; thus, the conclusions of the research on GROs are based largely on Ugandan experience. In Uganda, there are a few large apex NGOs such as DENIVA, but intermediary NGOs tend to pre-

Table 13.1 *Number and type of organisations surveyed*

Type of organisation	Tanzania	Kenya	Uganda	Total
Apex (Southern) NGO	7	7	7	21
Intermediary NGO	6	6	13	25
Grassroots organisations (GROs)	4	3	29	36
Donor (Northern) NGOs	7	6	–	13
Total	24	22	49	95

Source: Fieldwork data

dominate. The many GROs we visited in Uganda are also affiliated to apex and intermediary NGOs. In Tanzania (where the formation of NGOs is a more recent phenomenon), development work is dominated by the three major churches – Catholic, Lutheran, and Anglican. Thus, most of the discussions held in Tanzania were with church (or related) development programme officials in Arusha, Moshi and Dodoma.

Contextualising NGOs and development

Historically, most development programmes at community level in Africa have been dominated by the state. More recent intervention strategies are different, first, because they have been promoted largely by foreign or foreign-sponsored agencies; and second, because they rely on financial and material resources supplied from outside the country. This has important implications. Previously, most development initiatives were subordinated to state control; now they tend to be subordinated to foreign agencies. Both the design and implementation of development programmes are largely dominated by external development agencies. Fieldwork revealed that SNGO development programmes (whether service-delivery or otherwise) are heavily influenced by Northern NGOs. NNGOs have their own agendas and often specialise in particular activities or approaches: relief, environment, child sponsorship, health services, human rights, credit programmes, training and so on. Poor people themselves have little influence over most of these programmes, as in other areas of aid policy and practice. As Bratton (1990, p 90) has noted, 'poor people have no control over the material and institutional conditions under which they exist ... the poor lack the political "clout" to make their own preferences stick.' In addition, development programmes have tended to target individuals rather than community problems: poverty-alleviation programmes tend to target women as beneficiaries, but do not tackle women's subordination, nor do they transform 'the systems and structures which determine the distribution of power and resources within and between societies' (Edwards and Hulme 1994, p 13). The issue of women's empowerment is part of the larger process of social transformation, to which the response from the state remains muted at best and oppositional at worst.

The influence of NNGOs over development programmes has also meant that issues of accountability have been transferred from the realm of bureaucratic reports to state functionaries, to the realm of evaluation and monitoring reports to the headquarters of NNGOs in foreign capitals. Until recently, popular participation was not regarded as an essential component of NGO development programmes. The African Charter for Popular Participation, which was drawn up in Arusha in 1990, was in part a response to this situation. It called for a new era in Africa 'in which democracy, accountability, economic justice and development for transformation become internalised ... the empowerment of the people, initiative and enterprise and democratisation of development are the order of the day in every country.' Crucially, the charter noted that development cannot be divorced from the wider, economic, social and political process in African societies; that for development and transformation to take place, community initiatives must be placed at the forefront; and that the development process is inescapably a part of the democratisation process in Africa. These strictures have yet to be internalised in North–South NGO relations.

NGOs and donor-dependence in East Africa

The links between NNGOs and East African NGOs are mainly financial. Financial assistance is limited, however, to the better organised and more easily accessible apex and intermediary NGOs. Although some apex NGOs claim to have a paid membership, contributions from members are mainly token payments. Of the 62 NGOs and GROs in East Africa which responded to a questionnaire on their sources of funding, 36 reported that they depended on foreign donations for between 75 per cent and 100 per cent of their funding, and a further 7 received between 50 per cent and 75 per cent. The 18 organisations who received less than 25 per cent foreign funding are mainly GROs which either have limited access to foreign donors, or whose funding is mediated through apex and intermediary NGOs. Such high levels of foreign funding tend to deprive NGOs of a strong base in their own societies and contribute to their inability to plan for the long term.

Compounding this already difficult situation is the issue of accountability or, more precisely, the demand for strict accountability by external donor agencies. This comes in two forms. First, demands for strict financial accountability do not allow for flexibility in switching funds between alternative uses. Second, the demand for continuous monitoring reports of programme activities, implementation and the evaluation of achievements is extremely time-consuming. On the lack of flexibility, an official from one NGO in central Uganda complained thus:

> ... we want to start our own income-generating projects so as to sustain our programmes when the donors stop giving us financial assistance one day. The area we are in has rich fertile soils which can be used to grow food crops for sale in the main urban centres. Our donors cannot allow us to use part of the money they give us to purchase land and start an agricultural project. When donations stop this year, we would have wanted to be able to continue some form of assistance from our own sources but now it will be difficult. We shall have to close unless we get another donor.[4]

An official of another NGO (in Nairobi), who was involved in credit delivery, had this to say:

> They [the donor agencies] should give us money but should not dictate what we should use the money for. Sometimes we want to set up our own income-generating activities such as consultancies, training centres or services such as accommodation units but donors would not hear of it.[5]

Such views may appear Utopian, but they are not isolated. They pervaded most of our discussions with the numerous NGOs we visited in all three countries. To break their dependence on donors, KENGO (the Network of Kenya Environmental Non-Government Organisations) has acquired a plot outside Nairobi to construct a training centre and establish a business bureau to undertake consultancies to generate their own sources of funds in support of their environmental programmes. Nevertheless, demands for strict account-ability and adherence to rigid terms-of-reference limit the extent to which NGOs are able to shift development funds to related activities which are not specified in the initial programme document. Much of the disillusionment of SNGOs with donors stems from their lack of control over their financial resources. In the long term, this limits their ability to create an independent source of material support for their programmes. Above all, it reflects the influence of complex demands for financial accountability by Northern NGOs and official donor agencies (Edwards and Hulme 1994).

What is more difficult to explain is the level of bureaucracy which exists in many local NGOs, which donor agencies are also opposed to. Some donors insist that at least 75 per cent of project funds should go directly to beneficiaries or projects. However, evidence from the field revealed that salaries and other operational expenses often push the cost of administration to as high as 60 per cent. For example, analysis of one proposal by TANGO (the umbrella orga-nisation for NGOs in Tanzania) revealed that out of a total package required for a three-year training programme, only 20 per cent was directly allocated for training. Salaries and consultants' fees were allocated 14.2 per cent and 29.2 per cent respectively; equipment and travel 19.6 per cent; rent 3.0 per cent and other miscellaneous charges 15.5 per cent.

Apex NGOs, grassroots organisations and village level development

Apex NGOs are networks of member organisations formed partly at the initiative of NNGOs to co-ordinate development activities at grassroots level. However, the membership of apex NGOs in East Africa remains limited to GROs which are easily accessible or to intermediary NGOs which are more highly organised. Part of the explanation for the weak links which exist between apex NGOs and their members is that membership is based on co-option rather than being a response to pressure from below. Thus, NGOs such as the Network of Kenya Energy and Environmental Non-Government Organisations (KENGO), and the National Union of Disabled Persons of Uganda (NUDIPU), despite being membership networks, tend to operate more as national registration centres and clearing houses for other organisations. Other apex NGOs have been formed in response to hostility and pressure from the state. The Tanzania Non-Governmental Organisations Network (TANGO), which was formed in 1989, and the Development Network of Indigenous Voluntary Associations (DENIVA) in Uganda, which was formed in 1992, were both established to provide a protective shield and a united voice for their members.

In both TANGO and DENIVA, however, financial contributions from affiliates and member organisations represent only a token amount of their total budgets. This has important implications. First, it reduces the potential influence of member organisations on decision-making. Second, because they are themselves dependent on foreign funding, the activities of apex NGOs (such as networking, training and research) may be determined not by the demands of their members but by the amount of financial support available from outside. Accountability may not respond to demands for effective representation from below. Weak links between the grassroots and the apex body restrict the developmental impact of NGOs because of 'the failure of NGOs to make the right linkages between their work at micro-level and the wider systems and structures of which they form a small part.... In other words, small-scale NGO projects will never be enough to secure lasting improvement in the lives of poor people' (Edwards and Hulme 1992, pp 13–14).

Because most apex NGOs are dependent on donors, they are less able to support independent GRO initiatives, and tend instead to integrate them still further into the world of foreign aid. This is summed up by the comments of the Chairperson of a grassroots women's organisation in Mbale, Eastern Uganda:

> ... we were told to form a group so as to obtain financial support. We went for training seminars on project proposal writing, project planning and implementation. When we came we wrote a proposal. It is almost a year, we have not received any money.[6]

Further problems arise because of internal organisational, structural and institutional weaknesses in GROs. In most cases, GROs are too small, too poor and too weak institutionally to take on larger and longer-term development programmes. They are loosely organised and have little influence over the larger urban-based NGOs and institutions. Most are located in remote areas and are therefore unable to benefit from the information systems available to apex and intermediary NGOs. Small GROs also tend to take on a wide range of unrelated activities, thus stretching their own meagre resources too thinly.

Another disturbing aspect of GRO–NGO relations concerns the erosion of voluntary participation. Historically, the strength of village-based GROs has been their reliance on voluntary participation and contributions in the form of funds and/or labour from their members. This had several advantages. Accountability (in terms of decision-making and project implementation) had a popular mandate, and was to the membership and not to any outside authority. Projects acknowledged and built on existing initiatives within communities. As a result of externally derived initiatives, this perspective is slowly being eroded. Presently, most development programmes consist either of elaborate project proposals seeking foreign funding, or donor-derived projects such as credit schemes, income-generating projects, health or child sponsorship schemes, all seeking local participation. Membership lacks real strength and permanence. Out of the 29 GROs surveyed in Uganda, less than 10 (mainly savings co-operatives) could claim a membership of more than 10 registered and fully paid-up members. With such a limited membership, it is very difficult to move accountability from being donor-driven to being membership-driven.

The state, NGOs and development: collaboration or recognition?

Bratton (1990, pp 95–96) has argued that 'selective collaboration between NGOs and the state is likely to be more productive than confrontation'. Relationships between NGOs and the state in East Africa remain cold. Most African governments remain suspicious of any independent initiative which attempts to mobilise and provide services to disadvantaged communities without the direct involvement of the state. Because increasing NGO involvement in development has been conceived as a challenge to state hegemony and a response to state failures, this has intensified the suspicions which exist between the state and NGOs. In a report to a workshop on NGOs, an official of an Ugandan NGO commented thus:

> *In some cases relationships with government are characterised by suspicion and mistrust. Some government officials are fearful that as NGOs gain greater recognition by donor agencies, they will begin to compete with government for outside funds.... NGOs (on their part) lack knowledge of and access to government aid priorities and programmes due to the tight secrecy that surrounds them.[7]*

There is also a tendency to incorporate NGOs as collaborators of state functionaries. In Tanzania, TANGO also noted that:

> *The general attitude of government towards NGOs in the country is that these are collaborators in development and have a role to play ... it is held, from an official point of view, that NGOs will not work against government policies but will help in achieving the social goals and objectives which are pronounced from time to time.[8]*

Governments tend to see NGOs as an extension of state policy. They are expected to implement government policy instead of charting their own independent agenda. This undermines the social base of NGOs in their efforts to pursue an alternative development path for the poor and marginalised sections of East African societies, in the face of the failure of state-centred development. Generally, NGOs are not opposed to implementing government policy. Most, however, are opposed to deliberate frustration by state functionaries and to increasing state monitoring, control and direction. Sections of the state leadership have occasionally branded NGOs as 'foreign agents'. For example, at the height of multi-party debates in Uganda in 1992, the Foundation for African Development (FAD), an indigenous NGO, was accused by the President of Uganda in a statement to Parliament of serving 'foreign interests'. In their defence, FAD took out a newspaper advertisement on 28 August 1992, which stated that:

> *Our attention has been drawn to a statement dated 6th August 1992 presented to the National Resistance Council (NRC) ... also attributed to the President. In the statement reference is to made to 'Certain foreign groups, eg FAD' ... having persistently not heeded advice that the interim period be a time of national recuperation and of allowing the population of Uganda to chart their own future ... The Foundation for African Development is **not a foreign group** [emphasis in original]. It is an organisation which was founded in Uganda by Ugandans way back in 1979.[9]*

FAD further argued that:

> *Reference has been made about FAD receiving foreign assistance. This is not a secret ... This is not peculiar to FAD ... we do not need mention the so many Ugandan NGOs which depend entirely on foreign donations and assistance without being subjected to the kind of accusations FAD is constantly subjected to. The Government itself is depending on foreign assistance.[10]*

These are not isolated incidences. They depict the precarious situation under which NGOs work if they intend to pursue programmes independent of those sanctioned by the state. Some East African governments have turned suspicion and mistrust into an attempt to extend direct control over NGO activities. In Uganda, for example, all NGOs (both foreign and local) are required to register with the NGO Registration Board under the Ministry of Internal Affairs. The NGO Statute No 5 of 1989 states that 'No organisation shall operate in Uganda unless it has been duly registered with the Board'. One of the functions of the Board is 'to guide and monitor organisations in carrying out their activities'. The membership of the Board includes officials of the two major intelligence organisations. Statutory Instrument No 9 of 1990 further states that 'an organisation shall, in carrying out its operations, comply with the following: it shall not make any direct contact with the people in any part of the rural areas of Uganda unless it has given seven days notice in writing of its intention so to do to the Resistance Committee and the District Administrator of the area.' Compounding the complexity of control is the fact that co-ordination and monitoring of NGOs falls under the Prime Minister's office, where NGOs are 'expected to register and declare their project proposals and to require an endorsement for their correspondence with foreign donors to solicit for funds.'[11] Like most Ugandan government policies, however, these laws have not been implemented, largely because the Board 'has no resources to guide and monitor NGOs... There is one full-time officer and a clerk, no office equipment and transport, and an inadequate budget' (Ratter and Kwesiga 1994 p 17).

As a response to the power of the state, some NGOs have chosen the path of collaboration in order to survive both financially and politically. The co-opting of politicians on to NGO boards and management committees has been used to secure additional protection. In turn, NGOs are allowed access to information about government programmes and policies – for example, via NGO representatives at meetings of local and national planning authorities. Some of the large NGOs such as KENGO and 'Maendeleo ya Wana Wake' in Kenya; and the Community Development Trust Fund (CDTF) and UMATI (the Family Planning Association) in Tanzania, have appointed prominent politicians and senior public officials to their boards.

This research does not suggest, however, that the situation for NGOs in East Africa is hopeless. Indeed, to emphasise their independent existence, attempts are being made to forge regional linkages between NGOs in Eastern and Southern Africa, to 'harness the capacities of NGOs in the region to articulate and implement an African development agenda rooted in on-going experiences and analyses, with a sensitivity to both the realities and aspirations of African societies.'[12] The NGOs which participate in such networks are both indigenous and foreign. The extent to which such efforts can forge an economic, social and political development agenda for transformation, participation and democratisation remains to be seen, but seeking recognition from, rather than collaboration with, the state seems to be a better strategy for NGOs in the region.

Conclusion

There are a number of lessons to be learned from the research presented above. First, there is an obvious need for African NGOs to become less dependent on foreign initiatives, which tend to bring only short-term benefits. Second, NGOs and GROs in East Africa have yet to come to terms with a context of development assistance which emphasises projects and programmes to the exclusion of social and economic transformation. Development assistance which seeks to solve the immediate problems of individuals can only succeed in the short term. Long-term development requires that development be viewed as a process which seeks to overhaul the present social and economic structures which are responsible for the destitution and deprivation of poor people in rural and urban areas. For some time now, NGOs have merely responded to the crisis of poverty and deprivation; they now need to go beyond this narrow perspective.

Within this context, it is pertinent to note that NGOs are not a substitute for the State in the process of development in Africa. Nor are they to be conceived simply as partners of government. The State and NGOs have different perspectives on development. Development cannot ignore politics and in order to facilitate transformation, NGOs must pursue an agenda which seeks to democratise both economic and political power. Thus, the development of organisational capacity and skills among poor people should be enhanced within the NGO agenda. Lastly, NGOs need to enhance their struggle for recognition as independent organisations with a specific agenda of their own, and not organisations to be tolerated by the State or subordinated to its interests.

Notes

1. A more detailed version of this paper is published as a working paper of the Centre for Basic Research, Kampala.
2. 'Apex NGOs' are usually hierarchical, urban-based organisations formed (partly at the suggestion of donors) to act as a link between NNGOs and SNGOs. 'Intermediary NGOs' are dependent on donor funds and are often formed by university graduates, as a form of employment for themselves and as a response to the harsh socio-economic climate resulting from the structural adjustment programmes implemented in Africa since the early-1980s. 'Grassroots organisations' (GROs) are village-based groups formed to pursue the interests of their members.
3. Thirteen other organisations were included in the survey from government training institutes and trade unions in Kenya, Tanzania and Uganda. They do not form part of the analysis for this paper.
4. Fieldwork interview, the Administrator, Senyange Project, Masaka, Uganda.
5. Fieldwork interview, Credit Manager, Kenya Rural Enterprises Programme.
6. Fieldwork interview, Chairperson of Muyembe Women's Co-operative Society.
7. Report by Ssentamu-Makumbi, Executive Director, Joint Energy and Environment projects (JEEP), Kampala, 1992.
8. TANGO policy paper entitled 'Strengthening the Efficiency and Development Impact of TANGO and its member NGOs in Tanzania', Dar es Salaam, November, 1992.
9. The full-page statement appeared in *New Vision* of 28 August 1992.
10. Ibid.

11. *New Vision*, 16 May 1992. Statement by Dr Madraa, National Co-ordinator of NGOs in the Prime Minister's office to a meeting of indigenous NGOs in Lira, Northern Uganda. This directive has largely remained unimplemented. With more than 1000 registered NGOs by 1994, most of them seeking foreign assistance for projects, the administrative costs of such an undertaking would be very high.
12. This policy framework is contained in a workshop report titled 'Consultation on a Research and Advocacy Agenda for African NGOs', prepared by Mwelekeo wa NGO for a Vision for NGOs (MWENGO), an Eastern and Southern African Reflection and Development Centre for NGOs, held at Nakuru, Kenya, 26–29 July 1991.

Part III
Ways Forward

14
Assessing NGO Performance:
Difficulties, Dilemmas and a Way Ahead
Alan Fowler

1. Introduction

The 1990s have witnessed a significant increase in efforts to assess the performance of non-governmental, non-profit development organisations (NGOs). This trend can be traced to a number of factors. First, since the early 1980s a growing proportion of financial resources used by NGOs has derived from the official aid system, overtaking, in terms of rate of growth, their income from public giving (Fowler 1992a). Public funds are accompanied by more stringent 'contractual' demands for financial accountability and the realisation of agreed impacts (Hawley 1993). Second, the post-Cold War rationale for official overseas development assistance (ODA) is further accelerating shifts in donor priorities towards the institutional restructuring of recipient countries, with a corresponding push on NGOs to alter their role in society. Effective management of such organisational transformations requires sound and timely information about achievement. Third, NGOs tend to argue that they are more cost-effective than governments in reaching and serving people who are poor and/or marginalised and are now being called upon to demonstrate that this is indeed the case (UNDP 1993; van Dijk 1994). Fourth, there is a growing realisation that organisational effectiveness is positively correlated with an ability to learn from experience (Senge 1990). This insight is argued to be of particular relevance for NGOs because, as entities dedicated to social change, they predominantly function as natural open systems (Scott 1987, pp 105–115; Fowler et al 1992, pp 17–19), where performance is very dependent on and sensitive to instability and rapid change in the external environment. Such situations are common in both the South and the North. Learning requires data about all aspects of organisational functioning, prompting greater attention to the need to gather evidence of impact and assess the capacity to adapt.

NGOs have always understood the need to assess their performance. However, the growing internal and external pressures sketched out above are bringing to light serious inadequacies in past attempts to do so; inadequacies which stem from fundamental difficulties inherent to:

1. the development approach adopted by the aid system;

2.   the concept of performance when applied to non-profit organisations;
3.   the way developmental NGOs need to profile themselves in order to secure and maintain public support and funding.

This chapter reviews the difficulties and dilemmas which accompany attempts to determine NGO effectiveness, and charts some practical ways ahead. Section Two looks at the basic problems of performance assessment which arise as a result of contradictions between the principles which underpin international aid and the nature of sustainable change which aims to benefit poor people. The intrinsic difficulties of identifying performance criteria for non-public, non-profit organisations are examined in Section Three. This analysis identifies the challenges to be overcome in designing approaches to NGO performance assessment that are sound, practical and cost-effective, approaches which are the subject of Section Four. The concluding section of the chapter offers some speculative observations on ongoing attempts by NGOs to gain more insight into what they are achieving.

2.   Factors affecting the assessment of project performance

Figure 14.1 provides an overview of the factors which condition NGOs' ability to determine what impact they are making in terms of the people they are established to serve. It shows the interconnections commonly found in the project flow of international development resources; the interfaces where one organisation's ends become another's means; the factors that influence the flow of resources; and the different points at which performance can be assessed in terms of outputs, outcomes or impacts.

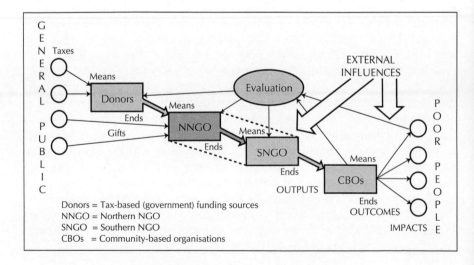

Figure 14.1   *NGOs in the aid chain*

Development as a linear process

The international aid system was initially premised on the notion of under-development as a 'deficit' in capital, knowledge and technology. The transfer of such resources from richer to poorer economies would, it was believed, enable or speed up economic growth, leading to an improvement in the material circumstances and well-being of poorer strata within recipient societies. Projects – discrete packages of resources and activities – were the mechanism chosen to achieve this outcome. The project mode of development, sometimes called the 'blueprint approach', assumes that it is possible to pre-determine a set of cause-and-effect relationships that will turn resources, knowledge or technology into desired and sustainable human change. In other words, that it is possible to predict and create a knowable future (Roling and de Zeeuw 1987).

The notion of prediction and a controllable future underpins 'hard' science and its application to the physical world. It also determines what is considered to be valid knowledge and dictates the methods by which such knowledge can be gathered and validated. Most critically, knowledge must be objective in the sense that it is derived from observation in the real world, which can be demonstrated to be independent of the person(s) doing the observing. Under these assumptions it should be possible to define and plan a project as a linear process of causes and effects, using resources in a pre-determined sequence of activities to produce the desired outcome. Logical framework analysis is an instrument now commonly used for designing this type of development.

Putting project development into practice requires action by a number of organisations which are tied together like a chain between the resource provider and those intended to benefit. Figure 14.1 shows this typical set-up for NGOs. From left to right in the diagram, resources move either directly (as gifts from constituents in the richer North) or indirectly (from taxes through governmental donors) to Northern NGOs (NNGOs), Southern NGOs (SNGOs) and then on to community-based organisations (CBOs) comprised of poor people and households. Each organisation obtains resources (or 'means' in the figure) to fulfil its role, while its processes and capacities are tailored towards goals (or 'ends') which are set in relation to an overall mission and the specific objectives of the project. If all goes well, the result of this joint endeavour is the realisation of a pre-defined impact on human well-being.

Despite attempts at rigorous study, there is far from unanimous evidence that project-based aid does achieve the intended effects reliably (Cassen 1986; White and Woestman 1994). In fact, some analysts argue that 60 per cent or more of such aid is ineffective (Korten 1991; Hancock 1989). If this is the case, there must be something essentially questionable about such an approach to development.

Development as complex, contingent change

Accumulated experience shows that the principle and practice described above is seriously flawed for most types of human and social change. First, the concept of a knowable future is highly questionable, as is the validity of the notion of objective knowledge (Long and Long 1992; Wolpert 1992). Second, the 'blueprint' approach requires an ability to control all the factors outside of the project which may influence its outcome. This degree of control is possible in a very limited number of instances, usually where technology is very dominant, as with road and bridge construction or telecommunications.

At least five other factors work against the linear approach realising what is intended. First, as one moves along the chain in the figure, the number of actors involved increases and each has their own perspective and set of interests which are not static. Second, in their turn, each actor's behaviour is conditioned to a greater or lesser degree on external forces, with NGOs particularly dependent on the vagaries of external finance for maintenance of their core functions (Hudock 1994). The increase of contingent factors on project progress gives rise to greater levels of uncertainty and unpredictability. Third, the time-scale required for observing effects or changes tends to lengthen. For example, reducing infant mortality rates cannot be seen from the life or death of one child. Only after a longer period does this type of change become apparent. Fourth, human well-being is determined by many external elements which are integrated within an individual. Improving access to potable water, while useful in itself, won't mean much if food intake is diminishing, nor will economic investment mean much if there is no political or financial stability, nor will education mean much if it cannot be applied to anything tangible. Finally, getting returns from external flows of financial investments, knowledge or technology is determined by how people use them (their behaviour), while who benefits is determined by people's ability to organise and by the basis on which power, influence and control over resources is distributed.

An example can help to illustrate what these factors mean in terms of practical impact assessment. Assume that a particular population group suffers from poor health due to inadequate nutrition. One reason identified for this is the high percentage of harvested crops lost in storage. A project is defined and designed by an NGO to introduce improved grain stores. The *output* of the NGO's work can be measured in terms of the number of stores built and at what cost. However, the *outcome* of the project will have to be measured in terms of the reduction of crop loss during storage (which may take more than one season to determine) which, in its turn, will be critically affected by how the grain stores are used from one season to the next – ie, by people's behaviour. The nominal value of the crops saved can be set against the cost of the store to calculate a financial cost-benefit, but this will only be possible some years after their completion. Project *impact* must be sought in the improved nutritional status of the population, which is unlikely to be determined by grain alone and will require distinctive non-agricultural or economic measures, such as improvement in anthropometric status and reduced incidence of nutrition-related illnesses such as kwashiorkor. Further, the spread of impact on human well-being will be determined by the differential ability of household members to gain access to the increased food supply, experience showing that women and children tend to have the weakest entitlements.

To all of the above must be added the fact that, while varying significantly between countries, overall international aid is only a tiny proportion of the flow of resources and knowledge between countries and levels within societies. For example, the World Bank's total lending in 1993 was the equivalent of the amount transferred by international capital markets in the space of nine minutes.[1] The idea that aid can, will or does 'make the difference' to world development or the distribution of poverty is illusory; far larger forces are in play.

Together these factors, and the interplay between them, reduce the validity of predictive change as an appropriate approach to socio-economic development. Indeed, it is increasingly argued by even the most hardened physical scientists and economists that development at all levels of the natural and social order is the product of complex and contingent processes which are only partially amenable to prediction and control (Anderson et al 1988; Waldrop 1992; Lewin 1994; Gell-Mann 1994). They point out that as component systems of the world evolve, they interlock and give rise to new ('emergent') properties. For example, computerisation and communication technology are creating new ways of organising, including 'virtual organisations!'. Similarly, localised environmental degradation caused by myriad individuals struggling to survive across all continents of the world can combine to destabilise whole patterns of weather or lifestyles of the better-off. Simple rules employed by billions of people operating in parallel can lead to dramatic, unexpected outcomes.

In sum, the basic linear principles on which development aid is allocated do not correspond to the complex, contingent way development actually occurs. This fundamental mismatch complicates performance assessment, particularly when it comes to attributing cause to effects and working out what would have happened anyway (the 'counterfactual' case). This realisation has increased the call for a new sort of development professionalism not premised on linearity (Chambers 1985, 1993). The gap between the principles of aid and the nature of poverty creation and alleviation makes life particularly difficult for NGOs, who need to convince their supporters and funders that they have 'made the difference' to people's well-being. Because they cannot levy taxes, NGOs (more than official aid agencies) face a major problem of public persuasion if performance assessment cannot attribute effects to causes.

3. Assessing NGO organisational performance

NGOs must contend with the fact that they belong to a category of organisation with no straightforward or uncontested measure of organisational, as distinct from project, effectiveness. In other words, unlike governments and businesses – which can be assessed respectively in terms of political support or financial returns – non-profits have no readily acknowledged 'bottom line'.

A 'bottom line' for non-profit organisations

By nature of their (social) function, NGOs provide services to a segment of the population who are unable to meet the full cost of what they receive; if they could afford them they could go to the market as consumers (Fowler 1989; Leat 1993). Financial returns, therefore, cannot serve as a measure of organisational performance. Likewise, as self-established entities not owned or mandated by those they serve, feedback from political processes which are intended to legitimise governments are not appropriate. What approach can be adopted to establish the standards against which non-profit organisational performance can reasonably be assessed?

Measuring the performance of non-state, non-profit development organisations, rather than of the projects they implement, is a relative newcomer as an issue in the development arena. Its arrival is tied to the growing concern, associated with increased aid from official sources, that their organisational capacity is inadequate for the expanding role they are expected and funded to play (Campbell 1990). For the present, therefore, analysis of the problems associated with measuring the organisational performance of developmental NGOs must draw mainly on work focusing on non-profits operating in the North.

Some fifteen years ago, the well-known organisational analyst, Rosbeth Moss Kanter (1979), reviewed the wide range of conceptual dilemmas, practical difficulties, contending principles and different methods adopted in attempts to determine non-profit effectiveness, productivity and performance. She concluded:

1.   That the measurement of effectiveness must be related to a particular context and life stage of the organisation.
2.   That rather than seeking universal measures, the need is to identify appropriate questions reflecting multiple criteria.
3.   That the concept of assessment of organisational goals should be replaced with the notion of organisational uses – in other words, to recognise the fact that 'different constituencies use organisations for different purposes' (op cit, p 36).

Drucker (1990) reaches essentially the same conclusions, namely that:

1.   Performance must be determined and interpreted contextually.
2.   Questions should form the base of the assessment approach.
3.   Standards must derive from the various constituencies that the organisation serves.
4.   The process of organisational assessment should be participatory.

Another approach to performance assessment of non-profits working in the North relates to the 'contract culture' which is shaping their role, position and behaviour (Smith and Lipsky 1993) and which is rapidly permeating into the aid system (OECD 1993). This approach focuses on the quality of service provided. Lawrie (1993 p 19) identifies four types of performance indicator in this respect: (per unit) cost; take-up or 'occupancy'; impact or result; and user reaction. Each has different applications and levels of difficulty in terms of definition, the ability to obtain the needed information, and degrees of precision and tangibility. He stresses the distinction between performance indicators as unambiguous (or what he calls 'dials') and as contestable (or 'tin openers').[2]

Lawrie notes the bias that funders have towards 'dials' and the insufficient time available to negotiate 'tin openers'. Organisational effectiveness, in terms of quality of service, is determined by measuring gaps which exist in the expectations and perceptions of different stakeholders. What might all this mean for development NGOs?

The bottom line for development NGOs

Each of the analyses noted above highlights the difficulties involved in identifying a non-profit bottom line, even when the purpose is reasonably straightforward – for example, providing a direct welfare service such as running a home for elderly people or a shelter for the homeless. Developmental NGOs are faced with an additional obstacle because, as shown in Figure 14.1, the 'product' of their endeavours (sustainable development for poverty alleviation) is not produced by NGOs but by (poor) people themselves (Lewis et al 1988). In other words, at best NGOs can facilitate and support the process of people's own development and need to be assessed in how well they do this, in addition to what their work realises in terms of material change.

Yet another complication arises because the funds that Southern NGOs employ are normally derived from foreign sources. This separates the political relationship between giver and receiver, and means that there is no recognised system by which the (dis)satisfaction of those served can be fed back to the funder independent of the NGO itself.[3]

This situation does not arise in the North, where local or national political processes can serve to monitor the performance of a non-profit organisation.

These problems have resulted in a situation where performance appraisal for most NGOs has remained stuck at the point of comparing outputs with intentions – ie, with (negotiated) plans such as the number of wells built, number of people attending training activities and repayment rates for credit. Crucial elements of development processes, such as people's degree of control over decisions, or the capabilities of community-based organisations (CBOs), are seldom assessed at all. There is a general consensus that this situation is neither adequate nor acceptable (Marsden, Oakley and Pratt 1994). How can this accumulation of obstacles be overcome? Is there a way forward?

4. A way ahead in NGO performance assessment

The problems recounted above are not new; for a number of years both researchers and practitioners have recognised them and have been actively looking for ways to overcome them. However, more progress has been made in the area of assessing project performance than the performance of NGOs themselves. These two strands are tied together, only weakly, if at all, with the measurement of project impact separated from organisational appraisal. However, a common principle underlying both is the need to involve stakeholders more systematically.

A unifying principle: engaging multiple stakeholders structurally and systematically

Attempts to reconcile the contradictions of linear versus contingent development, as well as to assess NGO effectiveness, share a common principle – that of structured multiple stakeholder involvement.[4] In relation to project performance, a promising direction for impact assessment appears to lie in the application of frameworks and methods which allow all interested parties to have a say in defining means and ends. Causes and effects are negotiated, monitored and evaluated from the perspectives of the actors who can be reasonably assumed to have an influence on both progress and impact. One approach of this sort which has been tested in practice is the marrying together of Logical Framework Analysis (LFA) and Objective Oriented Intervention Planning (OOIP) (INTRAC/South Research 1994). Over a period (which could extend to a year), the goals, objectives, existing context and processes to be used are discussed with the stakeholders whose involvement will be critical to a project's definition and implementation. Differences in motivation and perceptions underpinning what is to be achieved, how and who is likely to benefit, become more apparent early on, so that compromises can be negotiated. Rather than crippling a project later on, insurmountable conflicts can be identified and a decision made as to whether the pre-conditions exist for the initiative to be viable.

In terms of organisational appraisal, involving stakeholders in this way calls for some form of *social accounting of multiple interests* (Epstein, Flamholtz and McDonough 1977, p 76, quoted in Kanter 1979).[5] One recent application of these principles – known as a 'social audit' and derived from a process of independent social accounting – is being tested by Traidcraft and the New Economics Foundation (Traidcraft 1994; Zadek and Gatward, this volume). Here, performance criteria are negotiated with four key stakeholders: producers, staff, consumers and shareholders. In parallel with the financial audit, an independent person obtains feedback on stakeholders' views about the degree to which Traidcraft have fulfilled the standards agreed.[6]

More recently, OXFAM (UK and Ireland) initiated an 'assembly' of some 250 diverse stakeholders – partners, advisers, associates, volunteers, staff, senior managers, donors, 'friends' and others – to deliberate and provide advice on strategic issues facing the organisation, such as whether or not to work in the UK (Oxfam 1994). The assembly is advisory and not a formal part of Oxfam's organisation. Yet the step taken by Oxfam contains a clear moral imperative to take the assembly seriously or risk being publicly derided and written off as a dishonest organisation.[7] It is too early to ascertain what the influence of these initiatives will be for the overall performance of these organisations.

The importance of process

It is beyond the scope of this chapter to detail precisely how multiple stakeholder involvement is obtained in the two areas described above. However, some points are worthy of note. First, in both cases stakeholder input is not a one-off affair, but a continuous process within the organisation's functioning.

One option being adopted by some NGOs is to establish a permanent advisory body composed of different stakeholders whose task is to monitor organisational performance in meeting standards which have been agreed and modified by mutual consent.

Second, creating a systematic way of engaging multiple stakeholders is unlikely to be free of conflict and risk, especially where different levels of authority and power exist. In this situation, the weighting of different stakeholders is important. Additional pitfalls can arise where there is a significant disparity in understanding between donor, NGO and recipients about what development is or entails. For example, in NGOs funded by child sponsorship, a donor may wish their sponsored child to receive direct handouts, as may the child's parents. In these circumstances, how can the organisation justify a non-welfare, community-based approach? Bringing parties together as stakeholders invites organisational disturbance![8]

Third, the process of stakeholder engagement should help to build the capacity of the parties involved, particularly the poor and marginalised whose ability to put forward their interests is most likely to be constrained. In sum, to be useful and meaningful, obtaining stakeholder engagement must be matched by the right processes.

NGO performance assessment as combined social judgement

Multiple stakeholder engagement allows the performance of NGOs (as organisations dedicated to social change) to be defined as the – often contested – outcome of the social judgements of the parties involved, using criteria which are important to them. The methods set out above help to temper the shortcomings of 'linear' approaches by:

■ contextualising assessment and hence taking account of contingency;
■ making the interpretation of events more objective as multiple perspectives are brought to bear;
■ contributing to cost-effectiveness through combining capacity-building with performance-monitoring.

In sum, the key to NGO assessment appears to lie in identifying and using as performance standards the criteria or factors which relevant people are likely to use when making a judgement. Herman and Heimovics (1994) describe and examine how this can be done in practice by constructing and employing 'vignettes'. A vignette is a picture built up from criteria, and values attached to them, which relevant stakeholders would use to judge the organisation. For example, as measures of effectiveness, they may include: the percentage of income spent on fund-raising, the proportion made up by contributions from volunteers, the percentage of revenue coming from government, the profile of those whom the organisation actually reaches, the gender divisions within the organisation, and so on. Vignettes describing what interested parties consider to be signs of effectiveness, can help to construct a bottom line.

Uniting the strands: performance as an expression of organisational capacities

A key weakness in today's practice of NGO performance assessment is the separation of project evaluations from features of the organisation itself, as if each has relatively little or nothing to do with the other, which is patently not the case. For example, one recent comparative impact assessment of NGO work in credit-provision did not take organisational variables into account when explaining differences in performance (Riddell and Robinson 1992). One way of bringing together the major facets of NGO performance is to use the concept of organisational capacity. Neither NGOs nor donors have a uniform definition of 'capacity' (James 1994). However, current uses of the term imply that capacity can be understood as a number of core abilities, together with the means and relationships through which to express them. Analysis of the NGO sector in Africa indicates that to be effective three principal areas of ability are required. These are:

■ an ability *to be* – ie, to maintain its specific identity, values and mission;
■ an ability *to do* – ie, to achieve stakeholder satisfaction;
■ an ability *to relate* – ie, to manage external interactions while retaining autonomy.

When combined, these three areas of organisational ability determine the overall performance of NGOs as well as their role and institutional position as civic actors (Fowler 1992b; Fowler et al 1992). Figure 14.2 is a schematic presentation of the above.

A significant amount of effort is presently being applied to the identification of appropriate indicators of capacity and effectiveness within each of these areas, although endeavours are biased towards measures of achievement in various types of poverty-reducing sectoral investments (Carvalho and White 1993).[9] Progress in locating indicators of organisational capacity in terms of

Figure 14.2   *Types of performance as factors in NGO organisational capacity*

'being' and 'relating' is less advanced, partly because of the relatively recent concern about them and partly due to the inherent difficulties described above.

The design and practical testing of organisational assessment indicators and methods currently undertaken with NGOs reconfirms that question-based approaches are likely to be the most viable.[10]

Drucker (1993) believes that there are five key questions an NGO should ask itself. These are:

1. What is our business (mission)?
2. Who is our customer?
3. What does the customer consider valuable?
4. What have been our results?
5. What is our plan?

From these derive all sorts of sub-questions, which must be answered by the organisation in a participatory way involving all levels of staff as well as the board, facilitated by a skilled, independent outsider. However, interpreting the answers to these questions requires that users have a firm understanding of the nature of non-profit organisations. Bringing staff up to the necessary level of insight, often including the cross-cultural dimensions of organisational behaviour, requires significant investment and guided application. More often than not, it appears that time and other resource constraints present the major hurdle to Northern NGOs when carrying out a thorough organisational assessment of or with their partners. Although some Northern agencies have involved their partners in policy formulation and 'reverse evaluations' (with mixed success), there is little evidence to date to suggest that many NGOs are aware of the potential of, or are actively moving towards, a set of standards and measures for performance appraisal negotiated among their stakeholders.

Easing management tensions: linking performance and accountability

A final, and perhaps most significant feature of structured stakeholder performance assessment, is that it simultaneously resolves some of the difficulties faced by NGOs in satisfying the multiple demands for functional and strategic accountability which face them (Edwards and Hulme 1994). NGO stakeholders are commonly characterised by contrasts in their attitude towards, power over or reliance on the organisation. Typical differences include: understanding about purpose or role; perspectives on development; ability to sanction; levels of understanding about the organisation itself; and diverse expectations about responsiveness, acceptable levels of service, time-scales for results and impact. To some extent these differences derive from basic contradictions between the role of aid and the functioning of the global political-economic system, of which poverty and marginalisation are but one product. Perspectives in North and South certainly differ considerably.

In organisational terms, these and other differences translate into more or less permanent tensions which have to be managed; most cannot be 'developed' away or resolved solely by the action of the NGO itself because their origins lie deep within the institutional structures of society. Be that as it may, although not without risks in the short term, structured engagement with stakeholders can externalise, make transparent and hence ease the tensions and associated management stresses which NGOs currently internalise. Enabling stakeholders who seldom, if ever, meet to come together and listen to the incompatibility of the demands they are placing on an NGO can be both a salutary experience and a good education for all concerned. If located within the right process, such encounters can make a significant positive difference to NGO functioning, and can help to transform North–South NGO relationships into effective partnerships.

5. Speculative conclusions

There is little doubt that external pressure and internal concerns (both opportunistic and professional) will continue to push NGOs to demonstrate their effectiveness and hence their value as agents of development. Given the consistent trend to include more non-state actors in development, it is likely that the methods adopted will stretch along some form of continuum from simple participatory project-appraisal at one end to full stakeholder-determination of NGO performance criteria and judgement at the other. The factors which will determine which NGOs end up where on the spectrum are not easy to discern. A guess is that an NGO's position will be related to the profile of its funding, its ability to retain autonomy, and its particular ideology or analysis of the causes of poverty and marginalisation.

The rationale and expectations associated with tax-derived finances are more likely to make NGOs relying on this type of income adopt a contracting role than those financed by the gift economy (such as Oxfam) or their own market-oriented activity (such as Traidcraft; Fowler 1994b). In the former case, projects will probably remain the primary mode of operation linked to government agreements, treating beneficiaries as inputs rather than as actors central to the development process (World Bank 1994). Autonomy is a more complex factor because it is determined by an NGO's ability to maintain its own policy-development and decision-making processes unimpeded by other agencies. While sources of finance play their role, the strength and unity of the constituency which 'owns' the NGO is a significant factor in helping to maintain independence of policy and action. NGOs which benefit from greater autonomy are usually better able to include a broader range of stakeholders in any or all aspects of their work.

Surprising as it may seem, relatively few development NGOs have a coherent and well-articulated understanding of why the problems they seek to address actually arise. Put differently, they lack a theory or analysis of why poverty exists as a global phenomenon. Dealing with symptoms and effects is still a sufficient justification for the existence of many NGOs. This means that they are unlikely to consider or seek to counter the structural nature of impoverishment (in the North as well as in the South) in what they choose to do. This appreciation is more likely to be found in NGOs treating poverty alleviation as a global civic endeavour requiring international solidarity and mutual responsibility. The latter type of NGO may be more inclined to recognise the interests of stakeholders outside of a project framework.

The existing literature on NGOs and development, together with the few impact studies which exist, suggest that, by the end of the century, most NGOs will be found clustering between the 'people as project-input' end of the performance assessment spectrum and a middle point pivoting around the LFA/OOIP approach, which itself may have evolved to embrace organisational as well as project performance. It is doubtful that many NGOs will be found operating on the basis of performance criteria and standards negotiated with and between their diverse stakeholders, unless this is recognised as the real bottom line for demonstrating both performance and accountability.

Notes

1. Estimate of John Clark, NGO unit of the World Bank, Washington DC (personal communication).
2. 'Dials' are supposedly unambiguous standards and measures of performance, such as the temperature shown on a thermometer. 'Tin-openers' are measures of performance which are contested, such as the minimum acceptable waiting time for an operation, or for an ambulance to arrive at an emergency.
3. Independent evaluations are the normal way of providing funders with alternative feedback on the work of the NGOs they finance. There are many limitations on the utility of this instrument, among which are: (1) delay in gaining information; (2) contention on definition of terms of reference and competing paradigms used for interpretation of results; (3) critical dependence on who is selected to do the work; (4) difficulties in gaining 'objective' involvement of those served and (5) transience of staff involved over the duration of the project and hence consistency of ideas (Marsden and Oakley 1990; Howes 1992; Cracknell 1983; Carlsson et al 1994; Marsden, Oakley and Pratt 1994). There are now a number of initiatives, such as the Aga Khan Rural Support Programme in Pakistan, dedicated to improving on this situation using participatory and other people-centered mechanisms.
4. Stakeholders could be regarded as the groups or entities to which an NGO is accountable. For an overview of who they might be, see Edwards and Hulme (1994, pp 18–24). For a discussion on the principle of stakeholders in relation to (development) organisations, see Fowler (1994a).
5. Commercial co-operations appear to be rediscovering the merits of social responsibility and social change as components of their overall goals and strategies (Smith 1994).
6. More information can be obtained directly from Traidcraft Exchange, Kingsway, Gateshead, Tyne and Wear, Newcastle NE11 0NE, UK.
7. The (political) risk taken by Oxfam in constituting the assembly was highlighted when the gathering's advice to commence work in its home country made front page headlines in the *Guardian*, which argued that prevailing government policies had turned the UK into a developing country in need of Oxfam's attention (personal communication from Max Peberdy, assembly organiser).
8. I am grateful to Wendy Crane of Plan International for this observation.
9. In May 1994, the World Bank hosted a meeting with NGOs to compare notes on impact assessment which focused almost exclusively on technical interventions at the project level.

10. These findings result from experience in designing and running courses on orga-
    nisational assessment and organisational development with INTRAC attended by
    staff of over 50 Northern and Southern NGOs as well as in-house consultancy work
    and personal communications from Piers Campbell, Peter Baas, Rajesh Tandon,
    David Harding, Daudi Waithaka, Dr John Hailey and others of the growing but
    limited number of specialists in this area.

15

Painting Canadian Roses Red

Ian Smillie

This chapter deals with the strange phenomenon of a multi-billion dollar international endeavour that is poorly understood and, despite fast-growing interest in the subject, very poorly evaluated: the work of Northern non-governmental organisations (NNGOs). It draws in part on an extensive, twelve-country study in which the author participated, conducted by the Development Centre of the OECD in 1993 (Smillie and Helmich 1993), but focuses specifically on the case of Canada, where NGO evaluation is considerably more advanced than in most other OECD countries. The OECD study observed that NNGOs are in trouble. Collectively they spend an estimated US$9 to $10 billion annually,[1] but live with a level of financial insecurity that would drive most private-sector firms into bankruptcy. Increasingly criticised by governments for their lack of professionalism, they are accused of bureaucratisation when they do professionalise. With very few exceptions, governments refuse to contribute seriously to financing professionalism, insisting on unrealistically low over-heads, and on putting NGOs through long, inefficient approval processes. Many governments are locked into an out-dated project approach which also works against professionalism. Despite the fact that they spend tens of millions of dollars annually through their NGO communities, few governments have taken evaluation seriously, with the result that NGO survival has been almost completely delinked from performance.[2] Perhaps most fundamentally, NGOs have a growing identity crisis in relation to their increasingly effective Southern counterparts, most of whom want money rather than interference, and support rather than second-hand rules and regulations passed on from government donors in the North.

Just as the North–South NGO identity crisis began to peak in the early 1990s, it became clear that official development assistance itself was in serious trouble. Report after report on official development assistance scandals, such as the Pergau Dam affair in the UK, and World Bank performance (the 'Wapenhans Report') has damaged public opinion, encouraging recession-plagued govern-ments to cut aid budgets and retreat behind 'new' concepts of accountability, participation and the role of 'civil society'. Adding to the burden these shifts place on NGOs, many governments actively poach on Northern NGO territory, dealing directly with Southern NGOs as though they have nothing better to do with their overstretched bureaucracies.

Some Southern NGOs, tired of the paternalism and the financial limitations of their erstwhile Northern NGO 'partners', have welcomed the change. Adding to the confusion, many governments have restricted their matching or 'responsive' NGO funding programmes, while providing massive funding increases – on highly favourable terms – for emergency and refugee work. Most governments have also thrown in special funds for AIDS, women, democracy and a variety of other issues, as though NGOs – which first brought some of these issues to the attention of governments – needed special prodding to take them seriously.

A high proportion of NGOs, suffering from recession and dysfunctional competition, have flocked like swallows towards the easier money. Not content with the huge new sums available from government for emergencies, however, too many have turned up the 'starving baby' fund-raising, adding to a wide-spread Northern image of the Third World as a wholesale disaster area. The public, confused by highly competitive fund-raising appeals, unsubstantiated NGO claims and unremitting horror stories from the South, can perhaps be forgiven for its ignorance of what is going on, and for a growing antipathy towards any kind of aid but the most heart-wrenching.

The failure to learn from failure

In discussing NGOs, it has become fashionable to move quickly from their positive attributes (increasingly referred to as 'unproven')[3] to their obvious weaknesses. The 1993 UNDP Human Development Report, which devotes an entire chapter to NGOs, is one of the most recent and dismaying examples of this. Ten of its fifteen pages are devoted to debunking – with faint praise and outright condemnation – the effectiveness of NGOs in tackling poverty, providing credit to the poor, reaching the poorest, empowering marginal groups, challenging gender discrimination and even in delivering emergency relief.

Development is, or should be, a knowledge-based endeavour. The importance of learning what works, and why, is essential to success. Knowing what does not work is almost more important. Knowledge, however (too often confused with information), involves awareness, consciousness and the familiarity that develops with experience and learning. Just as messages sent are not always received, lessons *taught* – in school and in life – are not always *learned*. This is particularly true at an institutional level; the inability to learn and *remember* is an acknowledged and widespread failing of the development community as a whole. For NGOs it represents a particular dilemma, because there are few reasons (and no money) to disseminate the positive lessons of development, and many more powerful reasons to conceal the negative lessons than to institutionalise, remember and disseminate them.

Part of the problem has to do with the expectations of supporters – the public at large and governments. NGOs have long prided themselves on reaching the poorest quickly, effectively and efficiently. In the 1960s, when much NGO work was relief-oriented, this was certainly true. It is still true in emergency work today. As NGOs became more involved in development work, however, their advertising messages remained the same: speed, effectiveness and efficiency. As more NGOs came on to the Northern scene, competition for funding increased and promises escalated.

But development is not speedy and NGOs, working with the very poor in resource-deficient, marginal regions of countries in great distress, know that effectiveness and efficiency are far less easy to deliver and to measure than, say, infrastructure development. Having promised too much to the donor and the public, however, the NGO is trapped in a vicious circle. If funding is to be maintained or is to increase in the face of growing demands, success is essential. Often it is exaggerated, while failures are downplayed or concealed. Important lessons are not learned, and only successes – often highly situational – are disseminated, usually in a public relations format.

Part of the solution to this problem has to do with public perception. Much has to do with the development of transparency, accountability and, ultimately, greater credibility – through appropriate types of evaluation, research and the dissemination of findings.

Duplication at the expense of replication

NGOs repeat the same types of project time after time. There is little effective co-ordination at home and less overseas. NGOs pride themselves on, and are rewarded by, donors for 'innovation', but often innovation is simply a reinvention of old wheels. 'Pilot projects' and demonstrations demonstrate only that the NGO can do it. Uptake by others is limited. Despite the admirable push-start provided by the first Manchester conference on 'scaling-up' (Edwards and Hulme 1992), government support remains limited for the widespread replication of successful programmes – for the complex set of activities that Norman Uphoff calls 'extendability': institution-building, linkage to government services and broadly based empowerment.[4] This is in part because many NGOs are not interested in, or capable of, scaling-up. But the way in which NGOs are funded by governments is also a factor. NGO budgets in most government agencies have little flexibility, are often tied to a historical rather than a developmental reality, and have no capacity to help move real success stories to full-scale application.

Evaluation

The country studies in the 1993 OECD report (Smillie and Helmich 1993) demonstrate that although NGO evaluation is rising rapidly on the agendas of many OECD governments, it is still very much in the elementary stages in most countries.[5] In those where it has advanced to a relative degree of sophistication (such as the Netherlands, the USA and Canada), it is used more as a control and justification mechanism by the donor agency than as a tool for learning or for disseminating findings.

There are examples of attempts to expand and enhance approach as to NGO evaluation – for example, the Rapid and Participatory Rural Appraisal Techniques developed at the Institute for Development Studies (IDS) in Brighton and the International Institute for Environment and Development (IIED) in London; a NORAD study series; the Overseas Development Institute Working

Paper, 'Judging Success' (Riddell 1990). A handful of Northern NGOs have asked their Southern partners to evaluate *them*. Other suggestions include comparative cross-national and sectoral evaluations. Generally speaking, however, the relatively few serious NGO evaluations that do exist remain confidential. Government agencies, faced with the same public expectations as NGOs, with added and often conflicting demands from their legislators, become partners in the cover-up, burying their own failures and shortcomings in similar public relations exercises and obfuscation.

Development, especially human development, is not easy; it is not quick; it is not cheap. If it was, NGOs and foreign aid would have disappeared with the Marshall Plan. Failure should be regarded as a bad thing only if the same mistake is made over and over. But when evaluations are rare and secretive, when lessons are not shared, not learned and not remembered, repetitive mistakes are almost guaranteed.[6]

A related issue has to do with the conspiracy of silence that prevails within most NGO communities. NGOs rarely challenge each other openly; there is little, if any, regulation of NGOs by NGOs (unlike other professions such as accountants, architects and engineers); and the NGO codes of conduct that do exist (in Australia, the European Union and the USA) are usually not policed in any serious way.

Canada: Evaluation off the rails?

Hard choices in hard times

One of the findings of the OECD study was that both official and unofficial statistics on NGO funding are very unreliable. There is no doubt, however, that a very high proportion of the cash income of most Canadian NGOs is derived from the Canadian International Development Agency (CIDA). For some, such as Foster Parents Plan and World Vision, the proportion is low, but for most it is well over 50 per cent, and for some it is more than 80 per cent.[7] When CIDA sneezes, therefore, Canadian NGOs reach for their vitamin C.

The pace of change at CIDA since 1991 (including a series of major budget cuts, three presidents and three ministers) has been bewildering. Much of the change has focused on structures, systems and on what CIDA now calls 'stakeholders' – NGOs, the private sector and others with a financial 'stake'. This is perhaps understandable. CIDA's rapid budget growth throughout the 1970s and 1980s was not accompanied by a concomitant growth in its human resources. As development needs grew and became more complex, CIDA relied more and more heavily on others – consultants, the private sector, NGOs and professional institutions – to do the work its officers and contract employees once did. Gradually, much of the initiative for Canada's development work, especially in the social sector, seemed to fall away from CIDA.

In the early 1980s, CIDA began to place increasing importance on evaluation, and for most NGOs a comprehensive institutional review every three or four years became a feature of the relationship. These reviews, always conducted by external consultants, are lengthy and complex, delving into overseas programme effectiveness as well as questions of organisational management. Views on the quality and usefulness of the evaluations vary, according to the stance of the beholder. Because they are directly related to the renegotiation of a block grant, many NGOs approach them with considerable fear and loathing. For CIDA, however, they perform an important function. Because of declining human resources, CIDA officers can no longer examine their clientele in the depth they once did. In the almost total absence of any NGO self-evaluation, the institutional reviews provide the only serious government window into what an NGO does. The evaluations have rarely been used, however, to modify CIDA funding seriously, and certainly no evaluation in recent memory has resulted in the cessation of funding to an NGO. The evaluations are, in a sense, a corroboration of CIDA's decision to support an NGO in the first place.

Ultimately, most of the evaluations are weak when it comes to questions about an NGO's programme impact. This is partly because the generic methodology for NGO evaluation is weak. It also has to do with poor or non-existent baseline indicators around which an evaluation can be framed. And it is partly because – despite the large CIDA evaluation budget – the time and resources available for individual NGO reviews are usually inadequate.

Institutional funding

'Institutional funding', introduced by CIDA in 1993, is the newest approach to dealing with some of these problems.[8] Institutional funding means that CIDA funds the 'institution', rather than a collection of projects and programmes. It is assumed that mature NGOs, if well managed and founded on clear development principles, will have, as a matter of course, the sort of impact they and CIDA espouse. Much of the evaluative function can actually be carried out by the NGO itself. To put it simply, detailed, third-party overseas impact evaluation is not necessary. In principle, institutional funding makes sense. At first glance, it appears to reduce CIDA involvement in the routine administrative and programming work of the NGO; it places less emphasis on 'blueprint' planning; and it emphasises *development* work overseas and puts new emphasis on development education in Canada, merging this with regular programme approvals.

Institutional funding, however, means that the *entire* NGO will now be open to full CIDA scrutiny: its structure, management, programmes, policies and attitudes. Current institutional assessments do cover many aspects of an NGO's persona, but the new approach guarantees that *all* will now be addressed. While the implications for some NGOs are not great, and the sacrifice small, for others they are significant. Institutional funding represents a step forward in the ability of government to manage and control Canadian NGOs, and a step backward from the concept of NGOs as independent expressions of civil society.

The NGO must now spell out its 'understanding of the development challenge', work through its goals and objectives, establish a strategic approach, provide details on the scope of work envisaged, describe the implementation structure and the partnership relationship, and develop or describe a monitoring and evaluation plan. In return for much greater openness, the only actual promise from CIDA is a more critical application of its cost-sharing formula.

That CIDA wants to encourage greater self-evaluation and better strategic thinking among NGOs is a positive feature of the new arrangement. But CIDA still intends to conduct its own formal institutional assessments 'to thoroughly assess the organization and its continued eligibility' every three to five years. It may conduct mid-term reviews; it will do an 'annual financial assessment' (with the possibility of 'more extensive monitoring'). CIDA managers will continue to make field trips 'to review activities of organizations and their southern partners on the ground'; there will be regular discussions and contact with the NGO, and CIDA programme managers will attend the NGO's board meetings 'at least once a year to discuss issues of mutual concern'. In short, there is considerably more work for the NGO, more CIDA intrusion than in the past, and there is likely to be at least as much work as before for the CIDA manager, if not more.

How to evaluate a Canadian NGO

CIDA's new institutional funding arrangement is based on a comprehensive checklist of characteristics and practices which form the basis for evaluation and funding allocations. CIDA, of course, and any other institutional support agency, *should* have clear funding priorities for NGOs. These should be based on an organisation's developmental cost-effectiveness. In order for criteria to be used effectively, they must be clear and the application must be seen to be fair. A difficulty with the new CIDA approach, however, is uncertainty about its basic objective. It is no secret that CIDA is in a period of contraction; the irony is that contraction, rather than expansion, seems to have bred a stronger interest in good management and good programming. This makes the need for clarity and fairness essential if CIDA is to avoid the lobbying, grantsmanship and grandstanding that has marked the rise of Canada's 200–300 NGOs over the past 30 years. It is absolutely essential if good work is to be rewarded – if the intent is to create something more than a paring knife.

At this level, CIDA's new criteria largely fail. Take the simple question of governance, for example: one of the criteria is 'reasonable staff turnover relative to the needs of the organization'. What is 'reasonable'? Who will judge? In some categories, there is a clear requirement: defined evaluation plans, an explicit policy and strategy on gender, and training in environmental assessment. In others, despite a listing of categories, there is none – for example, 'nature and extent of the donor base; nature and extent of the volunteer base; nature and involvement of the constituency'. 'Nature' means what? What is good? What is good enough? What is bad? Who decides?

There are some excellent and innovative questions. Unfortunately, many of these are buried in vague and repetitive lists based on current aid enthusiasms: the environment, gender, sustainability, human rights, democratic development and 'good governance'. The imbalance in priorities is extreme: there are over two pages on the environment and gender, fewer than two explicit lines on poverty, and no description of what is meant by 'democratic development' or how NGOs might contribute to it.

Another confusion, common to most NGO support institutions, is the conflation of innovation and replication, as though they were the same thing. This criterion is a serious contradiction in terms. Replication means to make a copy of, to reproduce. 'Innovate' comes from *novus*, 'new'. It means to invent. This needs to be thought through. 'Innovation' appears on almost every list of funding criteria for NGOs, worldwide. Why? Innovation certainly has its place, and many accepted development lessons have come from NGO innovations. But too many NGOs reinvent too many wheels in the name of innovation. Ironically, there is less and less money available for replicating or taking the innovations to scale. Donors should think carefully about the trade-offs involved here, and they should make sure they know what they really want to foster.

The word 'sustainable' is used in the new CIDA policy 25 times. The words 'poor' and 'poverty' appear once. Although the word 'development' is used liberally, there is no definition for it, other than what might be inferred from the sum of the parts. If development is the intended whole, however (and there is no explicit assurance that it is), it comes off as considerably less than the sum of its parts.

In sum, Canadian NGOs now have a suggested and reasonably clear formula for good management, but of what? An NGO with competent staff, a good board and a constituency. An organisation that understands gender and environment, one that gets along well with its partners and whose staff work 'as a team'. In one document it is stated that 'development performance will be given the most weight' in determining budgetary allocations, but this is not borne out in the text. Programme impact is placed last, after governance, management and delivery, Canadian constituency and identity.

The section on impact is, in fact, the foggiest part of the new policy. It is as though we no longer know what development is about, as though long jargon-laden checklists about environmental or social sustainability are a substitute for the hard question: 'What is this organisation doing to reduce poverty in the short and long run?' The 'impact' section of one document uses the word 'sustainable' 19 times, breaking it up into a myriad of vague proxies which ultimately mean very little. For example:

> *Extent to which the organization has demonstrated an understanding of the key factors which contributed to social sustainability, such as improved income distribution, social equity (gender, class, race, religion, etc.), empowerment of women and men in directing their own growth, emphasizing participation of beneficiaries, and access to productive resources.*

> *CIDA policy statement, 1992*

Apart from the redundancy, this is a fairly tall order, one that has baffled and defeated many organisations, including the Soviet Union, the United Nations and CIDA itself. Many paragraphs in the new CIDA policy documents are like that, and yet there is something missing from all of them: NGOs have to *understand* empowerment, access, etc ('etc' is used seven times in one paragraph); they have to *demonstrate* an understanding of key environmental sustainability factors, of gender, of political sustainability; and they have to *incorporate* these into their policies and strategies. However, there is little suggestion anywhere that anyone really has to *accomplish* anything.

Funding criteria

The documents say that where an NGO's performance is deficient in two out of the sixteen new funding criteria, reductions in funding will be 'indicated'. The fundamental problem is that when lists of criteria are lengthy and vague, they can be taken to mean anything. How will reduced funding be 'indicated'? If an organisation does not have a strong environmental assessment capacity, for example, and if the 'nature and extent of its volunteer base' is deemed inadequate, would a 10 per cent reduction be indicated? 11 per cent? 30 per cent? Who will make this decision? Precisely how important are things like human rights and democratic development? In the absence of any real development performance indicators or comparative impact evaluation in the field, CIDA managers will end up with a stew which simply encourages the arbitrary decision-making that these documents seek to alter.

Conclusion

The dictionary defines a 'professional' as one who is extremely competent in a job. The voluntary sector has a number of inherent weaknesses that work against professionalism: a dependence upon what Salamon (1987) calls 'the particularism and favouritism of the rich', an inability to generate adequate or secure resources, and a proclivity towards self-defeating paternalism. Too often, however, governments tend to see professionalism in terms of their own standards and procedures. The more an NGO acts like government, the more 'professional' it is. Some NGOs have conformed, becoming as bureaucratic within themselves and with their Southern partners, as they are forced to be with their funders. Others, reacting against this trend, throw the baby out with the bathwater and refuse to take the issue of professionalism seriously.

Some constraints to NGO professionalism are a reflection of the NGO community as a whole. For example, the vast and increasing number of small, generalist Northern NGOs almost guarantees a high level of amateurism. The OECD Directory of NGOs listed 1600 Northern NGOs in 1980 and 2500 in 1990. In the 1993 12-country OECD study, some 2970 NGOs were identified, a number that is probably on the low side.

A strong concern expressed in many countries has to do with the growing level of financial dependence that many NGOs have on government. Governments are torn: they are eager for NGOs to do more, but want them to raise more from a public that may be unable or unwilling to contribute further. Governments want ready and compliant NGOs that can go where governments cannot, but they worry about amateurism, and they dislike the grasping, commercial mentality that seems to have infected many. Most governments claim to value NGO independence, but insist that NGOs conform to government norms and priorities, and are resentful of NGO criticism.

Several suggestions for consideration emerged from the OECD study, and they are compatible with the situation in Canada. The most basic is that the *learning* aspect of evaluation must be stressed. If evaluation fulfils this function properly, the other major function reassuring the donor (which until now has received top priority) will take place naturally. If learning is to take place, the implied financial threat that seems to accompany failure must be removed. This should not absolve NGOs from responsibility for preventable errors and inefficiencies; rather it would help to ensure that the preventable becomes more predictable and therefore more avoidable.

But evaluation is only part of the learning process. NGOs also have an important research function which is barely acknowledged and poorly supported. For thirty years, NGOs have been valuable laboratories for public health, credit for the poor, the involvement of women in development, environmental issues and a wide range of other initiatives which have gradually been taken up by governments and donor agencies. Much of this has happened, however, by osmosis and by accident, and with much needless trial and error. Research and dissemination could and should be a much greater part of the NGO agenda. A few positive examples stand out, but they are the exception, rather than the rule: *The Oxfam Field Director's Handbook*; *Making a Difference* (Edwards and Hulme 1992) and the research programmes of Save the Children-UK which spawned it; the Sustainable Agriculture Programme of IIED; and the publishing houses of the Intermediate Technology Development Group and Earthscan.

Only recently has the NGO phenomenon itself been seen as a subject worthy of academic research. Growing interest on the part of universities and research institutions will undoubtedly help to build awareness, understanding and support for the movement as a whole. Ultimately, however, the survival of an independent NGO community as a source of development learning and as a genuine weapon against poverty will depend on its own willingness to confront questions of quality, cost-effectiveness and impact head-on, openly and by itself. Evaluation in most countries has not been given the same priority as in Canada, but it is rising rapidly on the agenda of many governmental support institutions. If NGOs are to avoid the confusion, the contradictions and the hijackings that have occurred in Canada, they would be well advised to take the matter in hand themselves, before it is too late.

Notes

1. Accurate statistics on NGOs are elusive. This figure is therefore an estimate. Reasonably accurate US figures, however, which show a total flow of $5.8 billion for American NGOs in 1991, would suggest that a total of $10 billion is probably not an exaggeration.
2. This divorce between funding and performance is discussed by Singh (1987).
3. This sort of terminology can be found in reports that use Judith Tendler's largely

outdated 1982 study as a source, including the 1993 Human Development Report. While important in many ways, Tendler pulled a lot of wings off NGO butterflies by debunking what she called NGO 'articles of faith'.

4. See *Voluntary Aid for Development; The Role of Non-Governmental Organizations* 1988, p 57, OECD, Paris.

5. New evaluation procedures for NGOs are being developed in Britain, Canada, the US and Australia. Broad overview studies of the NGO community have recently been conducted or are under way in Norway, Sweden and the United States. A limited survey on NGO evaluation was conducted by the OECD/DAC Expert Group on Aid and Evaluation in 1992.

6. Sweden and Norway publish (in English, so beneficiaries can read them) a wide variety of often very critical evaluations of projects undertaken by their bilateral agencies, SIDA and NORAD. Ironically, both governments have only recently decided to undertake comprehensive reviews of their NGO sectors.

7. CUSO 1992: 48 per cent; Canadian Hunger Foundation 1991: 70 per cent; CARE Canada 1992: 71 per cent; CODE 1992–93: 83 per cent; CUSO 1992–93: 83 per cent.

8. The following sections are based on four CIDA documents: 'Institutional Review: Issues for Consideration' (1992); 'Eligibility Criteria for Partners' (1992); 'NGO Program: Program Criteria' (1992); 'NGO Division Allocation Process for 1994/95'.

16

Accountability and Effectiveness in NGO Policy Alliances[1]

Jane Covey

At the beginning of the last decade of the 20th century, there was much talk of the emerging advocacy role for NGOs in both North and South. Debates about the propriety, legality and safety of NGO lobbying were in the air. Now, only a few years later, advocacy activities with governments, donors, multilateral development agencies and publics is assumed to be a crucial ingredient in enhancing the position of NGOs as key players in the diffuse social movement loosely labelled 'sustainable development'. UNCED, in the summer of 1992, undoubtedly helped to turn the tide from the 'Should we?' line of questions regarding NGO roles in policy influence to the 'How do we do it?' discourse now emerging.

Democratisation, in its messy evolution in societies around the globe, tugs NGOs toward a more active policy-influencing role as more political space opens for people's voices in public affairs. The promise of democracy becomes a reality, however, when groups (especially marginalised sectors of society) participate effectively in the market-place of competing interests. Inclusion in political systems long dominated by élites depends on the institutional strength of policy newcomers and the perceived legitimacy of their participation. The challenge of building an effective policy-influencing organisation increases as groups seek to shape positive policy environments as well as to protest against negative ones. For example, winning policy advantages requires that mobilised public opinion be accompanied by convincing analysis that is at least on a par with the analytic capability of the decision-makers that NGOs are trying to influence (Clark 1992). The dual challenges of mobilising arguments as well as people are great. Arguments that gain the attention of policy-makers call for 'expert' knowledge of both the issue and the decision-making process; while public outcry and protest actions that constrain decision-makers' power call for an active and organised grassroots constituency.

Policy-influence efforts may or may not create conditions that foster greater popular participation in the future. A movement may not achieve its immediate policy objectives, but getting its issue on the public agenda expands the range of voices engaged in the political process and so expands political space. On the other hand, attempting policy reform through protest and advocacy that threaten vested interests too dramatically may engender a dangerous backlash from social and political élites, a problem of special importance in less open political regimes. Similarly, campaigns can be carried out in ways which strengthen grassroots organisations and their voice, or they can be implemented by intermediaries for whom the grassroots are 'clients'. The latter can lead to the evolution of a civil society with a strong professional advocacy sector and a weak grassroots base (Jenkins 1987).

The status of poor and marginalised groups is a poignant reminder of their lack of power in society. Grassroots organisations seldom, if ever, achieve policy change in their favour without the participation of other social groups such as NGOs, churches, professional groups and academia. The small literature on the policy influence work of NGOs in Southern countries reports a strikingly similar pattern of organisation. Some sort of alliance emerges to bring together grassroots groups, intermediary NGOs, allies from academia or the Church and, more frequently than perhaps expected, allies from the State or official development agencies. Hall (1992) notes, for example, that the success of the Itaparica hydropower campaign in north-east Brazil can be attributed to a combined bottom-up and top-down strategy involving local communities, a regional NGO formation, the Church, international NGOs and the World Bank.

Multi-organisational, multi-sectoral alliances are complex. Questions of how interests, participation and power are balanced among members typically arise in alliance-formation and during the course of a campaign. They reflect the challenges inherent in forging alliances across groups which differ in wealth, class, culture and resources. Fundamentally, these questions have to do with finding the right balance between bottom-up and top-down forces in an alliance. The process of finding this balance is directly related to the questions central to this book: what does an alliance need to be effective? How is alliance accountability to its members maintained, especially to the grassroots interests it purports to represent? This chapter explores the questions of effectiveness and accountability in policy alliances. It is a preliminary exploration of data from two Institute for Development Research (IDR) studies, one looking at national policy-influence campaigns promoting a wide variety of development issues, and another examining transnational NGO alliances formed to influence World Bank projects.[2]

The concepts: effectiveness and accountability

Looking at policy alliances in terms of effectiveness and accountability is important for NGOs that seek to promote sustainable development and more open societies through popular influence on decision-makers. Together, effectiveness and accountability reflect the character of a policy-influence campaign and the nature of relationships among the parties in an alliance. By developing clarity about what effectiveness means and understanding how and to whom accountability flows, those who pursue development through policy-influence may achieve greater success and avoid some unintended consequences of their actions.

Effectiveness of policy alliances

Basically, the success of a policy alliance is measured by the degree to which its stated policy goals are achieved. Did the alliance win desired policy advantages for those it represented? How significant were its compromises? Even if the gains were small, were they consistent with longer-term objectives or was the alliance co-opted? Is the bureaucracy implementing the policy as it was designed? Answers to these questions depend on one's interests, point of view and subjective judgement. Nevertheless, they are the measure of the alliance's policy achievements.

A second dimension is less explicit. It is often assumed that policy efforts intended to benefit under-represented groups also strengthen the capacity of these groups to advocate for their own interests. Expanding people's consciousness and empowering community-based organisations is not an automatic outcome of policy work. However, strengthening community-based institutions so that grassroots groups can be more effective actors in the policy arena is crucial to long-term alliance effectiveness.

Analyses of the Southern development experience conclude that, while presumptions of grassroots association presence and strength are often ill-founded, institutions for popular participation are essential for sustainable development (Cernea 1987; Bratton 1989). Likewise, policy alliances must strengthen grassroots participation if people are to develop the 'staying power' required to build democratic societies. A second set of questions emerge from the role of policy alliances in strengthening civil society. To what extent has the alliance, through its organisation and campaigns, strengthened the institutional base for citizen action? Has it nurtured informed grassroots participation for the long haul, not simply mobilised groups for acts of protest? Has it contributed positively to an inclusive political culture and to public resolution of conflict through peaceful means?

Accountability in policy alliances

NGO policy alliances typically include a constellation of community-based organisations; organised social movements such as peasant federations; local, national and international NGOs; and allies from the Church, academia, business, government and official agencies. A set of cross-cutting social and power relationships are therefore established which form a bridge between the grassroots and élite groups. Structurally, alliances incorporate many of the inequalities in wealth, power, knowledge and resources they are trying to reshape (Brown and Tandon 1993). Where many actors are involved, to what and to whom is the alliance accountable? Each member has unique interests in addition to those encompassed by the shared agenda. Competing interests must be negotiated and renegotiated in some fashion as the alliance carries out its campaign. As the alliance interacts with policy-makers and opponents, goals and tactics must be changed. Decision-making reflects the power dynamics of the alliance itself. To what extent do these dynamics perpetuate existing patterns of influence in society, albeit in the service of a shared purpose? To what extent is the alliance internally democratic?

Alliance accountability rests partly on formal representational and decision-making structures that characterise membership-based community organisations. However, even when representative democratic structures exist, organisations may not be democratic because over time the 'iron law of oligarchy' presses for bureaucratisation and concentration of power at the centre (Fox 1992). Accountability between NGOs and the communities they work with is similarly elusive. Despite the growing consensus that people's participation is a hallmark of good development projects, NGOs are seldom formally structured to ensure their accountability to grassroots organisations. In fact, NGO accountability procedures are most often designed to meet donor needs rather than grassroots objectives. Edwards and Hulme (1994) point to 'the paradox of organizations promoting democratization which are themselves only weakly democratic'. Carroll (1991), on the other hand, offers alternatives to direct or representative democracy by which NGOs can be held accountable to the grassroots. His findings suggest that an open collegial NGO style and an ethos that encourages community participation, can help to create sensitive and accountable organisations.

The following analysis asks two questions:

1.   What factors increase the effectiveness of policy alliances in achieving policy outcomes and strengthening civil society?
2.   What factors enable alliances to be accountable to their members, especially grassroots groups?

The cases

The analysis is based on two cases of national-level policy change in the Philippines and two cases of transnational alliances which aimed to influence World Bank projects. The cases were chosen from a larger body of IDR work to illustrate how structures and processes within alliances lead to different levels of effectiveness and types of accountability. Both national and transnational alliances are examined because each has important consequences for the lives of people in developing countries. The Philippine cases involve community-based organisations, NGOs, NGO coalitions and other allies. The transnational cases involve all these actors plus international NGOs focused on World Bank environmental policy reform. Together the four cases offer contrasting examples of alliance effectiveness and patterns of accountability.

The Philippine campaigns

The first Philippine alliance, the Urban Land Reform Task Force (ULRTF) arose from more than twenty years of community efforts to protect the rights of the urban poor. It is the first attempt by urban people's organisations to influence policy through the parliamentary process rather than through open confrontation and mass protest. The alliance, which also included policy-oriented NGOs, a progressive church-related business group and leaders of the

Catholic Church, came together in 1991 when a weak Urban Land Reform Bill was drafted by the legislature. The task force's goal was to improve the quality of this legislation. It built on the strength of its key players: the mass base of urban people's organisations; the business council's experience with and access to the legislative process; the bishop's political clout; and the NGO secretariat's technical and professional expertise. Governance and decision-making in the alliance were fairly loose. Over the course of the campaign, trust and flexibility increased significantly within the alliance as more ideologically radical community groups withdrew. The alliance won passage of an amended legislative agenda and enhanced the legitimacy of urban land concerns of the poor. Furthermore, participation strengthened the ability of grassroots member organisations to negotiate with powerful groups.

The second case is the Task Force for a Total Commercial Log Ban (TCLB), formed in about 1990 when a small number of Manila-based environmental groups, concerned with the rapid depletion of Philippine forests, came together with related NGOs and community organisations to launch a co-ordinated legislative campaign to protect the remaining forest cover. As it reached out to other groups around the country, the alliance incorporated grassroots economic concerns about equity and community use of forest resources. As a result, its initial call for a total ban on logging was modified to call for a ban on commercial logging. The national campaign was co-ordinated by a secretariat and a set of operational committees run on a part-time basis by staff from the Manila-based groups. Diverse community and regional log-ban campaigns functioned simultaneously, but autonomously from one another. The task force succeeded in placing environmental concerns on the national agenda and strengthened NGO commitment to the issue. However, its limited resources and a lack of effective co-ordination among members reduced its ability to influence outcomes.

The transnational campaigns

The Sierra Madre Forestry Project involved protest against a World Bank–Mexican Government venture intended to modernise the forestry industry of northern Mexico. A local church-based human rights organisation began tracking this project because of concerns over its environmental and social impact on the indigenous groups in the area. This group initially worked with a Texas-based policy group and an environmental advocacy group in Washington. Later, other US regional and national NGOs exerted pressure on the World Bank to cancel the project due to concern about its effect on the Rio Grande watershed and plant and wildlife populations. The aim of the local NGO was to redesign the project to increase economic benefits for the area. However, after a second environmental impact assessment was released, international NGOs increased pressure on the bank to cancel the project altogether. Meanwhile, macro-economic factors associated with trade liberalisation undermined the project's financial viability, and at this point it was cancelled. The forest dwellers (Tarahumara Indians) were largely absent throughout this campaign, even though the Mexican Department of Indigenous Affairs secured extra funds to consult them, and the local NGO had previously worked closely with them on human rights and land tenure issues.

The Mount Apo Geothermal Plant Project was also contested by local, national and international groups whose goal was to persuade the World Bank not to finance a large-scale energy project in Mindanao (Philippines). In 1983, the Department of Environment and Natural Resources (DENR) denied the Philippine National Oil Company's exploration request on the grounds that this type of development was prohibited in national parks. However, in 1985 the Bureau of Energy Development issued an exploration permit without an environmental impact assessment or public hearing. DENR declared the action illegal. In spite of this, the project got underway.

The concerns of indigenous people centred on the desecration of sacred sites and the violation of tribal self-determination, while local farmers were worried about down-stream pollution. Joined by the local Catholic church, these groups formed a task force that took the initiative in opposing the Mount Apo project. They solicited assistance from regional advocacy NGOs and obtained help from Manila-based national advocacy groups. Through their various solidarity networks, this alliance of local, regional and national groups brought the project to the attention of counterparts in Europe and North America. The project was suspended in 1989, but resumed in 1992 as pressure to meet growing energy needs mounted. At the suggestion of a US environmental NGO representative, a campaign began to pressure the World Bank and the IMF through close co-ordination between the Manila-based NGOs and a Washington-based advocacy network. The World Bank rejected the environmental impact assessment approved by DENR. Subsequently, the government withdrew its loan request, but is seeking alternative funds to complete the project.

Analysis of alliance effectiveness

This section examines the four cases with respect to their effectiveness on policy outcomes and their impact on civil society.[3] Policy effectiveness involves the extent to which the alliance achieved its policy goals through either direct or indirect influence on decision-makers. The civil society dimension of effectiveness involves two measures: the alliance's impact on the strength of local institutions, and the nature of community participation in the process of policy influence.

Policy outcomes

In none of the cases was there total victory. Influence often comes through compromise, as in the urban land reform case. The task force modified its goals during the campaign and, as a result of these compromises, won solid, but only partial reform. When multiple policy goals are pursued, outcomes are likely to be mixed – the alliance wins some, but loses others. In the Mexican forestry case, project abandonment achieved the alliance's environmental goals, but simul-

Table 16.1 *Policy alliance effectiveness*

The cases	Policy/project outcomes	Civil society outcomes
Urban land reform	Achieved its legislative goals	Involved urban poor in legislative and bureaucratic advocacy
Logging ban	Concrete gains at local level; no national reform	Built environmental constituency
Sierra Madre Forest Project	Project cancelled	No involvement of local people
Mount Apo Geothermal Plant	Philippine government withdraws World Bank loan request; project will probably be completed	Increased strength of existing local and regional groups and their relations to support networks

taneously made the economic development goals of the local NGO impossible to achieve.

The log ban case illustrates that policy outcomes often occur at various levels. The coalition failed to get national legislation passed because the national campaign was technically and politically unable to counter the weight of the commercial logging lobby. However, local groups did succeed in stopping some commercial logging and in gaining some reforestation projects. When alliance members pursue different levels of policy action (local, national and international), gains at one level do not necessarily flow to others. Determining when to compromise and balancing trade-offs among different goals and different policy levels, pose major challenges to NGO policy alliances.

Finally, effectiveness in influencing multiple actors also needs to be considered. The Mount Apo campaign skilfully pressured the World Bank to reject the environmental impact assessment performed by the Philippine government, which caused the government to withdraw its loan request. In this instance, however, the alliance did not gain sufficient bargaining power to dissuade the government from going forward with alternative funding.

To what extent are the alliance's efforts responsible for the policy outcome? In the urban land reform and community level log ban campaigns, the alliances can clearly take credit for the outcomes. However, positive outcomes are not always a direct result of alliance activity. Even though the result for some alliance members in the Mexico forest case was positive, the alliance's efforts were secondary to economic and political forces that made the project undesirable to the Mexican government. When policy gains are not achieved (as in the Mount Apo and national-level log ban campaign), larger forces tend to overwhelm the interests of grassroots groups. For example, energy demands carried great economic and political weight with the new Philippine government elected on a platform of economic success 'by the year 2000'. Similarly, the economic and political clout of commercial loggers outstripped the influence of environmentalists whose ideas were not firmly rooted in broad public acceptance.

Impact on civil society

There are clear positive outcomes in two of the cases. Local organisations were strengthened in some fashion in the urban land reform and Mount Apo cases. The presence of pre-existing grassroots organisations is a critical element in both. In the Mount Apo case, locally initiated action was reinforced and linked to provincial, national and international resources. This was made possible in part by the active role played by the federation of indigenous people's organisations at the national level. Because the federation was co-ordinating national and international lobbying efforts, grassroots leaders were able to keep attention focused on community issues during the course of the campaign. The Urban Land Reform Task Force also included strong grassroots organisations, but some of them left the alliance in protest against compromise. During the legislative campaign, local organisations were active, citizen participation was high and grassroots leaders developed new skills. However, when the task force later took on the role of monitoring implementation, local organisations became overextended and had difficulty in delivering basic services and benefits to their members. None of the cases illustrates a clear negative impact on grassroots groups. However, in the Sierra Madre case, the indigenous people affected were used briefly to lend legitimacy to the environmental campaign. They felt exploited and withdrew from further involvement, and so lost an opportunity to pursue their interests.

Seeking impact on both policy and civil society

Figure 16.1 depicts the degree to which each alliance changed policy and strengthened civil society. The four cases plotted on the two dimensions show strikingly different patterns. The urban land and Sierra Madre campaigns are

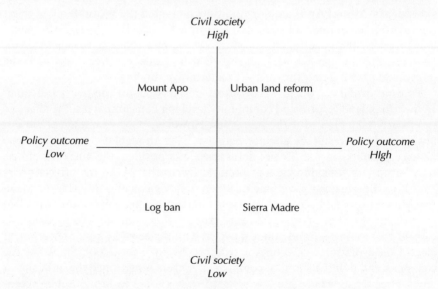

Figure 16.1   *Effectiveness in achieving policy gains and strengthening civil society*

more effective in terms of policy gains, but differ on the degree to which they promote stronger grassroots groups. In contrast, the Mount Apo and log ban cases are both lower on policy outcomes, but Mount Apo supported greater local involvement, while the national log ban campaign was unable to engage with local groups successfully.

Because the ebb and flow of a successful campaign must match the rhythm of the political process, it often appears that trade-offs must be made, at least in the short term, between policy gains and strengthening grassroots associations. Lobbying actions sometimes cannot wait for slower-paced grassroots education and participation efforts. Sometimes, the strategies preferred by the grassroots frame the issues so that they are hard to win. However, the urban land reform example shows that effectiveness on both dimensions is possible. It illustrates the potential for educating and involving grassroots groups in campaign decisions and strengthening alliance capacity to achieve policy outcomes. The alliance's strategy simultaneously:

1. increased the commitment of the poor to support legislation through mass action;
2. expanded their understanding of political decision-making processes;
3. increased their confidence and repertoire of skills for dealing with the government.

Through the active involvement of grassroots and other members, the alliance had the ability to influence at many points of leverage and through multiple channels.

At the other extreme, the log ban alliance achieved neither its policy goal nor a positive impact on civil society and citizen participation. In fact, efforts to engage local organisations in the commercial log ban campaign were unsuccessful, largely because the national environmental NGOs could not forge a genuine alliance with grassroots groups. They were unsuccessful at forging a campaign to encompass both livelihood and environmental issues. There were, in fact, two campaigns being waged: one at the national level, which had little popular support, and another at the grassroots in which people struggled with some measure of success to secure more control over their livelihoods.

Characteristics of alliance effectiveness

Among the many factors that influence the outcomes of a policy alliance, four alliance characteristics stand out from these cases as fundamental to success. Two influence effectiveness in terms of policy change; two others affect strengthening civil society. Fundamental to the accomplishment of policy gains is a coherent campaign strategy coupled with adequate resources to influence decision-makers. The Urban Land Reform alliance included a policy research centre capable of critiquing legislation and offering sound alternative proposals. Businessmen lobbied the realtors and developers; Cardinal Sin lobbied key players in Congress; and the community groups mobilised their constituents at critical junctures. The task force brought together excellent access and strong technical capability, with well-organised and well-informed, active grassroots constituents. In contrast, the Total Commercial Log Ban Alliance had too few organisational resources to design and implement a campaign strategy or to build a coalition successfully. It was particularly limited because it failed to build a strong grassroots constituency and so was vulnerable to charges that it represented the interests of élitist conservationists.

Secondly, a campaign's ability to win policy advantages depends on its ability to counter the forces of opposition. Framing a winning issue requires that the alliance defines the debate in terms compelling to grassroots groups and which limit the opposition's ability to mobilise its own forces. In the log ban case, the alliance modified its initial stand from a call for a *total* logging ban (which directly threatened forest dwellers) to a *commercial* logging ban. However, community groups had difficulty grasping the difference, and the opposition successfully portrayed the issue as one of 'jobs versus environmental conservation'. The Log Ban Task Force was also not able to gain favourable media coverage – a crucial ingredient to successful framing of any issue.

Third, a commitment to strengthening civil society and democracy is essential if an alliance is to have a positive impact on citizen participation and building grassroots institutions. This is particularly clear in the international alliances. The Mount Apo case represents a network that was strong on commitment to citizen participation and close co-ordination of campaign strategies with grassroots groups. This alliance cared deeply that affected people be centrally involved. Consequently (and fourth), Mount Apo offers a clear example where grassroots groups had significant influence on the structure, goals and strategies of the alliance. Other alliance members followed the lead of the local groups because of the quality of their organisations and their legitimacy as primary stakeholders. In contrast, the Tarahumara in the Sierra Madre case were powerless. They expressed disapproval and dissent by withdrawing after being used to lend legitimacy to the campaign. In some circumstances this 'exit' option can limit the effectiveness of an alliance. However, the NGOs were not limited by the Tarahumara's absence since their primary target (the World Bank) did not require local representativeness when considering the merits of environmental issues.

This analysis suggests that an alliance can achieve successfully both policy and civil society outcomes if it aspires to do so, includes the appropriate social groups and has access to the necessary resources. Perhaps the most important element is whether or not the alliance *actively seeks* both policy outcomes and increased citizen participation.

Analysis of alliance accountability

Policy alliances involve multiple members who each expect the alliance to be accountable to their interests. Since there is never a perfect fit among the expectations of alliance members, the task of being accountable to all is challenging. As microcosms of the larger society, alliances can easily replicate unbalanced patterns of influence and so give their grassroots members short shrift. This section identifies how alliances are accountable to the grassroots as well as to other members. Indicators of accountability include: inclusion in decision-making; access to alliance resources, especially information; and division of roles and responsibilities (for example, who the spokespersons are).

Figure 16.2 shows the four cases arrayed on a continuum of accountability to the grassroots. High accountability is associated with alliances in which grassroots groups have access to key information; participate in strategic as well as tactical decision-making; and play leadership roles in the alliance.

The Mount Apo case has high levels of grassroots accountability. It was structured so that the regional, national and international task forces and networks supported the goals defined by indigenous people and farmers. Where alliance members held different institutional priorities – for example, environmental protection versus indigenous people's rights – they resolved conflicts arising from these interests in an agenda set by indigenous people's and farmers' concerns. In contrast, in the Sierra Madre case, there was little accountability to affected people. NGOs pursued their own priorities and solicited only token input.

In the urban land reform case, local groups were active decision-makers and implementors of the national campaign strategy – a task relatively easy to accomplish logistically since Manila was the focus of the national campaign. The secretariat was strongly committed to inclusion of all parties and especially sensitive that legislative proposals be put forward only when they had strong grassroots support. Grassroots outreach and education enabled active and informed participation by grassroots leaders in decision-making. In addition, the secretariat was highly accountable to all through direct member participation in key decisions.

In the log ban campaign, the rural members of the alliance were geographically, organisationally and ideologically diverse, with no framework or mechanism for common representation in Manila. Local groups did not have an active presence in Manila where national campaign decisions were made. This, coupled with the task force's limited resources and its inexperience with the concerns of local groups, produced significant gaps between the intentions of the task force concerning inclusion and accountability, and its actual performance.

Factors affecting alliance accountability

These cases suggest several factors that affect an alliance's accountability. Inclusion is the prerequisite for accountability to the grassroots and so the composition of the alliance is a fundamental defining characteristic. The diversity of interests and organisations within an alliance also affects its accountability. If the alliance has many and diverse members, the task of accountability is more complex. The Urban Land Reform Task Force illustrates

High	Moderate	Moderate	Low
Mount Apo	Urban land reform	Log ban	Sierra Madre

Figure 16.2 *Alliance accountability to grassroots groups*

a heterogeneous alliance which cuts across many sectors of Philippine society, from poor urban communities to the highest ranks of the Catholic Church. Significant differences in wealth, culture and power existed among these groups. Even though they came together to seek benefits for the urban poor, their inherent social differences made accountability a complex task. From the beginning, the alliance recognised that community groups had important resources to contribute as well as the primary stake in the outcome of its work. This realisation, coupled with a strong community empowerment ethos, led it to seek high levels of accountability to the grassroots.

The Sierra Madre alliance excluded indigenous people, but it included a Mexican human rights organisation, US regional environmental organisations and a Washington-based advocacy NGO. Despite differences among these NGOs, the alliance remained unisectoral. It left out other interests such as business, the Church and professional groups. Balancing accountability in this type of alliance is simpler than in one which includes NGOs, community-based organisations and representatives of other social sectors.[4]

The legitimacy and resources each member brings to the alliance shape the power dynamics of the alliance itself (Brown 1995). Where the grassroots is organised, respected and has considerable resources, it has power relative to other members. In this instance other members are likely to be more accountable to grassroots interests, as in the Mount Apo and urban land reform cases. Where grassroots groups cannot assert their legitimacy or other groups hold most of the resources, as in the log ban and Sierra Madre cases, grassroots accountability will be minimal. The power of each member also depends on their role and function in campaign strategies. In the Sierra Madre case the Tarahumara lent symbolic legitimacy to the campaign. There was no need for them to be active participants since the target of the campaign, the World Bank, was interested in the technical merits of the argument rather than the political base from which it came. The strategies of the Mount Apo and urban land reform cases, however, relied heavily on demonstrating to the Philippine government that a political constituency demanded a response to their concerns. Community groups in these instances had resources critical to success.

Institutional mechanisms for information-sharing and decision-making are fundamental to fostering accountability to the grassroots. In the urban land reform alliance, the secretariat played a pivotal role. It was an ideologically neutral, technically competent, professional NGO secretariat committed to supporting grassroots participation. This secretariat was instrumental in negotiations between community organisations and the business group on specific legislative strategies and goals. It helped to balance power in these negotiations by informing the community about options and by educating the business group about the core concerns of the community. The Mount Apo alliance involved a series of sub-coalitions at local, regional, national and international levels, each with different roles and decision-making responsibilities. National groups had primary responsibility for linking local, national and international strategies, but this was done with strong local representation in Manila through the indigenous people's coalition and through systematic consultation with all parties.

The log ban case illustrates that resources and experience in managing multi-organisational, multi-level alliances are necessary for the successful inclusion of all parties in decision-making. Lapses in consultation with the grassroots and in the formulation of a cohesive strategy resulted from limited time, personnel and skills in the co-ordinating bodies. Alliances which were more successful in accounting to all their members, especially the grassroots, had both formal and informal mechanisms to ensure good information flows and the inclusion of all members in decision-making. Some form of structured representation of grassroots groups in decision-making structures, coupled with a secretariat that had commitment and resources to encourage community participation, seem to be essential for accountability to the grassroots.

Conclusion

NGOs have growing opportunities to be involved in policy alliances as states gradually open themselves to greater citizen participation and as donors learn the value of including the grassroots as a legitimate stakeholder. NGOs also can take an active role in supporting grassroots involvement in situations where the state and donors are not open to popular participation. In these instances, confrontation is the likely course of events. Whether the context is co-operative or confrontational, alliances may take one of three basic forms, characterised by different goals, influences and accountability: grassroots-centred alliances, NGO-centred alliances and mixed alliances.[5]

Grassroots-centred alliances, such as the Mount Apo coalition, define the policy question from the grassroots point of view. NGOs and NGO coalitions join the alliance based on their affinity with the issues framed by the grassroots and their willingness to play a supporting role. Established primarily on principles of solidarity, these alliances may forego policy gains to strengthen civil society. For example, NGOs with expert resources may defer to goals and strategies devised by the grassroots, even when their skills and insights could improve strategies for policy change.

NGO-centred alliances are exemplified by the log ban and Sierra Madre cases. In these alliances, NGO definitions of the problem shape the alliance agenda and strategy. If grassroots groups are involved, they play a supporting role to NGOs (providing information, staging local protests or lending legitimacy to NGO-designed actions). Accountability to the grassroots tends to be weak since the alliance is formed primarily to achieve NGO-defined policy goals. These alliances are well suited to achieving policy change with institutions which themselves have low levels of public accountability, such as multilateral development banks. They may also be useful for incremental policy change (Jenkins 1987), but they have little positive impact on deepening civil society and broadening democratic participation.

Mixed alliances, such as the Urban Land Reform Coalition, link poor people, middle classes and élites in pursuit of a common objective. They have the potential to build civil society and to enhance policy outcomes simultaneously. However, this type of alliance offers the greatest challenge as well as the best promise for combining concrete policy benefits with increased participation in the institutions of civil society for marginalised groups. Success requires the alliance to have a bridging mechanism capable of spanning ideological differences and balancing power.

In a study of NGO roles in community-government partnerships in several Asian and African countries, Brown (1995) draws lessons which are highly relevant to mixed alliances. He concludes that NGOs balance power in multi-organisational alliances 'by controlling important resources, shaping participants' awareness of their own and others' interests, and defining and enforcing the rules of the game to promote mutual influence'. The Urban Land Reform Task Force NGO secretariat played this role by being an honest broker between grassroots and élite groups. The secretariat's sensitivity and respect for the interests of all members is largely responsible for the alliance's success in balancing local needs with the interests of the business community and church. In the urban land reform alliance, the NGO secretariat had important resources itself – for example, technical and policy analysis skills – but it also provided others with access to resources they did not have – for example, information about political processes to community members and 'expert' community knowledge to businessmen. The secretariat urged the urban groups to understand their interests in new ways that enabled them to reframe their demands. It also facilitated the creation and implementation of decision-making rules that increased mutual influence.

Brown (1991) suggests that this 'bridging' function is extremely demanding of the organisations and individuals who perform it, and that NGOs are uniquely able to fill the role. In a policy alliance, not only must the bridging agent help others to establish mutual goals and reconcile differences; it must also manage its own interests and priorities. The bridging agent must have strong skills to facilitate mutual influence and to assist alliance members to find common ground. When the bridging agent has a strong stake in the alliance's policy outcome (as did the environmental NGOs in the log ban case), those interests may undermine its ability to balance information and decision-making processes. However, the urban land reform and Mount Apo cases illustrate that it is possible for NGOs to be effective intermediaries in developing multi-sectoral and international policy alliances that influence policy *and* strengthen civil society at the same time.

Notes

1. The paper draws heavily on the joint analysis of the Philippines cases done by Valerie Miller, Dina Abad, David Brown and myself. Their contributions are crucial. I am also indebted to Scott Kennedy for his editorial assistance in preparing this paper.
2. IDR is researching NGO policy influence efforts at the national level in several countries in Asia and Africa. A comparative analysis of cases in the Philippines is underway, and new case studies are beginning in Indonesia and India. The study of

transnational NGO influence efforts looks at large projects with environmental consequences as well as World Bank operational policies. These studies work with NGO communities to identify and build capacities necessary for effective and accountable policy influence. Support for these case studies comes from the Ford Foundation, the Moriah Fund, the Joyce Mertz Gilmore Foundation, the Asia Foundation, the Social Science Research Council, and the Canadian International Development Authority (CIDA).

3. The analysis of alliance effectiveness draws on Miller 1994.

4. Differences between the desired outcomes of the Mexican and US advocacy groups undoubtedly affected accountability. This analysis will be refined when the final draft of the Sierra Madre case is completed.

5. A second form of grassroots-centred alliance, not represented in the cases here, is the grassroots movement that has little, if any, direct involvement of NGOs. National federations of peasants, unions or women's groups often fit into this category.

Participatory Methods for Increasing NGO Accountability: a Case Study from India

Parmesh Shah and Meera Kaul Shah

This chapter explores the participatory methodologies used to increase the accountability of one NGO to the village institutions and communities which it professes to support and serve. The case study used is the Aga Khan Rural Support Programme in India. The problems which are likely to occur in using these methods are highlighted, and mechanisms are explored which may help NGOs to introduce and increase accountability to grassroots institutions.

Accountability: multiple dimensions

Accountability is generally understood as a means by which individuals and organisations report to authority (Edwards and Hulme 1994). However, in development programmes at the grassroots level, accountability relates to the wider process of information exchange, decision-making, management, nego-tiation and bargaining that takes place between different stakeholders. Accountability exists between peer groups and operates at many levels. For example:

Membership organisations	Members
Community organisations	Community
NGOs	Community organisations
	Membership organisations
	Village institutions
	Local government
	State and central government
	Donors
	Other competing and complementary NGOs

This chapter focuses mainly on the accountability of Southern intermediary NGOs (or grassroots support organisations) to community organisations and membership organisations (Carroll 1992). It also examines the suitability and relevance of participatory methods tried out at grassroots level for introducing accountability at other levels – between Southern NGOs, Northern NGOs and official donor agencies.

In the past, accountability has been used to introduce control mechanisms linked to hierarchy and authority. In contrast, we consider accountability to be a reciprocal process in which multiple actors are accountable to each other. Accountability does not just mean reporting; it means a process of information exchange, consultation and joint decision-making.

Current experience shows that accountability is mostly upwards, toward donors and governments. In the context of development programmes, NGOs have undertaken limited consultation with community institutions before taking strategic decisions which affect them. We use the term 'reverse accountability' to emphasise the need to reorient the flow of accountability, reporting and decision-making towards community institutions. An overemphasis on mechanisms for introducing upward accountability has led to weak links between accountability, performance and impact in Southern NGOs. If Southern NGOs have limited personnel and scarce resources, they should spend more time on introducing mechanisms to increase accountability to community institutions. However, evidence shows that the time and resources spent by Southern NGOs on improving accountability to donors (including Northern NGOs) has reduced their capacity to do this. Participatory methods provide fertile ground for increasing the accountability of Southern NGOs to the community institutions and membership organisations they support.

Participatory methods to increase accountability

Participatory methods have been used by NGOs in development programmes to increase the participation of local communities in the development process and to support the formation of accountable local institutions. NGOs have used methods like Participatory Rural Appraisal (PRA) to increase the accountability of office bearers and leaders in community institutions to members, and of members to each other. However, these methods have rarely been used by NGOs to develop accountability mechanisms to the local institutions they support or to undergo peer evaluation of NGO performance. Most NGOs are happy to involve community institutions in programme monitoring and evaluation, but are less active when it comes to evaluating the performance of the NGO itself as a support institution. There is considerable scope for using participatory methodologies to develop reciprocal accountability between NGOs and community institutions.

The Aga Khan Rural Support Programme, India (AKRSP)

AKRSP is an NGO which has been working in western India since 1985 to create an 'enabling environment to enable local communities to develop and manage their local natural resources in a productive, sustainable and equitable manner through their own local institutions'. It has catalysed the formation of a range of village membership organisations by agencies with elected office bearers and leaders. AKRSP has been using Participatory Rural Appraisal to enable communities to participate in programme appraisal and planning, and to develop their own institutions and para-professionals to manage development programmes.

The programmes implemented by village institutions involve watershed management, forestry, small-scale irrigation, the rehabilitation of tanks, agriculture, savings and credit, animal husbandry, marketing and energy conservation. AKRSP provides training, and technical, financial and management support to the community institutions, based on the appraisal and planning process carried out by the villagers. Budgeting is carried out by the programme, based on a participatory planning process at village level. AKRSP is currently funded by a number of donors, including State and Central Government, and bilateral agencies.

The initial strategic planning and budgeting exercise for preparing proposals for funding was largely carried out by AKRSP professionals, based on limited consultation with the community. The donors to AKRSP relied heavily on an external evaluation to determine their support and funding for the next phase. The internal review of the first phase clearly showed that many assumptions made by NGO staff and the external evaluation team were not valid, and that inadequate consultation had led to unrealistic planning. AKRSP therefore decided to involve village institutions (VIs) more actively in strategic planning and the evaluation of its performance. It also decided to precede any future external evaluation of the programme by an internal evaluation of AKRSP carried out by community institutions. The areas to be covered in any internal evaluation were to include not only programme performance, but also NGO management, the process of decision-making and the nature of support provided by AKRSP. Community institutions were asked to develop criteria for assessing the effectiveness and performance of AKRSP as a support organisation.

The development of performance criteria for AKRSP through evaluation workshops

The Village Institutions (VIs) were asked to devote one session of their regular meetings to brainstorm criteria for evaluating AKRSP's performance. This exercise was carried out with all VIs to avoid selecting institutions with a bias. The discussions varied considerably among VIs and the criteria evolved after animated discussion. The major criteria developed by VIs were as follows:

Process of consultation.
Management style of NGO (bureaucratic, participatory).
Relationship with VIs (authoritarian, consultative, collegiate).
Speed of decision-making.
Structure of NGO (hierarchical, decentralised).
Ability to act and use information provided by VIs.
Regular presentation of the information to the community on key decisions (reporting).
Transparency in decision-making.
Sensitivity of NGO staff.
Timeliness of support.
Quality and nature of technical and management support.
Participation of VI representatives in key policy decisions of AKRSP.
Ability of the NGO to influence government operations and policies (lobbying).

Attendance of VIs jointly with NGOs in decision-making fora at the district and state levels through seminars and workshops.

Programme performance.

As can be seen, these criteria relate to processes of decision-making, the management style of AKRSP, reporting and action on information, the nature of programme support, and support in gaining access to external institutions and decision-making fora. This laid a good framework for evaluating the performance of AKRSP.

Ranking AKRSP as a support organisation based on the agreed performance criteria

In order to assess AKRSP's performance based on the criteria evolved by the VIs, they were asked to rank AKRSP on each of the criteria through a matrix-ranking exercise. VIs were also asked to justify the ranking by recalling a critical incident which could support their decision. Thus, both quantitative and qualitative information was collected during the process. This information was used subsequently in external evaluation and in training AKRSP staff and village-institution office-bearers. It was also used to take corrective action during subsequent planning and review exercises. An example of such a ranking is given in Table 17.1.

Some of the critical incidents recalled while ranking AKRSP's performance are as follows:

1. Regular presentation of information to the community on key decisions

AKRSP supported one VI to initiate a lift-irrigation co-operative and through

Table 17.1   *Ranking of AKRSP as a support institution by Village Institution in Bharuch district*

(1 = Best   2 = Good   3 = Medium   4 = Poor)

Criteria	Rank
Process of consultation	2
Management style	3
Relationship with VIs	2
Speed of decision-making	1
Structure of NGO	3
Ability to act on information provided by VIs	2
Regular presentation of information to community on key decisions	4
Transparency in decision-making	3
Sensitivity of NGO staff	2
Timeliness of support	1
Quality and nature of technical and managerial support	2
Participation of VIs in key decisions	3
Ability of AKRSP to influence government operations and policies	2
Attendance of VIs in decision-making fora of government	3
Programme performance	2

mutual discussion agreed to support the management costs (the salary of a water distributor) on a progressively declining basis for the first three years of operation, to enable the co-operative to stabilise its operations. This was agreed on the basis of estimates of additional income for members, evolved jointly by VIs and AKRSP. The performance of the programme was reviewed after the first two years. Studies undertaken by AKRSP showed that irrigation in some villages had resulted in a higher and more rapid increase in income than had been envisaged. AKRSP discussed this issue with some, but not all, the VIs, and decided to reduce the amount of management support, providing it only in the first year of operation. The decision was communicated to office bearers in an annual review meeting and they were asked to tell their members.

Many members were surprised at this decision, since they were never presented with the relevant information. They were not against the assessment of viability and the rationalisation of management support, but felt that AKRSP should have presented the information directly at the VI meetings. They felt that the decision had been taken by AKRSP in its internal fora without adequate consultation with VI members. They also indicated that each VI required different support and that AKRSP should have made regular presentations to *all* VIs. After all, this was a key decision affecting the viability of the farmers' livelihoods.

2. Timeliness of support   During one particular year, VIs were facing a drastic shortage of groundnut seeds in the 'kharif' season, since nearly all the stocks had been cornered by the Groundnut Growers' Federation. The VIs were concerned that most members would not be able to sow good-quality seeds at the right time and would thus lose out on potential income in a good rainfall year. During one of the review meetings, they raised this as a concern and asked AKRSP to help. AKRSP approached the Groundnut Growers' Federation in Ahmedabad (the state capital) and asked whether they would be able to earmark a stock of seeds for the VIs supported by AKRSP. The Federation requested a deposit of 20 per cent of the value of the seeds as a precondition for reserving the stock. AKRSP knew from past experience that VIs had already collected deposits from their members, but to save precious time, AKRSP itself deposited the money and asked the VIs to reimburse it from their funds. The timely delivery of seeds was linked to a credit and marketing programme planned by the VIs. The VIs got their seeds delivered on time and performed significantly better than other villages in the area. During a subsequent review exercise, they appreciated the speed of AKRSP's response and have encouraged AKRSP to respond to similar contingencies in the future.

Institutional (Venn) diagramming to assess the comparative performance of AKRSP vis-à-vis other development institutions in the area

Since discussing relative performance is a sensitive issue, VI members are asked to represent institutions by circles ('chapatis' in the Indian context) and indicate their relative performance by arranging them in different sizes and colours.

They are also encouraged to develop criteria for assessing comparative performance, and to indicate the closeness of the external institution to the VI by arranging the 'chapatis' at different distances. Subsequently, this method was also used to enable VI members to evaluate the performance of the VI in relation to external institutions.

VIs were also asked to illustrate the levels of co-ordination and overlap between the different institutions with which they interacted. They were then asked to indicate any improvements required in the workings of these institutions in relation to the VI and to each other. In this process, AKRSP generated useful data on its performance *vis-à-vis* other institutions (including the government), and developed greater downward accountability by enabling VIs to compare AKRSP with other institutions.

'Chapati' diagrams revealed that there were a number of other informal institutions which provided support to the village community by enforcing rules and regulations about common property resource management – for example, in forest protection. AKRSP had not involved these institutions in the consultative process adequately during the initial stages, and in some cases had provided incentives to VIs to set up parallel institutions, thus increasing the cost of management. VIs indicated that AKRSP should build on informal institutions and processes before catalysing the formation of new ones. As a result, AKRSP has now included an assessment of indigenous institutions as an integral part of the participatory appraisal process.

AKRSP has also supported the development of an animal husbandry programme for VIs. However, the quality and frequency of AKRSP support has been minimal, since it has not been able to recruit high-quality staff in this area. In one region, people indicated that the staff of the government Animal Husbandry Department were very competent and provided good support to the VI in spite of resource constraints. The VI therefore suggested to AKRSP that it should wind up its operations in animal husbandry and provide resources to the VI so that it could provide logistic and transport support to the government, enabling them to provide services to VIs in a timely manner.

Evaluation workshops to discuss the results of the ranking exercises and steps for corrective action

The results of the ranking process and institutional assessment were compiled jointly with VI representatives and presented to workshops, which discussed results and agreed on steps and mechanisms for corrective action in the future. These workshops were organised on a regional basis with all VIs participating in smaller group discussions and indicating areas for corrective action through presentations to each other. AKRSP also made presentations on the action it would like to take, based on the evaluation exercises. Decisions taken at the end of the workshops included:

- A workshop to review AKRSP performance by VIs every six months.
- AKRSP to make a presentation of its annual plan to the VIs in February and March.
- A group of VIs to undertake a performance audit of AKRSP.

- AKRSP to invite VI representatives to its strategic planning meetings on a rotating basis.
- VIs to be provided with training in programme management and communication skills, to enable them to make presentations at external fora.

All these measures have contributed significantly to the enhancement of reciprocal accountability between AKRSP and VIs.

Participation of VIs in strategic planning exercises prior to external evaluation

Before an external evaluation takes place, AKRSP now asks VIs to undertake an internal evaluation of their programmes and of AKRSP (using some of the methods described earlier) and to present the results to the AKRSP management. They are encouraged to produce a document summarising their findings in the local language, which is used as an important input to the external evaluation process. This document is also used as a guiding framework for strategic and annual planning exercises. This ensures that AKRSP seeks the opinion of VIs before any external evaluation is undertaken, and that subsequent funding of AKRSP is based on feedback from VIs.

Development of local monitoring and Management Information Systems (MIS)

Village Institutions are in the process of developing their own federation and will assume more of the responsibilities currently handled by AKRSP. VIs have therefore been encouraged to develop local monitoring and information systems which enable them to develop accountability with external institutions and to increase their capacity to provide feedback and communicate with members. These systems include the development of simple participatory methods to facilitate performance-assessment in other agencies and the training of VI functionaries in using these methods. The methods have enabled the VIs to be proactive in evaluating AKRSP and other agencies. Some VIs do not wait for AKRSP to take the initiative in developing feedback mechanisms. However, all VIs are not equally interested in evaluating the performance of AKRSP. AKRSP is working towards developing a core group of village leaders who can take the initiative lead in monitoring and evaluating the performance of external agencies (including government), and so help to change the direction of accountability (downwards) in the long run.

Participation of VI office-bearers in the recruitment of NGO staff, training and performance appraisal

This sort of involvement has only been tried out on an experimental basis, since it is a sensitive step and should be taken only after careful consultation with all concerned. It ensures that VI leaders take more responsibility at the initial stage of a programme and assume a proactive role in ensuring staff performance and accountability. It also ensures that AKRSP staff are oriented early on towards the concept of management by the VI. Subsequently, VIs are given a major role in training new staff, who are attached to VIs. VIs are encouraged to provide feedback about the performance of staff, to develop criteria for performance appraisal and periodically to assess their performance. These inputs are incorporated into the formal staff appraisal process used by AKRSP.

Problems encountered

Of course, the use of participatory methods in this way encounters many problems. The major problem is the change in power relationships which VI participation implies. People working for AKRSP sometimes feel threatened, and may be defensive because the methods used bring uncertainty in their jobs and evaluation by multiple stakeholders. A second problem relates to changes in management style. Many issues raised in assessments by VIs lead to a transition from management styles based on hierarchy, inhibited communications, and 'command-and-control' relationships, to more organic styles that encourage lateral communication, collegial authority, and flexible rules and procedures. This transition is not easy.

A third problem relates to a common fear of making mistakes and a lack of suitable opportunities within NGOs to learn from experience. The use of participatory methods depends to a large extent on prioritising learning as an objective in organisational development. Fourth, these methods imply a change in programme management and implementation procedures, particularly in resource-allocation, financial decentralisation and decision-making mechanisms. Many institutions which start by using participatory methods are not ready to make corresponding procedural, structural and policy changes and thus are unable to sustain their use. The use, operationalisation and integration of new methods within both VIs and AKRSP is a long-term process which requires iteration and adaptation. Most NGOs, VIs and donors lack the patience to introduce such a process, and so continue to initiate programmes without adequate consultation.

For NGOs and others who want to try to use participatory methods, the experience of AKRSP suggests the following lessons:

- Do not try using these approaches on a large scale. They require a significant amount of iteration and experimentation. Pilot them first in a region or a group of village institutions, discuss the results, and institutionalise lessons learned from experience.
- Spend enough time initially in explaining the purpose of the methods to key NGO staff members and office-bearers from village institutions. Seek the commitment of top management for using these approaches and sustaining their use.
- In the initial phase of introducing these methods, the results of any evaluation process should be delinked from financial support to village institutions and incentives to staff members. This is essential to ensure that both VIs and NGO staff learn from the process. Subsequently, feedback can be used to make decisions about resource allocation for VIs and performance appraisal for NGO staff.
- It is important to involve VIs in the assessment process before seeking their feedback on performance. VIs are not interested in participating in the process if they have not been involved at the beginning.

■ Participatory methods should be used only if the NGO is interested in changing its decision-making mechanisms and accountability structures.

Implications for practice and policy

The experience of AKRSP shows that participatory methods can be used by NGOs to develop reciprocal accountability to community institutions. We feel that there is a strong case to apply the same principles in other contexts, including in relations with Northern NGOs and donors. Building both upward and downward accountability require major reversals in the mindsets of donors, NGOs and community institutions. Any external evaluation by an external donor or a team comprised of external professionals should be preceded by a reciprocal evaluation by the recipient of funds. The process should start with community institutions being evaluated by their members, followed by an evaluation by the institutions of the nature and performance of NGO support. Southern NGOs should have an opportunity to evaluate their donors (Northern NGOs or other aid agencies). Northern NGOs who raised funds from official agencies should develop similar processes. External evaluation should incorporate the results of these processes into their outputs. In many cases, the role of the external evaluation itself would become peripheral, perhaps limited to combining the outputs of the process at all these levels.

There is already considerable dissatisfaction with so-called 'experts' and short-term consultants who spend very little time with programmes and make recommendations based on their impressions which might affect significantly the development process in an area. We are not making a case for the eradication of external evaluation, but feel that it should form a small part of the evaluation process and the process of accountability. NGOs should make more use of participatory methodologies for interactive learning and corrective action. Many NGOs continue to use hierarchical, top-down control systems to exert authority and to demand accountability in their own institutions, and in the process may become as bureaucratic as their counterparts in government. NGOs should also earmark increased time and resources to institutional development in the first two years of the programme cycle, to enable the development of consultative and participatory evaluation mechanisms. Any overemphasis on financial accountability should be replaced by a process of joint decision-making, evaluation and governance.

Participatory methods can be an important step in introducing more appropriate accountability mechanisms. However, the use of these methods alone does not guarantee increased or reciprocal accountability. To do this, NGOs need to make major reversals in their own institutions and to be prepared to carry out structural changes in the long run. The question is, will NGOs be proactive or will they be forced to make such changes only under external pressure?

18

Transforming the Transnational NGOs: Social Auditing or Bust?

Simon Zadek and Murdoch Gatward

What are the possible futures for NGOs? Are they to become 'little more than' the organisational mechanism for an international welfare system, as Fowler (1994) fears? Is the level of co-option into state agendas through funding and joint initiatives as advanced and problematic as Farrington et al (1993) have intimated? Are they doomed to become the new 'lords of poverty' despite Hancock's (1989) plea to the contrary? What will be the leading edge of local, national and international 'third sector' organisations as we move into the 21st century? Will NGOs have the flexibility and efficiency that they claim to underpin their effectiveness, and the vision they claim as their 'speciality' (Clark 1991; Edwards and Hulme 1992)? Most important of all, will NGOs have the *legitimacy* to represent those they claim as their constituents and the forms of *accountability* which ensure effectiveness in relation to their needs?

These questions need to be considered in the broader context of development, which includes:

- Extensions in economic globalisation.
- Continued environmental decay.
- Increases in material absolute and relative poverty.

Northern, or 'transnational', NGOs (TNGOs) face an additional set of issues specific to their current institutional situation:

- *Gradual deoperationalisation from the South.* A pattern of change that on the surface has been welcomed and encouraged by Northern NGOs, as their Southern 'partners' become increasingly effective and anxious to take on the operational roles previously fulfilled by Northern NGOs. Beneath the surface, however, has been enormous resistance to this change from some Northern NGOs, many of which have evolved around an operational focus. Few of them have come firmly to grips with the enormous implications of these changes in terms of their future size, form and relationships.
- *Decline in income.* This is partially attributable to economic recession, but also marks a more fundamental shift that will eventually undermine traditional sources of NGO financing, requiring more radical changes in approach than traditional marketing perspectives can offer. One trend

which may continue is a shift in public support from development to relief. Another trend is a reduction in state funding as bilateral links develop between Northern funders and Southern NGOs. The intermediary role which funded much of the institutional growth of the larger TNGOs during the 1980s will more or less disappear over time.

■ *Concern over accountability.* Development NGOs in the North have acquired a habit of saying 'we represent', but do not do so in any clear sense. This habit is being increasingly challenged, partly as a consequence of the withdrawal of NNGOs from operational work in the South, partly because of the parallel growth in the international voices of Southern NGOs, and partly because of a changing environment in both North and South which will increasingly question the moral high-ground that NGOs achieved during the 1980s.

■ *Policy inertia.* NGOs have increased their national and international policy advocacy at an extraordinary rate over the last ten years. Increasingly, they are consulted by the major development institutions, which have responded to pressure by creating a complex maze of consultative fora. However, the actual successes of policy advocacy are few and far between; the effect of engaging in consultation is often limited, yet they are costly uses of scarce time and money (Edwards 1993).

A crisis?

Do these issues add up to an impending crisis? Casual evidence from our ongoing involvement with TNGOs and others in both North and South suggests that a combination of ideological ruptures, concern about personal futures, funding shortfalls and broader institutional shifts, are combining to create considerable disorientation within the NGO community. There is, of course, much thinking and planning going on in NGOs in order to cope with these issues. However, the disorientation is highly dissipated and therefore tends to emerge in the context of one-off 'fire-fighting' or ubiquitous 'reorganisation' exercises. As Landry (1994) and others have argued, 'there is nothing as yet resembling a strategic response, or indeed a long-term vision, of how the non-profits should adapt'.

One view of this situation is that there should be no generalised strategic approach, given the diversity of the NGO community and its culture of institutionalised pluralism. The 'community' clearly has neither one form, aim or voice. It is certainly reasonable to expect, and desire, that it will continue to evolve in many different forms and different directions. This diversity, however, does not obviate the need for debate and policy, and for the development of some cohesive common ground in terms of insight and direction. Indeed, such diversity makes the need for coherence all the more important.

At the same time, the dilemmas facing major parts of the NGO community and its constituents are rooted in patterns of social and economic upheaval that may not wait for quiet contemplation or piecemeal responses. NGOs need to forge new directions in the future if they are not to become increasingly impotent, or indeed – worst of all – if they are not to become part of the problem.

Ways of seeing

It can be difficult to see problems clearly, let alone ways to resolve them and move forward. This is not because of ignorance or malice. We often prefer to hang on to redundant Utopias rather than risk letting go and falling free into the unknown. This is particularly relevant today, as much to social activists and intellectuals as to bureaucrats, politicians and the business community. The certainties of what is wrong are not matched by the clarity of how to achieve what is right. This state of 'perplexity', as Manfred Max-Neef (1991, p 1) describes it, is the 'outcome of a situation for which we cannot recognise a precedent, which has kept us in a dead-end alley and barred the road to imaginative, novel and bold solutions'. The only route forward, Andre Gorz (1989, p 8) confirms, is to 'find a new Utopia, for as long as we are the prisoners of the Utopia collapsing around us, we will remain incapable of perceiving the potential for liberation.' As John Maynard Keynes similarly argued, there is no shortage of new ideas, just a problem in letting go of the old.

One way of letting go of the old and grasping the new is to 'look forward', to envisage what it might be like in the future. Many of us may have personal experience of this approach in working at grassroots level in community-led planning processes. Community 'visioning' is an established part of the toolbox of participatory research. Few of us, however, have tried the same techniques in planning our own futures, or the future of the organisations for which we work. Looking forward to the future, or imagining ourselves looking back from that future, may be a useful way of thinking about the issue of NGO accountability. What might the NGO community look like if it continues along its current path, or if we make certain assumptions as to what might occur over the coming years?

On the other hand, visioning can have its limitations. It can become detached from what is really going on, and therefore from what is likely or possible. These pitfalls can lead to the kinds of unrealistic visions that give those with Utopian leanings a bad name. It is equally important, therefore, to root vision in concrete processes, possibilities and practice. In particular, what practical examples are there of attempts to evolve and institutionalise new forms of accountability?

Both visioning and practical examples can offer insights into the issue of NGO accountability. However, these are complements not substitutes. Together, they root the analysis in practical possibilities, while seeking to evade the constraints of focusing purely on the past and present. The main part of this paper therefore explores both approaches simultaneously. The left-hand column sets out one possible future scenario in which to consider NGO accountability. This scenario extrapolates from the earlier analysis of the current situation, trying to find a middle path between Utopian and dystopian leanings. The right-hand column sets out one particular example of a practical approach to increasing accountability that is currently being tried out by a number of organisations with support from the New Economics Foundation, particularly the UK-based fair trading organisation, Traidcraft plc.

Looking back from 2010: forced shifts in accountability

Context

It all came to a head in the second half of the 1990s, although the roots of the crisis have a far earlier origin.

After a period of rapid growth, many of the larger NGOs found themselves in increasing difficulties. Money was seen to be at the heart of the problem, although, in the event, it proved to be just the tip of the iceberg. When they had it (money, that is) there seemed to be more and more strings attached. When they didn't have it, their enormous bureaucracies (and their many dependent sub-contractors) grew hungry, angry and frightened. A real addictive dependency had set in. More and more of the stuff was needed, even though it was clear that the more they had, the more the values and other strengths of the NGOs were compromised in its use.

The Northern transnational NGOs (TNGOs) had a further particular set of problems. Their Southern partners had by the early 1990s outgrown their subordinate status and were demanding a more than equal share of the cake to make up for lost time and their sense of grievance. The TNGOs found themselves limited to an ever-diminishing set of activities. Funding from governments and international agencies flowed directly to the growing cadre of Southern NGOs. The Southern NGOs took the international stage by storm, insisting on direct representation rather than relying on the earlier indirect routes to power through their Northern colleagues. Some Southern NGOs launched their own fund-raising organisations in Europe and North America.

Looking forward from now: a practical approach to accountability

Context

Traidcraft plc is a public limited company registered in England, with some 3,750 shareholders. Its main activity is the purchase and resale of products produced by small companies and community enterprises in Africa, Asia and Latin America. It currently trades with over 100 such organisations, covering a wide range of crafts, fashion and household goods, and foodstuffs. It has an annual turnover of about £6 million, of which about 60 per cent arises from sales of goods from the South. This allows payments of about £1.5 million in 1992–93 to its producer-suppliers in the South.

Although it is not an NGO, Traidcraft's objectives focus on benefits to people other than shareholders, particularly the small companies and community enterprises in the South from which they buy most of the products which they trade. Traidcraft is also rooted in the Christian faith, and therefore places its ethical aims in that context. Thus, Traidcraft's 'Foundation Principles' specify the overall objective of the company as being: to establish a just trading system which expresses the principles of love and justice fundamental to the Christian faith.

Traidcraft, like most NGOs and a few commercial organisations, makes its ethical aims explicit in all of its relationships. Thus, although it does not raise grants or sponsorship, it has raised investment capital and sells its products to consumers in the UK on the back of a commitment to trade

Most of all, however, the legitimacy of the TNGOs was challenged. At the liberal end of the spectrum, they were seen as overbloated bureaucracies, where well-meaning ethical and political initiatives increasingly became buried under a snowstorm of paper and a sweaty morass of circular consultation. At the more cynical end, they were seen as a self-serving élite, unwilling to submit themselves to the very forms of accountability that they advocated for others.

These issues did not come to a single head, although some have pointed to the renowned 1994 Manchester conference on NGO accountability as a key turning point. But it would be true to say that there was a wave of changes that started in the mid-1990s and took more or less a decade to work themselves (more or less) fully through.

The changes that took place occurred largely *despite* the efforts of many NGOs, particularly the transnationals. There were a few cases of medium-sized NGOs moving towards new forms of accountability. But these cases had no real ripple effect because of the obstinacy of the largest NGOs, the so-called 'Seven Brothers'. Unfortunately, this resistance meant that the first real changes came about through the emerging crisis, rather than through opportunities for change being grasped positively.

The crisis comprised a series of disclosures about malpractice, shoddy performance and outright cynicism in high profile TNGOs (quite unrepresentative disclosures, as many of those in the know have since argued). These disclosures led to a dramatic collapse of funding from state and public sources, and a withdrawal from a number of TNGOs of accreditation

'fairly' with producers in the South. Furthermore, its Foundation Principles commit the company to 'fair' and 'participative' relationships with staff, the network of representatives who sell products, and the shareholders.

By consciously placing itself in the trading sphere, Traidcraft seeks to demonstrate that such principles are compatible with sustainable economic activity. It is committed to working out, and being a working example of, a more just system of international trade between the North and the South. International trade is, however, a demanding discipline even for those who do not bring to it an overriding set of ethical principles. As Traidcraft has felt more keenly the pressures of trying to run an effective business, it seemed increasingly important to be able to measure social and ethical performance, as well as reporting on financial results. This was important for the company to see whether it was being effective in relation to its aims and to be able to make adjustments where necessary. It was also critical to be able to show those to whom commitments were being made – particularly producers, customers, staff and shareholders – whether Traidcraft's practice matched those commitments.

Traidcraft recognised that its continued success depended on being able to demonstrate that it was trading 'fairly' with these various groups. Without some proof, support would eventually fall away, and with it the sustainability of the company and the gains that it felt it was achieving. Furthermore, the proof that ethical trade was possible was necessary if Traidcraft was to provide a demonstration which might give courage and direction for other businesses.

rights to major national and international policy fora.

Seeking ways forward

The TNGOs were in a shambles, as a domino effect tore through their ranks. The Seven Brothers met in closed sessions but, by then unaccustomed to real collaboration, they failed to reach any agreement on how to meet this challenge together. Parallel to this process, all of the Brothers (as well as many of the smaller NGOs caught up in the crisis) were busy making bilateral deals in an attempt to survive (as well, to be fair, as wanting to maintain the very real quality of work that they had achieved).

The main, and certainly most publicised, outcome of this process was a series of mergers between key TNGOs and Southern NGOs. Five of the Seven Brothers chose this route as a way of rebuilding their damaged reputations. Others attempted, with varied success, to transform themselves internally in such a way as to regain credibility. Some, including the other two of the Seven Brothers, tried to ride it out.

This strategy failed, as they found themselves subjected to predatory 'asset stripping' of people, programmes and funding sources by other NGOs from the North and the South. Most of those with the 'ride it out' philosophy eventually had to change tack, with a number leaving it too late and having to close their doors for good.

These mergers and internal transformations were in most cases sufficient to move the new organisations on to a new plateau of stability. However, in some cases the basis for change took on more confrontational

Seeking ways forward

In the early 1990s, Traidcraft explored possible routes for assessing social impact and ethical behaviour, and for communicating this information. The extensive experience of many organisations in the evaluation of development work gave a rich source of principles and methods. The whole 'participative' paradigm, in particular, seemed to resonate with Traidcraft's own organisational culture and aims.

However, these approaches remained inadequate for Traidcraft's needs in a number of respects. In particular:

- Traidcraft wanted to take account of all its relationships as far as was practical.
- Traidcraft wanted this to be a regular, institutionalised activity.
- Traidcraft wanted both the process and the outcome to be public.
- Traidcraft wanted the process and the outcome to have the same weight (as far as possible) as the statutory financial audit.
- Traidcraft wanted the process to be usable by other trading organisations, particularly commercial companies.

Thus, while Traidcraft did not want to reinvent existing wheels, it felt that it needed to mould together elements of existing approaches to form a model that would fulfil the above criteria. To achieve this, Traidcraft approached the London-based research and lobbying NGO, the New Economics Foundation (NEF), to assist in the development and trialing of the method, and also the dissemination of the lessons learned to a wider audience. Furthermore, a steering group was formed to provide critical inputs forms. The experiences in the mid-1990s of mass demonstrations against GATT in India, and the uprising in Chiapas following the signing of NAFTA, provided a model for one form of resistance to what was seen as the high-handed approach taken by TNGOs. The embarrassment caused by these demonstrations, as well as the small-scale but well-publicised loss of lives of TNGO officials and demonstrators (particularly in that one awful case where the officials at one office turned out to be armed and fired on a peaceful demonstration in a fit of fear), pushed those transnationals which were proving to be slow on their feet towards change more quickly.

Another factor in this transformation was the law. A number of legal cases against the TNGOs were launched by community organisations through the international courts. Most focused on the argument that TNGOs had expropriated personal and community-based information in order to raise money. Others took the approach of arguing that 'false promises' had been made. Legal history was made in a number of cases where peasant and urban communities made effective use of legislation that was intended originally to protect famous people and profitable trademarks. Many of these cases were settled out of court. However, the writing was on the wall for all to see, and legal precedents played a key role in the TNGOs' decisions to shift the onus of ownership – and, of course, legal liability – elsewhere.

Accountability and ownership

The issue of accountability therefore became inextricably linked with the issue of ownership. It became widely in the development of the method, which included people from business schools, campaigning and research organisations, and representatives from some of Traidcraft's stakeholders.

The outcome of this process was the Traidcraft Social Audit. Traidcraft is now in its third year of auditing; other commercial companies are trialing it or evolving their own method; other versions relevant to community enterprises are being developed and trialed in the UK, Tanzania and South Africa; and interest has been shown by NGOs and international agencies for organisation and project-level assessments (Zadek and Evans 1993; Zadek 1994).

Social auditing

Social audit offers a method of accountability that involves all stakeholders and is neither prescriptive nor bureaucratic. Buzz words that are in vogue at the moment, such as 'transparency' and 'good governance', are easy to use but difficult to implement. How can NGOs or community businesses ensure transparency and measure themselves against something other than static objectives which, though out-of-date within six months of being introduced, become the yardstick of any future evaluation?

For any organisation to have ownership of its outputs, the indicators by which it is measured must be relevant to everyone involved, not just to the key players such as directors and senior management. Read any up-to-date management text-book and the philosophy of taking decision-making to the lowest point will be preached. The same applies to the measurement of success or failure: the accepted that the traditional model of NGO ownership – which was, basically, no formal ownership at all, leaving effective ownership in the hands of unelected officials – was inadequate. In 1996, drawing partly from a government-sponsored in-depth analysis of the voluntary sector in the UK, a Private Members Bill passed through the English parliament, marking the end of charitable status for all but a few (rather archaic) cases. This was soon followed by European legislation to the same effect. By the turn of the century, the whole notion of 'non-governmental' as a form of (non)-ownership was effectively over.

Forms of TNGO accountability

It would be great to be able to say that a 'new' form of ownership arose phoenix-like from the ashes to support appropriate forms of accountability for NGO-like organisations. This did not happen, although there was a period of intense and often very creative innovation in new forms of accountability and ownership. Rather, a range of existing models of accountability were taken up by different NGO-like organisations.

(1) Institutional-federal model

Probably the most common form adopted was what became known as the 'institutional–federal' model. This approach tended to be quite similar to the model being adopted by the European Union at the time. Each part of the newly-merged organisations (often including parts of the old ones, following the 'Europe of the Regions' philosophy) had a vote according to various possible measures of size. The more con-

indicators must be set at the lowest point of the organisation. By developing a methodology for social as well as financial auditing, an organisation is able to set its own indicators and respond to changes within its social structure. All stakeholders have a say in developing indicators as the methodology evolves, as well as in applying the indicators. Managers have regular access to information regarding social as well as financial developments which enables them to respond in a timely manner, rather than when it is too late to do anything.

Key stages of the social audit process

Traidcraft's social audit was constructed on the basis of a carefully designed process of consultation across stakeholder groups. The key stages of this process are summarised below.

(1) Identify stakeholders   The
first stage of the Traidcraft social audit was to identify key 'stakeholder' groups. These groups included over 100 producer-suppliers, its many thousands of customers, its 100-plus staff and 2,000 voluntary representatives, and, of course, its 3,000 shareholders.

(2) Identification of stakeholder aims and indicators   The second
stage was to initiate a process of consultation with each stakeholder group that allowed them to establish criteria against which they felt Traidcraft's social impact and ethical behaviour should be judged, and then to assess the organisation's activities on this basis. Thus, the social accounts of Traidcraft reflected the aims and concerns of its key stakeholders, as

servative organisations tended to opt for measures based on financial contributions, whereas the more radical organisations went for some measure of how many people each part represented. This federal structure was different from the decentralised model employed by some TNGOs in the 1990s, in that the heads of the parts (many of which were in the South) made up the Board of Directors.

(2) Block-vote model Some NGOs went for a variation of the block-voting formulas adopted by UK trade unions and other movements in an earlier era. World Plan (International), for example, created a voting structure that gave funder stakeholders an aggregate block vote of 25 per cent, community organisations (the intended beneficiaries) about 55 per cent, and staff the remaining 20 per cent. While this should have given the community organisations effective control, the staff and funders managed from the outset to operate a divide-and-rule approach which gave them effective power. When this no longer functioned, the staff themselves organised a workers' buy-out (with support from the funders), leaving WPI in its current well-known form as the only TNGO workers co-operative. WPI now provide a range of services, in practice doing a lot of cheap subcontract work for other NGOs.

(3) One-person-one-vote model Of the large TNGOs, TransFam adopted the most radical approach of all, a one-person-one-vote system across their 1 million members. This was not, sad to say, because they were the most radical organisation prior to the period of change. It was Trans-Fam, some may recall, that became

well as its own stated social and ethical aims.

This stage required consultative approaches tailored to the characteristics of each stakeholder group. Extensive face-to-face discussions were held with representatives of the shareholders and voluntary representatives. Following this, postal questionnaires were used to contact and solicit the views of the entirety of these two groups. Two rounds of discussions were held with staff, one to establish how they wished to carry out the assessment, and then, on the basis of their stated preferences, a set of group workshops. In addition, basic data on staff conditions, including wages and equal opportunities, were collected and analysed. Finally, a sample of producers was selected for in-depth consultation, which in this accounting cycle involved spending several weeks with Traidcraft's Filipino producer-suppliers.

(3) Production of draft social accounts The third stage was the production of draft social accounts. These were produced jointly by Traidcraft and the NEF, discussed with the Traidcraft board, and again circulated to some stakeholders for comments. In producing these accounts, there was a real difficulty in compressing the enormous amount of information generated into a small number of readable pages. This information included not only statistics, but a vast body of qualitative data, often in the form of narratives about particular events or perspectives on Traidcraft. In selecting information and the format of presentation, it was necessary to get a balance between 'hard' ('objective') data, such as income to producers,

the focal point of mass demonstrations in the late Nineties, and that had to cope with the largest number of litigations. Eventually, faced with imminent bankruptcy, TransFam signed the famous Delhi Accord in 1999. The 3000-plus closely typed pages of the Accord boiled down to a relatively simple deal whereby Trans-Fam would become owned by all those people who had directly received financial assistance through them over a specific period.

In return, the various litigations were dropped, and the relatively widespread intimidation of TransFam's officials ceased. It was really quite a depressing affair at the time, seen as a low-point in the collapse of the TNGO dinosaurs. It is somewhat ironic, therefore, that the TransFam model is now seen as the most radical to emerge from that period.

Many of the new forms of accountability and associated ownership described above arose from the survival instincts of the large TNGOs when faced with extinction. These changes were applauded by the more visionary people within these organisations. However, it would be inaccurate to suggest that this minority played a major role in catalysing the changes.

The 'NICs': accountability and organisation

There were, however, a set of organisations that voluntarily embraced radical transformations in accountability and ownership over that period, the so-called 'New Internationalist Conglomerates' (NICs). These were a motley group of organisations that acquired the name 'NICs' along the way. Some of them

and qualitative information which revealed the complex fabric of social and ethical issues relevant to constituents and Traidcraft.

(4) Auditing the accounts The penultimate stage in the social accounting process was to audit the accounts. It was the NEF's role to 'sign off' the accounts, with whatever qualifications were deemed necessary. At the same time, the NEF's involvement in both the development of the methodology and the draft social accounts meant that there was a danger of a conflict of interest, or simply the loss of objectivity. For this reason, the NEF invited a group of people with some expertise to represent the various stakeholder concerns and interests on an audit group, to discuss and comment on the accounts, and to advise the NEF on the appropriate position to take.

(5) Publication of the accounts The final step was to sign off and publish the accounts. Publication of the social and financial audit occurred concurrently, highlighting the importance of the former. All stakeholders received a copy of the audit, as well as copies being available as a matter of public record for experts, traders, producers and the media. Traidcraft are currently undertaking the 1994–95 audit, which will be published and can be compared with the previous year's results, and are committed in future to undertaking a social audit annually.

Accountability and effectiveness

Accountability does not equate to effectiveness and therefore is not sufficient in itself. Social auditing is not, therefore, just about accountability.

were originally Northern NGOs which did operate on the international scene, but were rooted within their own communities and countries. This in itself gave them a different sense of accountability from the outset. Most of the NICs tended also to be relatively smaller and younger. This meant that there was less institutional inertia to constrain change due to bureaucratisation and internal vested interests.

Also interesting was the fact that many of these NGOs were of the information age. Their main functions concerned the movement of information rather than the raising and disbursement of money. They were involved in development education, research, lobbying and campaigning, rather than funding projects that had physical manifestations. This gave them an altogether different organisational form, one that did not need to have the same patterns of hierarchical authority.

Their relationships with each other and the communities they related to tended to far more open-ended, involving less dependence, fewer reporting structures, and in general a far higher level of voluntarism. All of these features supported the transformation process.

There was a further sub-grouping within the NICs known as the New International Traders (affectionately abbreviated to the 'NITs'). The main feature of these organisations was that they traded actively in goods and services.

The background to the changes that took place in this latter grouping was equally, if not more, complex than for the TNGOs, and again varied a lot between the organisations. However, I will give just one example, that of the

By undertaking social audits on an annual basis, an organisation's objectives cease to be static and become more responsive. The project evaluation cycle encourages measurement by someone else on behalf of a third party. Furthermore, it usually identifies problems out of context, in relation to out-dated aims, and in any case much too late. A social audit, on the other hand, is undertaken by an organisation for its own benefit; the results are therefore owned by that organisation and are taken on board as part of the strategic planning process.

Social auditing therefore offers a form of accountability that is integral to on going planning. It recognises the intimate relationship between allowing the voices of stakeholders to be heard and taken into account, and the effectiveness of decisions made and actions taken.

Conclusions and lessons

Can social auditing really make an organisation more accountable? After all, it does 'little more' than make information available about what has happened in relation to those who are most affected by the organisation's activities. The case of Traidcraft suggests that social auditing *can* 'make a difference'. To date, the social audits of Traidcraft have thrown up a range of issues about the way the company goes about its activities, and the ways in which different stakeholder groups are affected as a result. Generating this information, recognising the views of stakeholders and publicising the audit so widely, have undoubtedly led to Traidcraft refining and questioning the validity of key aspects of its approach, as well as developing ear, nose and throat products organisation, Facing the World. Facing the World had grown to be an enormous, worldwide, franchise-based retail chain by the mid-1990s. Its reputation was based on good products and 'fair trading' relationships with its suppliers. Facing some criticism for its secrecy, the organisation agreed to undertake a social audit, a technique that was at that time at an experimental stage. But it was too late for such a conciliatory gesture. 'Open season' was declared on Facing the World. Sales collapsed (a bit like with the water giant, Perrier, in the early 1980s), and the organisation faced extinction.

It was at this stage that a deal was cooked up aimed at re-establishing a sound financial basis and of rebuilding its public image. The organisation issued shares to all of its franchises and its suppliers. The franchises had to pay according to their likely losses if the organisation collapsed (and their likely profits if it did not).

The suppliers, on the other hand, received free shares based on the level of the trading relationship. The existing shareholders retained a small proportion of the shares – about 10 per cent. Given the extraordinary success of the renamed Facing our World, which is a well-known story to you all, I am sure, this small shareholding proved to be far more profitable than the original holding.

Conclusions and lessons

The history of the last 20 years has been remarkable. Looking back, it seems quite obvious that the changes should have been expected. However, all the historical documents reviewed, and the extensive interview pro-

new tools and processes for securing the interests of key stakeholders still further.

This success has depended, of course, largely on the receptivity of those who run Traidcraft, particularly the managers and the board. Traidcraft started on the route towards a social audit because these groups decided that they really did want to be accountable to stakeholders. Other organisations thinking about social audits need to ask the same question: 'Do we really want accountability to all stakeholders and, if so, which ones?'

The social audit carries no statutory or indeed mandatory weight, unlike the financial audit and, gradually, elements of the environmental audit. One day this may change, but not yet. At the same time, the publication of the social audit can create considerable pressure on the organisation concerned to take note of its contents. This is particularly the case for organisations whose continued existence depends in part on the belief by its individual and institutional supporters – including staff and volunteers – that it is ethical according to some set of explicit principles. However, even the more cold-hearted commercial organisations cannot always ignore clear evidence of moral malpractice, even where it is entirely legal.

Social auditing is an approach, not a solution. It allows organisations to move towards new forms of accountability without major shifts in ownership and organisational structure. It allows for an evolutionary process of taking stakeholder interests more directly into account, and having to report on activities according to their interests. Finally, through the information thrown up by social auditing, gramme underpinning this historical overview, confirm that it was all pretty unexpected. Even those most committed to change had got stuck in a visionless vision, one that was able to see what was wrong, but just could not unravel what to do. Everyone seemed to be looking for the 'big story' and missed the massive events that were unravelling on their own doorstep. That is, until these events stood up and slapped them in the face.

This story is a lesson for us all. We may be pleased at the changes that have taken place; the new forms of TNGOs, the NICs and the NITs. But history challenges us all not to repeat the incredibly myopic behaviour of the late 20th century. After all, it might have turned out very differently, and may still do so in the future.

and its open publication, it can be effective in reorienting the organisation's activities toward stakeholder interests.

19

The Primacy of the Personal[1]

Robert Chambers

Experience with Participatory Rural Appraisal (PRA) suggests that a reversal of the normally dominant behaviour and the attitudes of outsiders is crucial for participatory development. Personal behaviour and attitudes, though, have been neglected in seeing how to do better. The development enterprise is oriented 'North–South' by patterns of dominance between 'uppers' and 'lowers', and by funding, pressures to disburse and upward accountability. These patterns increasingly affect NGOs, which may then become more like government organisations in scale, staffing, hierarchical culture, procedures and self-deception.

Policies, procedures and organisational cultures are determined by individuals, especially those in positions of power. To stem and reverse trends of dominance and deception requires personal change and action by them: to shift emphasis from upward to downward accountability; to resist pressures to disburse; to stress trust and to reward truthfulness and honesty; and, above all, to enjoy giving up the normal exercise of power, enabling lowers to do more and take more responsibility. Participatory field experiences and training can help these personal changes. These in turn require a new professionalism of training, and for some NGOs a redefinition of roles. The question then is to what extent such changes would resolve the problems of performance and accountability which currently and correctly concern so many NGOs.

'Discovering' behaviour and attitudes

In the early stages of the coalescing of approaches and methods which led to Participatory Rural Appraisal (PRA) and its relatives, it was participatory methods that seemed the key: participatory mapping and modelling; matrix ranking and scoring; seasonal calendars; trend and change analysis; causal, linkage and flow diagramming; wealth and well-being ranking; time-use analysis; the identification and ranking of best bets; and so on. The failure for so long to recognise the capabilities of local people to conduct their own analysis, especially but not only visually, tended to be attributed to the fact that methods such as these and their combinations in sequences, had previously been underdeveloped and little used by local people. In the early 1990s, though, field experience showed that the beliefs, behaviour and attitudes of outsiders explained more of this earlier failure than did the lack of methods.

The belief that such methods could only be used by outsiders was self-validating. When dominant outsiders did not believe that local people could map and diagram, they lacked the encouragement and occasion to find out for themselves that they could. When the incapacity presented by local people – 'we do not know how to make a map' – fitted the preconceptions of outsiders, it was not challenged but reinforced by acceptance; yet I know of no case where local people, despite initial disclaimers, have been unable to map. The confidence that 'they can do it', that local people could map, diagram, list, estimate, compare, rank, score, prioritise, plan, act, monitor, evaluate and themselves facilitate and train others, proved to be an enabling precondition for outsiders to facilitate activities of which local people themselves often did not know they were capable.

Outsiders' normal behaviour also confirmed the incapacity of local people. Worldwide, when interacting with local people, outsiders tended to lecture, interrupt, criticise, suggest and dominate both verbally and non-verbally. A key learning was a PRA training in Karnataka in 1990 where a participatory planning session was monitored. This found that the villagers spoke for only 11 out of 45 minutes and were interrupted 45 times. The most difficult lesson for outsiders in PRA training was then understood to be learning to shut up: not to dominate, not to interview and not to interrupt while local people were doing their own analysis. More and more, PRA field-training exercises have come to stress outsiders' behaviour and attitudes more than methods.

Necessary behaviour and attitudes include outsiders sitting down, listening and learning; relaxing and not rushing; 'handing over the stick' (or pen or chalk); embracing error and failing forwards; being transparently clear about who they are, their purposes, and what can and cannot be expected; and 'being nice to people' (see for example, Mascarenhas et al 1991; Chambers 1994). Rigid rules are replaced by 'using one's own best judgement at all times'. Most recently, in late 1994, experience in Sri Lanka has added the principle of 'ask them': asking local people not just what they know and how they would like to show it, but also how they advise outsiders to behave and to become better facilitators.

Normal North–South dominance

These insights extend naturally into examining wider patterns of dominance and submission, seeing one dimension of social relations as being between uppers and lowers (Table 19.1) and then, by analogy with a magnetic field, as oriented North to South (Figure 19.1).[2] The stronger the top magnets, the stronger the North–South orientation of the low magnets. Any person can be an upper in some contexts and a lower in others; and some are multiple uppers (male, old, senior, white, wealthy...) and others multiple lowers (female, young, junior, black, poor...). Complete revolutionary reversals, as in Robespierre's France, Lenin's Russia, Mao's China and Mengistu's Ethiopia, are 'slot-rattling', retaining the patterns of dominance, but putting different people in power.

Table 19.1 *North–South upper-lower relationships*

Dimension/context	North Uppers	South Lowers
Spatial	Core (urban, industrial)	Periphery (rural, agricultural)
International and development	*The North* The IMF World Bank Donors Creditors	*The South* Poor countries Recipients Debtors
Personal ascriptive	Male White High ethnic or caste group	Female Black Low ethnic or caste group
Life-cycle	Old person Parent Mother-in-law	Young person Child Daughter-in-law
Bureaucratic, organisational	*Senior* Manager Official Patron Officer Warden, guard	*Junior* Worker Supplicant Client 'Other rank' Inmate, prisoner
Social, spiritual	Patron Priest Guru Doctor, psychiatrist	Client Lay person Disciple Patient
Teaching and learning	Master Lecturer Teacher	Apprentice Student Pupil

Democratic empowerment entails reversals which neutralise forces of dominance and liberate, allowing freedom for relationships in all directions ('free to spin' in Figure 19.1). For this to happen requires changes in the behaviour and attitudes of uppers in how they relate to lowers, and how they encourage lowers to be and to behave.

Contemporary change in NGOs

Participatory rhetoric notwithstanding, the whole enterprise of development can be seen to be oriented by this metaphorical North–South magnetism of dominance, with uppers and lowers. In the internal hierarchies and external relations of funding agencies such as the World Bank, multilaterals, bilaterals and Northern NGOs (NNGOs) which provide funds, and in the organisations of the South which receive them, the relationships are repeated and reinforced downwards. Four dimensions stand out.

First, pressures to disburse drive donor staff to dominate. The cultures of large multilaterals like the World Bank, the European Union and the Asian Development Bank encourage and reward the commitment and disbursement of large sums of money. In donor-speak, the 'absorptive capacity' of recipients

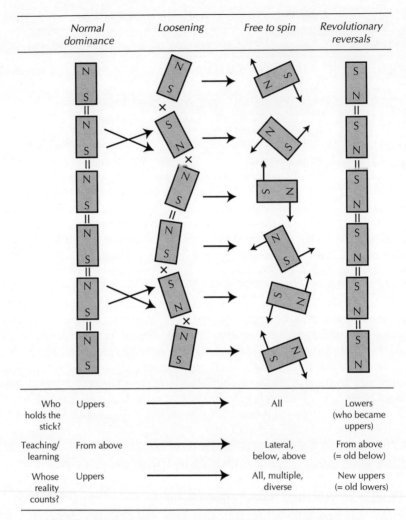

	Normal dominance	Loosening	Free to spin	Revolutionary reversals
Who holds the stick?	Uppers	⟶	All	Lowers (who became uppers)
Teaching/ learning	From above	⟶	Lateral, below, above	From above (= old below)
Whose reality counts?	Uppers	⟶	All, multiple, diverse	New uppers (= old lowers)

Figure 19.1   *Dominance, reversals and freedom, North–South*

is a constraint which hinders and delays expenditures. In Sri Lanka in 1994, the directors of three IFAD projects were said to be subject to meetings every quarter at which their expenditure record was reviewed. Nor are bilaterals and NNGOs always free from these pressures. When NNGOs raise large sums, they feel embarrassed to hold surpluses in the bank, fearing criticism from their supporters for the slow use of their contributions. So often with large donors, and sometimes with small, Northern staff on mission are impatient and insistent. The incentives are to spend, and for uppers to pressurise lowers to spend more and faster.

Second, rushing reinforces dominance. Participation takes time, but time is always short. For convenience, field visits are brief. Projects are appraised and prepared in a hurry. The more the rush, the less the consultation, and the greater the imposition of the reality of the uppers – donor agency and senior staff on that of the lowers – field staff and local people.

Third, demands for accountability upwards are believed to require systematic planning. Rightly or wrongly, those who receive funds are not trusted to plan well. So donors demand the use of Logical Framework Analysis, and its sub-species GOPP (GTZ 1988), ZOPP and the like. Whatever the participatory rhetoric, it is rare indeed for poor local people to be involved in these processes.[3] But, as endlessly documented, what outsiders think people will want or will be good for them is often not what they want and need.[4] To take a recent example, when an IFAD project in the North Central zone of Sri Lanka used PRA approaches after it had been planned, it emerged that people wanted cattle, not the goats prescribed by a consultant economist. Preceded by top-down planning, however logical, participation becomes submissive: 'they' participate in 'our' project. Even when monitoring and evaluation are demanded to assure that the money has been well spent and impacts have been good, the criteria and methods used are determined from above. Logic forces the local to fit its imperious frame.

Fourth, power deceives. The patronage of funds, pressures to disburse, rushing, Logical Framework Analysis and accountability upwards, all strengthen North–South hierarchies. They also give rise to top-down standardisation and packages, with misfits between central programmes and local needs. Prudent staff then provide misleadingly positive feedback.[5] The more the need or desire for funds, the greater the dangers of deception. NGOs with savings and lending programmes for the poor report ever better repayment rates, competing with others in reporting figures which constantly improve. The deceiving and self-deceiving state has long existed; it is now being joined by the deceiving and self-deceiving NGO.

As bilateral and multilateral donors divert more of their funds to NGOs, and as higher proportions of NGO funding come from these official sources,[6] so NGOs become more prone to these influences. It is commonplace that a top-down disbursement drive impedes and negates participation. The cultures and procedures of organisations are affected. As NGOs become bigger and undertake more of the service functions previously performed by governments, so they become more like hierarchical government organisations. This threatens the loss of some of the real and supposedly comparative advantages of NGOs. These include sensitivity to local conditions, commitment to the poor, honest reporting, ability to vary actions according to needs, and staff with the will to serve and to work hard and long hours.

The primacy of the personal

Many prescriptions for development mean that people in power – uppers – should do something different. It is embarrassing to make such an obvious point. Yet we are so trapped in the search for universals which fit normal concepts and criteria and which are part of our professional tools of trade, that we can easily not notice or discuss what stares us most in the face. This is the fact that individual personal choice of what to do and how to do it mediates every action and every change. Policy, practice and performance are all outcomes of personal actions. What is done and not done depends on what people chose to do and not to do, and especially on the choices and actions of those with more power.

If, for example, all managers and staff in all multilateral and bilateral agencies, NGOs and GROs abandoned their North–South orientation tomorrow, adopted a participatory philosophy and behaviour, and supported each other in these changes, the world of development would be transformed. The drive to disburse, the rushed visits, top-down logical planning, upward accountability, and many deceptions would diminish or disappear. Each level would empower and trust the levels below to exercise discretion, to foster diversity and to learn from mistakes.

Or if, to take another example, all development professionals were tomorrow to become aware, committed, honest and courageous in serving and empowering the poor, and enabling others to do the same, most field programmes would be transformed.

Homeostasis

What stops changes like these are 'the system' and the self. The system includes organisational cultures, inertia, procedures, precedents, punitive management, criteria for promotions, confidential reports and corruption. The self is ego, ambition, family-first motivation and the illusion of impotence. The individual appears powerless. One person cannot change, it is said, unless others change, unless the whole system changes.

This is a convenient but false position. In reality, every person always has *some* room for manoeuvre; and for every upper there is scope to make space for lowers. Alliances can be formed upwards, downwards and laterally with others who are like-minded both inside and outside an organisation. By expanding and exploiting spaces, by seeking and supporting allies, many brave people have had the vision and the courage to make changes and to help others to change.

The mystery is that such obvious points need to be made at all. Personal beliefs, behaviour and attitudes are an odd blind spot in development. Training (now graced with the ungainly economists' label of 'human resource development') is given prominence, but it is designed more to teach, to impart knowledge and skills, than to provide opportunities for experiential learning. Training or HRD is usually didactic, in a top-down transfer of technology mode. The trainer is an upper who is presumed to know; and those taught or trained are lowers who are presumed not to know. The teacher or trainer transfers to the trainees not only knowledge and skills, but also the upper-lower orientation. So trainees leave their courses to become uppers in turn. Armed and authorised by their certificates, they then transfer knowledge and technology to new lowers. Training thus reproduces and reinforces the North–South field.

Where, in contrast, training is itself participatory, a process of helping people to learn through experience and to find things out for themselves, enabling personal change towards egalitarian, democratic relationships, the North–

South field can be expected to weaken. Options for more trust, freedom and choice in relationships and actions will open up, allowing and encouraging more local and individual diversity.

Reasons for neglect

The neglect of the personal may be partly explained as follows:

- *Academic values.* Any discussion of personal change risks the charge of evangelism. Academics affect to abhor moralising. They tend to reward appearances of dispassionate scientific detachment, rigour and objectivity.
- *Fear of over-hypocrisy.* Almost all development professionals (and certainly myself) are hypocrites and at some level many know it. But we do not like to parade our hypocrisy too publicly by saying what ought to be done at the personal level, because we know we will not do it ourselves.
- *Missing disciplines.* Psychology is a missing discipline in development. Psychologists are rare among development professionals, and where they are found working in development, it is often not as psychologists or trainers but in some other capacity.
- *Low calibre and commitment of training staff.* Many staff are posted to training institutes as punishments or in the hope that in training, their incompetence or indolence will do less harm.[7] In consequence rather few trainers are interested, willing or able to innovate by conducting training for personal change or to work outside office hours.
- *The challenge of participatory training.* Participatory training is not easy. Helping people to learn for themselves rather than teaching them in a North–South manner often requires personal reorientation by the trainer, plus risk-taking, effort, long hours, at times discomfort, and tolerating uncertainty. The dominant mode of teaching and training, in contrast, is the lecture or discussion, where the instructor maintains control and implements a closed-ended blueprint instead of facilitating an open-ended process, allowing him (most are men) to go home at 5pm, if not earlier.

Even after these explanations, a residual mystery remains: why are personal change and training concerned with behaviour and attitudes such Cinderellas of development, when they are such potent and universal variables amenable to change?

An agenda for personal action

If policy, practice and performance depend on personal action, and personal action depends on personal experience, learning and commitment, an agenda for action can be sought. Many actions imply reversals of the conditions normally found. Here is a list:

- *Accountability:* shifting emphasis from upward to downward accountability for performance.
- *Behaviour:* respecting, listening to, learning from, 'handing over the stick

to', and empowering, one's lowers, and encouraging and enabling them to do the same.

■ *Management:* instituting and supporting democratic and participatory management.

■ *Disbursements:* refraining from and resisting pressures to disburse big sums fast, and changing procedures, values, indicators and rewards to stress quality, participation and sustainability.

■ *Trust, error and truth:* trusting lowers to exercise responsible judgement, encouraging them to fail forwards, acknowledging and reporting error, and valuing unpalatable truths as opportunities to learn and do better.

■ *Diverse experience:* deciding where best to work and seeking a mix of locations, posts, responsibilities and experiences (South and North, lower and upper, periphery and centre) in the interests of learning, improving judgement and seeing what best to do.

■ *Experiential learning:* seeking opportunities for experiential learning for oneself and for one's lowers.

■ *Reversals of power:* learning (as an upper) to enjoy giving up power and (as a lower) to enjoy accepting and exercising responsibility.

An agenda for experiential learning

The thrust of this argument is that personal learning and development should be high on the agenda for all development professionals, with scope for evolution and change in beliefs, behaviour and attitudes. Much of this concerns helping uppers to learn how to learn from lowers, and helping lowers to learn from and with each other. These have been amazingly neglected. Most university staff still lecture and know little about participatory learning. Since the time when they took up their posts, most donor agency staff have never spent unconstrained, unrushed, unofficial time exposed to and learning about field realities, if indeed they have ever done so. Many NGO staff believe that they can speak for the poor, but rather few have facilitated participatory analysis by poor people, or if they have, have tended to dominate without realising the misleading effects of their dominance.

The power and the potential of the family of approaches and methods now known as PRA must not be exaggerated. PRA, like any other participatory approach, can be done badly, and is being done badly on a growing scale. But where PRA has been done well, it has often brought personal change for those who facilitate it. Those who have managed to alter their normally dominant behaviour, to hand over the stick, to facilitate, to take time, to sit down and listen, and not to dominate, have found, quite simply, new pleasures, satisfactions, insights and interests – in short, that they enjoy and learn from the experience, and that things change for them.

Several elements have proved powerful: living and sleeping in villages; taking the role of novice in being taught and performing village tasks; video feedback of personal behaviour; facilitating and observing group visual synergy which shows how well 'they can do it' (Figure 19.2); sharing food; and personal and group reflection.

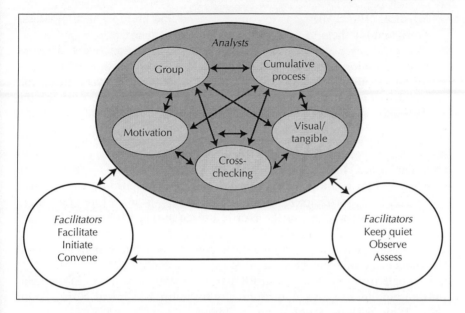

Figure 19.2   *Group-visual synergy in Participatory Rural Appraisal*

All this suggests a four-point agenda for experiential learning and change:

1. *New policy and practice in agencies.* This means rethinking and reorganisation by uppers in NGOs, governments and donor agencies to provide
   field learning experiences for themselves and their lowers, and setting aside
   time authoritatively for these activities. This is not a new idea. It has already
   been pioneered by the German organisation Justitia et Pax (Kochendörfer-
   Lucius and Osner 1989; Osner et al 1992).
2. *Multiplying, supporting and releasing good trainer/facilitators.* More good
   participatory trainer/facilitators are needed. The PRA experience is that
   this is a specialised activity requiring a rather special personal orientation
   and stamina. Most of the PRA training expertise is in the South. There is a
   danger in North and South alike of trainers setting up who are not right for
   the job. Some good PRA trainers in the South have been and are being
   enabled within their organisations to devote more time to participatory
   training. Others, sometimes frustrated by line responsibilities, have left to
   become full-time independent trainers or to found their own NGOs. Given
   current demand and need, the case is strong for supporting and releasing
   good trainer/facilitators wherever they are. For all concerned, the question
   of quality of training and learning remains.[8]
3. *Organisations for learning experience (OLEs).* New organisations are needed, or changes in existing organisations, to provide interactive learning
   environments and experiences (Pretty and Chambers 1993). In other fields,
   such as humanistic and gestalt psychotherapy, such organisations exist. The
   difference in development is that the interactive learning environment is at
   best the village or slum, which poses problems which are both ethical and

logistical. The challenge is to found, expand and multiply such organisations, and for them to gain and share more experience.

4. *New approaches and methods.* Scaling-up requires the discovery, development, adoption, sharing and spread of effective approaches and methods for behaviour and attitude change. Many are known in diverse fields and could be brought together. More could and should be invented for the development context.

These four directions, actions and sets of questions imply a new professionalism, with reversals of the normal top-down, centre-outwards, and upper to lower tendencies. Instead, the balance of the new directions is bottom-up, periphery to centre, and lower to upper. These reversals also turn the normal North–South donor-recipient relationship on its head. More and more development professionals in the North are requesting PRA experience and training for themselves in the South. Demand exceeds supply. The South already has a donor role in enabling those from the North to gain more general development experience. This could be extended and deepened by providing more people from the North with PRA-type learning experiences in the field, contributing more balance and reciprocity to South–North and North–South relationships, with the South being the donor.

The final questions refer back to the challenges faced by NGOs. Does the personal provide a point of entry? This is as obvious a question as it is relatively neglected. If those working in NGOs pursued an agenda of personal and institutional change, with alliances and mutual support by uppers and lowers alike, would the practical and ethical problems of management be reduced? If primacy were accorded to the personal, would the problems of performance and accountability largely be resolved?

Notes

1. I am grateful to Jenny Chambers for discussions and insights which have contributed to this paper, and to Charity Kabutha and Mallika Samaranayake for comments on a draft. Responsibility for opinions and errors is mine.
2. Table 19.1 and Figures 19.1 and 19.2 are from an earlier paper entitled 'Paradigm Shifts and the Practice of Participatory Research and Development', *IDS Working Paper*, no 2, April 1994. To any reader with *déjà vu*, I can only apologise. I am using them again because they fit the theme and illustrate the points in a different context.
3. No doubt there are other cases, but I know of only one where local people have been involved. This is in Urapulayagama village, Kurunegala District, Sri Lanka, where, as part of a programme of the National Development Foundation, supported by the Self-Help Support Programme of Interco-operation, the village displayed a logical framework chart and monitored implementation against a bar chart for activities. The normal practice outlined in the GTZ manual (GTZ 1988) is not only pathologically reductionist (forcing analysts to identify just one core problem, one overall goal and one project purpose) but also top down: the five ZOPP exercises (ibid, p 27) do not involve those who are described as 'the target group'.
4. See, for example, Leach and Mearns (1988), Starkey (1988), Bernadas (1991), Porter et al (1991), SPWD (1992).

5. For evidence and elaboration see three papers 'Bureaucratic Reversals and Local Diversity', *IDS Bulletin*, vol 19, no 4, pp 50–56; 'The Self-Deceiving State', *IDS Bulletin*, vol 23, no 4, pp 31–42; and 'All Power Deceives', *IDS Bulletin*, vol 25, no 2, pp 14–25.
6. NNGOs committed to long-term programmes but with volatile income from the public are continuously tempted into heavier reliance on official funding.
7. There are outstanding exceptions, of which at least half-a-dozen could be named in India alone; but I believe this to be sadly true for most training institutes.
8. See 'Participatory Methods and Approaches: Sharing Our Concerns and Looking to the Future' (IDS/IIED 1994), a statement by some 20 practitioner/trainers of suggested principles and precepts, available free on request from PRA, IDS, University of Sussex, Brighton BN1 9RE, UK.

20

Beyond the Magic Bullet? Lessons and Conclusions

Michael Edwards and David Hulme

A huge amount of information and experience from a wide range of contexts has been reviewed by the different contributors to this book. Clearly, any attempt to identify common conclusions and implications runs the risk of over-generalisation, particularly given the difficulty of disentangling the effects of official aid and the New Policy Agenda from pre-existing or other related influences. It is clear from the pictures painted by the contributors that NGO and GRO performance, accountability and legitimacy are tremendously complex areas. The situation of Sudanese migrant associations described by Pratten and Ali Baldo in their chapter provides a particularly good example of these complexities, with all sorts of 'checks and balances' between GROs and their members mediated by history and culture, and dependent on 'contemporary reconstructions of community identity'. Nevertheless, there are some clear and common threads which run through previous chapters which do seem to indicate that similar influences are at work. At least five sets of conclusions present themselves.

1. The influence of the New Policy Agenda – real or imagined?

There is certainly evidence from the case studies in this book that official aid to NGOs and the roles adopted by NGOs under the New Policy Agenda can distort accountability upwards and overemphasise linear approaches to performance-measurement, with damaging effects on the ability of NGOs to be effective catalysts for social change. Desai and Howes' account of Apnalaya in Bombay, and the chapters by Gariyo (on NGOs in East Africa) and Hashemi (on NGOs in Bangladesh) provide some such evidence, but in each case the influence of official aid and external agendas is only one of many factors at work. With or without the New Policy Agenda, strategic accountability is nearly always weaker than functional accountability and downward account-ability nearly always weaker than upward accountability. Even among very large NGOs (Southern or Northern) there is to date only limited empirical evidence of a significant fall-off in quality consequent on the growth of official funding, or of an incompatibility between service-provision, advocacy and 'development-as-empowerment'. Certainly, there are individual examples of negative trade-offs – for example, Perera 1995 – but perhaps as Howes and

Sattar (1992, p 117) put it for BRAC in Bangladesh, 'when attention is given to building organisational capacities to support programme expansion, there is no inherent contradiction between quality and scale. Bigger can be better.'[1] Such conclusions may simply reflect the fact that we still have insufficient evidence of the impact of current trends to conclude very much at all, and/or that the New Policy Agenda constitutes a *potential* threat to NGO performance and accountability whose real influence is yet to be fully felt, and/or an indication that it is in other areas, such as broader state-society relations, that the real issues will emerge (Hulme and Edwards 1995). But the evidence we do have suggests that there are certainly no universal relationships between official funding and the 'corruption of NGOs', nor any necessary correlations between NGO size, growth, function and funding.

Overall, the case studies show that it is the *quality of the relationships* between GROs, NGOs, donors and governments that determines whether patterns of funding and accountability promote or impede the wider goals of all these organisations in development. Issues of quantity and size are less important (Fowler 1991). A partnership approach, which emphasises participation, learning, reciprocity and transparency, may permit the problems that accompany organisational growth and donor funding to be managed: GRO/NGO performance, legitimacy and accountability need not be eroded. Donors (whether official or NNGO) must therefore be encouraged to move towards funding arrangements which provide stability and predictability in the long-term, and timeliness and flexibility in the short term (Van der Heijden 1987). Long-term institutional support requires a 'continual dialogue about objectives and strategies, rather than simply a specification of outputs and targets' (Carroll 1992, p 164) and hasty evaluations by overseas consultants. This is very different from the cut and thrust of the contract culture which (contrary to current thinking in official agencies) may ultimately disable organisations and compromise long-term quality of impact. It may be better to channel official donor funds to NGOs and GROs via an independent public institution which can protect them from undue donor influence, as recommended for the USA (Hellinger et al 1988, p 114) and in other countries (Smillie 1993; Baron 1993), or via local NGO networks which can ensure quality control through self-regulation and peer pressure, as in the Philippines (Constantino-David 1992). Official donors, such as the European Union, CIDA and the Overseas Development Administration, who are considering more direct funding of NGOs and GROs in the South, need to reflect on the alternatives available to them in this respect, rather than simply expanding their own offices in Southern capitals (Crombrugghe et al 1993).

2. The importance of negotiation

One of the most striking conclusions to emerge from earlier chapters is the emphasis that so many place on *negotiation among stakeholders* as a guiding principle for improving NGO accountability in the future. Indeed, Fowler, Shah and Shah, Biggs and Neame and others make it clear that there can be no improvements without such negotiations, supporting Marsden et al's (1994, p 1) earlier understanding of evaluations as 'negotiating points in the process of development'. Increasing the involvement of grassroots constituencies (beneficiaries and supporters) is the only way to correct the weakness of downward accountability which is such a common characteristic of the case studies in this book. 'Structured involvement' of a wider range of stakeholders can help to resolve many of the dilemmas facing NGOs and GROs in performance-assessment and accountability, although it will not make these dilemmas disappear. As Parmesh and Meera Shah show in their chapter, increasing the involvement of grassroots stakeholders also opens up the prospect of major changes in roles, responsibilities and accountabilities, and should not be undertaken by agencies who have no serious commitment to reform in their own institutions and structures. But wherever there are multiple constituencies, negotiation may be the only way to deal with differences over performance standards, 'bottom lines', and evaluation results. Since the short-term objectives of different stakeholders are likely to differ, such negotiations should focus on long-term aims and mission if any consensus is to be generated (Drucker 1990, p 110). The concept of 'stakeholders' is not, of course, uncontroversial. Poor people's development is 'their' process, which they must control; to this extent they are 'shareholders' in development, not 'stakeholders' – a situation analagous to Tandon's distinction (in his chapter) between the legitimate involvement of donors in NGO accountability but not in NGO governance.

A related conclusion concerns the importance of informal mechanisms in maintaining legitimacy and accountability. As the chapters by Pratten and Ali Baldo, Uphoff and others show, these mechanisms can often be very effective – more so than formal (democratic, representative) mechanisms introduced from the outside. This resonates with Carroll's (1992) conclusion that an open, collegial style, and attitudes which encourage bottom-up participation, can help to build organisations which are responsive and accountable to grassroots constituencies, even when they are not formally membership organisations. The possible erosion of such indigenous and informal systems by foreign aid (a danger cited by Gariyo and Hashemi in their chapters) is therefore very worrying.

As Biggs and Neame point out in their chapter, the key issue for NGOs in the New Policy Agenda is not how to preserve a 'mythical autonomy', but how to strengthen multiple accountabilities and 'room for manoeuvre' so that they can negotiate more effectively. The 'social audit' methodology described by Zadek and Gatward; the Aga Khan Foundation's participatory monitoring and evaluation framework presented by Shah and Shah; and the checks and balances analysed by Covey in her chapter on policy alliances, are practical mechanisms for promoting stakeholder involvement in performance-assessment and strengthening downward (and sideways!) accountability. Their example deserves to be followed by other NGOs, governments and official aid agencies.

3. The 'baby and the bathwater'

It is impossible to read the chapters in this book without being fully-appraised of the sheer complexity of NGO performance-assessment and accountability.

Clearly, this is an area which is full of difficulties – the problems of identifying impact when individual NGOs and projects are such a small part of the overall picture; how to measure qualitative changes in the strength of institutions or the awareness of individuals; how to deal with the many and often conflicting pressures for different forms of accountability from different directions, and so on. Faced by such a daunting range of problems, there is sometimes a tendency (reflected in some of the contributions to this book) to abandon completely the search for more rigorous performance measures or to establish more sophisticated systems for tracking impact. In our view, this is a mistake, equivalent to 'throwing the baby out with the bathwater and refusing to take the issue of professionalism seriously' (Smillie, this volume). Despite the complexities and uncertainties involved, all agree that the current state of NGO and GRO accountability is unsatisfactory. The search for improvements must go on, even if as Rondinelli (1993) concludes accountability has to be restricted to the ways in which NGOs and others use their resources rather than the long-term impact of resource use on development. This poses particular problems for 'strategic accountability' as defined in our Introduction, an area which the case studies in this book show to be particularly, and unsurprisingly, weak.

Finding accurate links between causes and effects is a problem for all development agencies, not just NGOs, and indeed poses a dilemma for social science as a whole as it struggles to emerge from the limitations of its positivist 'Newtonian paradigm' (Uphoff 1992). But even if individual NGOs find it impossible, for good reason, to measure the long-term impact of their work on broad development trends, they can still improve significantly on their current performance in evaluating learning, institution-building, levels of participation, gender equity and so on. As Desai and Howes conclude in their chapter, 'it may be very difficult to prove success conclusively, but the easier task of demonstrating that (NGOs) have not failed in key areas would in itself represent a considerable advance on the present state of affairs'. There is certainly no room for complacency. If NGOs do not improve significantly in this area, they run the risk of being 'sidelined to a backwater of carping utopianism ... [to be avoided only if they] ... further develop their capacity to identify concrete steps and achievable targets, and to agree on reasonable ways in which these can be measured' (German and Randel 1995). Drucker's (1990) advice, 'always ask how can we do what we already do better', is a useful reminder of the need to look for practical and incremental improvements even where 'reality is contingent' and impact is so difficult to establish.[2]

4. Accounting for what?

Although functional specialisation is clearly not essential for efficiency, some of the problems concerning NGO performance and accountability identified in earlier chapters do seem to be related to an inability among NGOs to decide what they really want to do, or to a mix of functions and tasks that may conflict with each other. The potential contradiction between the organisational characteristics required to perform effectively as a service-provider and as a catalyst of social change and institutional development was highlighted in our Introduction. Similar conflicts may exist between accountability and effectiveness in policy alliances (as Covey shows in her chapter). Equally, however, the reverse may be true, given the need for 'empowerment' approaches to bring material benefits if people's interest is to be sustained. The chapters in this book by Ramesh (on the Working Women's Forum in India) and Karim (on Proshika in Bangladesh) provide good illustrations of how different functions can be married together successfully. The same is true for NGOs who need to have solid field experience of the issues on which they lobby if they are to remain authoritative and credible (Edwards and Hulme 1992). This is the key to what Alan Fowler (1993, pp 334–335) calls the 'onion-skin approach' – an 'outer layer of welfare-oriented activity that protects inner layers of material service-delivery that act as nuclei for a core strategy dedicated to transformation'. Whether such an integrated strategy would be openly supported by donors or tolerated by governments is another matter, with important implications for the degree of transparency afforded to different accountabilities. Such combinations of functions are explored in more depth later in this Conclusion, but they do clearly complicate the issues of performance and accountability for NGOs.

5. The management of accountability

Because stakeholder perceptions inevitably differ and NGOs are subject to so many conflicting pressures, the dilemmas of accountability identified above cannot be 'solved' – they have to be *managed*. For example, Northern NGOs will always remain accountable to their donors and supporters, as well as to their partners, and, to some extent, to the beneficiaries of their work. As the example of Apnalaya in Bombay shows, managing multiple funding sources and therefore accountabilities is already normal practice in many NGOs (Desai and Howes, this volume). Official aid agencies, while they may move towards less 'linear' approaches to development, will have to satisfy the demand for 'results' which comes from their political paymasters. Many NGOs *choose* to work across national boundaries, sectors of work, service-delivery and other approaches to development; they do not see these choices as mutually exclusive. In other words, these are management issues rather than issues of principle. As Commins (1995) puts it, 'it is possible to remain operationally accountable to governments in terms of use of funds and yet remain accountable to the low-income communities where the NGO is carrying out programmes'. Chief among the factors which enable NGOs to manage these dilemmas effectively are: a strong sense of mission and attachment to values and principles; effective learning and action research (Hasan 1993; Wils et al 1993); local-level institution building and high levels of participation (Riddell and Robinson 1992); effective management, strategic planning and accountability mechanisms; skilled and committed staff; and a favourable external environment (progressive donors, open governments and strong links with other NGOs). This in turn requires organisational structures and cultures which encourage learning, accountability and experimentation – organically-structured organisations which are decentralised, problem-solving and task-oriented (Wierdsma and Swieringha 1992; Fowler 1988; Edwards 1994; Beets, Neggers and Wils 1988).

Underlying these characteristics are some deeper traits, which include a willingness by NGO staff to hand over more control to partners and/or beneficiaries, and an ability to live with non-standardised responses and procedures in order to promote flexibility and experimentation – the 'open systems' approach to development work recommended by Chambers, Uphoff, Fowler and others in this book. With these features in place, NGOs can analyse strategic choices about co-operation with donors or governments, or indeed any decision on programming, and identify those that are likely to weaken their comparative advantages or relations with beneficiaries (Fowler 1988, p 22). They will also be in a better position to prevent a 'law of diminishing returns' from setting in when increasing bureaucracy threatens to reduce the value added by each increment in funding.

The future of NGOs?

What implications do these findings have for the future of NGOs and their role in development? The first point to make is that without effective performance-assessment and strong, multiple accountability mechanisms, no NGO is likely to be able to find its way through the increasingly complex maze constituted by the world of development assistance, nor find and maintain the right balance between the opportunities and dangers afforded to NGOs as the 'favoured child' of official aid. Weak or distorted accountability, and an inability to demonstrate impact and effectiveness in a reasonably rigorous manner (where this is possible) are likely to leave NGOs more vulnerable to co-option into the agendas of others, or simply to lead them into areas where they are not doing very much that is useful. Improving performance-assessment and accountability is not an 'optional extra' for NGOs; it is central to their continued existence as independent organisations with a mission to pursue. However, judged by the meagre level of resources devoted to organisational development in these areas and the reluctance of NGOs to innovate, an independent observer would have to conclude that most were not seriously concerned with accountability at all. Despite record increases in income between 1984 and 1994, very few NGOs (North or South) have invested sufficiently in evaluation, learning, research and dissemination; nor have they become more transparent or accountable to their different constituencies. This is despite the fact that their 'continued existence depends on the belief by staff and supporters that they are ethical according to explicit values and principles' (Zadek and Gatward, this volume).

Second, many of the problems facing NGOs in this field (less so GROs) arise because NGOs are *problematic organisations*. By their very nature, NGOs must live and work in situations of necessary ambiguity. Some of these ambiguities are the result of the characteristics of NGOs as a form of organisation – accountable to trustees in one country but working with communities in others; committed to fundamental reforms but funded by donors and supporters who (by and large) demand short-term results; wanting to 'democratise development' but forbidden from entering formal politics. Others are a matter of choice, as, for example, when an NGO decides to work across a range of approaches embracing service-delivery, institutional development and advocacy, each of which may require different funding mechanisms, organisational structures, skills and time-scales. Faced by these potential contradictions, it has become fashionable to conclude that NGOs must choose to be one thing or another – either they are 'public service contractors' or 'citizens' movements' (Korten 1990); a 'first force' which 'harnesses independent energy for a moral purpose' or a 'third force' acting as sub-contractors to the state (Knight 1993); organisations which are 'market-led' or 'values-based' (Robinson 1995).

However, there is good reason to believe that such conclusions are misplaced, though no doubt there will be certain NGOs (as there already are) which do fall clearly and consciously into one category or another. Social justice requires that people be liberated from the conditions of material poverty as well as being able to organise themselves to defend their rights, and different sorts of organisation will be more, or less, effective in promoting these goals according to context and circumstance. The scale of material poverty and the size of gaps in access to basic services in many of the world's poor countries requires that NGOs continue to play a significant role in service-provision and 'welfare', although clearly this cannot be in permanent substitution for the state if progress is to be equitable and sustainable. At the same time, it is perfectly possible (though perhaps increasingly difficult) to innovate, and to retain a sense of mission, a high level of independence, and an attachment to values and principles. There are many NGOs which play a major role in social organisation, awareness-raising and advocacy; just as there are many GROs which aim to support material improvements in their members' lives. Indeed, there are strong arguments (some outlined above) to suggest that these functions are best combined together. If this is true, then the future of NGOs and GROs may be dominated by two developments: the rise of the 'legitimate hybrid', to use Korten's (1990, p 105) terms; and the evolution of national and international networks, alliances and federations in which organisations with different roles and characteristics work synergistically to achieve common long-term goals.

In this sense, the future of Northern NGOs may resemble the 'new internationalist conglomerates' envisioned by Zadek and Gatward in their chapter. The lessons generated by the Institute for Development Research's work on international policy alliances, and the importance of the 'bridging role' for NGOs which their research highlights, are extremely relevant here (Covey, this volume). This does not mean that difficult questions of legitimacy and accountability can be ducked – differences in these areas between, for example, membership and non-membership organisations will remain, and the dilemmas of performance and accountability highlighted earlier will still have to be managed. However, variations in needs, context, funding sources, organisational competences, legal and regulatory systems, supporter profiles, donor attitudes, tradition and politics point to a necessary focus on partnership, effectiveness and learning, rather than on particular organisational forms which are deemed 'right or wrong', 'good or bad'. The chapters in this book by Covey, Bejar and Oakley, Zadek and Gatward and others seem to point in this direction. As Nielsen (in Keating 1994, p 73) puts it, 'the landscape of the third sector is untidy but wonderfully exuberant. What counts is not the confusion, but the profusion.'

These observations do not mean that 'all is well' in the world of NGOs, particularly NGOs based in the North. Far from it: criticisms of Northern NGO performance and accountability surface regularly throughout this book, and they cannot be ignored. The complacency born of ten years of relatively easy fund-raising between 1984 and 1994 must give way to more serious reflection and openness to change. As Southern NGOs grow in number and authority (opening their own offices 'overseas', as BRAC has done in Kenya and as Filipino and African NGOs are doing in Washington), and as an increasingly integrated global economy throws up new challenges to NGOs in their own 'backyard', Northern NGOs are bound to come under increasing pressure to take partnership and accountability more seriously. As Bebbington and Riddell (1995) put it, the challenge to NGOs in the North is to 'define a role that can help to enhance the impact of the work of their Southern partners, and define it *with them*'. Joint advocacy, 'fair trading', facilitating access to specific expertise and information, and domestic development work, are examples of what these roles might be, redirecting Northern NGOs to address those parts of the global problematic of exclusion which they can tackle most effectively. As Béjar and Oakley (this volume) put it, the key task is to 'abandon unequal relationships between donors and recipients in favour of an effective South–North dialogue around common and practical tasks: to move from accountability to shared responsibility'. Much more effort must go into support to local fund-raising and other means of promoting the financial independence of NGOs in the South, which Karim, Biekart and other contributors to this book see as central if legitimacy and accountability are to be strengthened in the longer term. As in all 'open systems', to achieve real impact NGOs must focus more on changing relationships between people and institutions, and the values on which they are based, and less on shifting small, but growing, amounts of funding from one part of the world to another. The changes implied by such a shift will be slow and difficult, not least because of the need to bring NNGO constituencies along to provide consistent and independent support to this transition. If NNGOs have not already started to do this (and most have not), then they need to do so *now*.

In this process the questions of legitimacy, identity and governance take centre-stage; these questions are even more demanding than issues of performance and accountability, for they go right to the heart of the NGO and its mission: most obviously, 'What are NGOs for in the 21st century?'. Clearly, there can be no one answer to this question, but thus far few Northern NGOs have even faced up to the question itself, preferring instead to decentralise their management functions within existing, Northern-controlled, structures of governance. Of course, NGOs will adapt to the demands of a changing world, as they have done in the past, but will they adapt enough? Unless Northern NGOs begin to face up to the challenges of a new millennium quickly; unless they begin to redefine a role for themselves which recognises what is happening in the world around them; and unless they begin to take accountability much more seriously, they are likely to be bypassed in the future by governments, official agencies, citizens' movements, and perhaps even by their own supporters. NGOs have spent too much time criticising others and not enough time 'putting their own house in order'. Despite their rhetoric, no Northern NGO is seriously trying to 'work itself out of a job', and, sadly, most give the impression that only a financial crisis will be enough to enforce more fundamental changes in this direction. No matter how effective NGOs are technically in monitoring and evaluation, strategic planning, or managing multiple accountabilities, hard decisions will still need to be made about future roles and responsibilities. Moving away from operational work (and the large official grants that come with it) will inevitably mean a reduction in income for Northern NGOs. But perhaps a recognition of the 'limits to growth' is no bad thing, if it provides NNGOs with the room they seem to need for more profound reflection on their future, a greater commitment to issues of quality in their work, and the courage and vision they need to rethink and reform their roles into the 21st century.

In this task personal accountability is going to be essential, given the inertia which characterises all large NGOs, the resistance they will put up to change, and the temptations for NGO managers provided by organisational growth and the status of size. All organisations, and all individuals within them, possess some 'room for manoeuvre', which can be used to promote incremental reform, transparency, learning and sharing. As Chambers (this volume) puts it, 'if primacy were accorded to the personal, would the problems of performance and accountability largely be resolved?'. Perhaps not, given the dilemmas which face NGOs and the inherent difficulties of measuring performance and managing multiple accountabilities, but without an acceptance of personal responsibility and the determination to be accountable individually, there will be no resolution of these dilemmas and certainly no improvement in NGO performance. Moves in this direction, towards the 'open systems' mode of thinking and acting recommended by Uphoff and others in this book, would be in the very best NGO tradition – innovation, solidarity and humility.

The focus of this book on the New Policy Agenda and the influence of official aid may have led us to underestimate the influence of endogenous factors, and to overestimate the negative impact of donor funding, but it is on this basis that we posit that the modes of programming of NGO and GRO operations, of defining performance indicators, of claiming legitimacy, and of accounting for achievements, are being reshaped. From a neo-liberal perspective, the emergence of NGOs and GROs is desirable for its contribution to economic efficiency and political pluralism, although it may only be transitional as the commercial sector evolves and effective interest groups crystallise. From a radical perspective, it may be co-option: the abandonment of a mission for social transformation to become the implementer of the New Policy Agenda. If this *is* what is happening, then perhaps the best that can be hoped for is that the bubble will burst and that NGOs and GROs may then return to their former position – smaller and less lauded, but more independent and effective as agents of social change. The present popularity of NGOs with donors will not last forever: donors move from fad to fad and at some stage NGOs, like flared jeans, will become less fashionable. When this happens, the developmental impact of NGOs, their capacity to attract support, and their legitimacy as actors in development, will rest much more clearly on their ability to demonstrate that they can perform effectively and that they are accountable for their actions. It is none too soon for NGOs to get their 'houses in order': rethinking and reforming accountability – moving 'beyond the magic bullet' – is central to this challenge.

Notes

1. In reality, it is difficult to know whether such conclusions are accurate, since independent empirical evidence is very scarce. There is anecdotal evidence that the credit repayment rates and other impact indicators publicised by large NGOs in South Asia, including BRAC, are exaggerated, but insufficient evidence exists to confirm this view. Independent evidence in this area is urgently needed.
2. The key here is to experiment in practice with as wide a range as possible of different techniques for monitoring and evaluation, and learn from these experiences. Save the Children-UK has recently published a 'toolkit' on assessment, monitoring, review and evaluation which provides a useful foundation for such a process.

References

Chapter 1

Aga Khan Foundation Canada/Novib (1993) *Going To Scale: the BRAC experience 1972–1992 and beyond*, Aga Khan/Novib, The Hague.

Arellano-Lopez, S, and Petras, J (1994) 'NGOs and Poverty Alleviation in Bolivia', *Development and Change*, vol 25, no 3, pp 555–568.

Avina, J (1993) 'The evolutionary life cycle of non-governmental development organisations', *Public Administration and Development*, vol 13, no 5 (December), pp 453–474.

Bebbington, A and Riddell, R (1995) 'New Agendas and Old Problems: Issues, Options and Challenges in Direct Funding of Southern NGOs', in Hulme, D and Edwards, M (eds) *Too Close for Comfort? NGOs, States and Donors*, Macmillan, London.

Bebbington, A, Thiele, G (eds) with Davies, P, Prager, M, Riveros, H (1993) *NGOs and the state in Latin America: Rethinking roles in sustainable agricultural development*, Routledge, London.

Bratton, M (1989) 'The Politics of Government – NGO Relations in Africa', *World Development*, vol 17, no 4, pp 569–587.

Bratton, M (1990) 'Non-governmental organisations in Africa: can they influence government policy?', *Development and Change*, vol 21, pp 87–118.

Brett, E (1993) 'Voluntary Agencies as Development Organisations: theorizing the problems of efficiency and accountability', *Development and Change*, vol 24, pp 87–118.

Brown, D and Tandon, R (1992) *Public–NGO Financing Institutions in India: An Exploratory Study*, World Bank, Washington DC.

Carroll, T (1992) *Intermediary NGOs: the Supporting Link in Grassroots Development*, Kumarian Press, West Hartford.

CIVICUS (1994) *Citizens Strengthening Global Civil Society*, Civicus, Washington DC.

Clark, J (1995) 'NGO–State Relations: a review of the principal policy issues', in Hulme, D and Edwards, M (eds), op cit

Colclough, C and Manor, J (1991) *States or Markets? Neo-liberalism and the development policy debate*, Clarendon Press, Oxford.

Commission on Global Governance (1995) *Our Common Neighbourhood: the Report of the Commission on Global Governance*, Oxford University Press, Oxford.

Constantin– David, K (1992) 'The Philippine Experience in Scaling-Up', in Edwards, M and Hulme, D (eds), *Making a Difference: NGOs and Development in a Changing World*, Earthscan, London.

Drucker, P (1990) *Managing the Non-Profit Organisation*, Harper Collins, New York.

Eade D (1993) 'Editorial', *Development in Practice*, vol 3, no 3, pp 161–162.

Edwards, M (1993) 'Does the Doormat Influence the Boot? Critical thoughts on UK NGOs and international advocacy', *Development in Practice*, vol 3, no 3, pp 163–175.

Edwards, M (1994) 'NGOs in the Age of Information', *IDS Bulletin*, spring 1994, IDS, Sussex.

Edwards, M and Hulme, D (eds) (1992) *Making a Difference: NGOs and Development in a Changing World*, Earthscan, London.

Edwards, M and Hulme, D (eds) (1994) *NGOs and Development; Performance and Accountability in the 'New World Order'*, background paper to the workshop on NGOs and Development, SCF/IDPM, Manchester, 27–29 June 1994.

Esman, M and Uphoff, N (1984) *Local organisations: intermediaries in rural development*, Cornell University Press.

Farrington, J and Bebbington, A with Wells, K and Lewis, D (1993) *Reluctant Partners? NGOs, the State and Sustainable Agricultural Development*, Routledge, London.

Farrington, J and Lewis, D (eds) with Satish, S and Miclat-Teves, A (1993) *NGOs and the State in Asia: Rethinking Roles in Sustainable Agricultural Development*, Routledge, London.

Fisher, J (1994) 'Is the Iron Law of Oligarchy Rusting Away in the Third World?', *World Development*, vol 22, no 2, pp 129–143.

Fowler, A (1988) *NGOs in Africa: achieving comparative advantage in relief and micro-development*, IDS discussion paper no 249, IDS, Sussex.

Fowler, A (1991) 'The Role of NGOs in Changing State–Society Relations: Perspectives from Eastern and Southern Africa', *Development Policy Review*, vol 9, pp 53–84.

Fowler, A (1992) *Distant Obligations: speculations on NGO funding and the global market*, paper presented to the annual conference of the DSA, Nottingham, September.

Fowler, A (1993) 'NGOs as Agents of Democratisation: an African Perspective', *Journal of International Development*, vol 5, no 3, pp 325–339.

Fox, J (1992) 'Democratic Rural Development: Leadership Accountability in Regional Peasant Organizations', *Development and Change*, vol 23, no 2, pp 1–36.

Fox, J and Hernandez, L (1989) 'Offsetting the Iron Law of Oligarchy: the ebb and flow of leadership accountability in a regional peasant organization', *Grassroots Development*, vol 13, no 2, pp 8–15.

Friedmann, J (1992) *Empowerment: The Politics of Alternative Development*, Blackwell, Oxford and Cambridge (Massachusetts).

German, T and Randel, J (1994) 'Trends in Official Aid and the Implications for NGOs', paper presented to the Workshop on NGOs and Development, SCF/IDPM, Manchester, 27–29 June 1994.

Ghai, D and Vivian, J (1992) (eds) *Grassroots Environmental Action: People's Participation in Sustainable Development*, Routledge, London and New York.

Good, A (1994) 'Paying the piper, Calling the tune? Present and future relationships among Northern NGOs, Southern NGOs, and the ODA', paper presented to the SCF/IDPM workshop on NGOs and Development: Performance and Accountability in the 'New World Order', Manchester, 27–29 June.

Guba, E and Lincoln, Y (1989) *Fourth Generation Evaluation*, Sage, London.

Handy, C (1993) *Understanding organisations*, Penguin (4th edition), Harmondsworth.

Hasan, A (1993) *Scaling-up the OPP's low-cost sanitation programme*, OPP/RTI, Karachi.

Hashemi, S and Schuler, S (1992) *State and NGO support networks in rural Bangladesh: concepts and coalitions for control*, Centre for Development Research, Copenhagen.

Hellinger, D, Hellinger, S and O'Rogan, F (1988) *Aid for Just Development*, Lynn Rienner, Boulder and London.

Howes, M and Sattar, M G (1992) 'Bigger and Better? Scaling-up strategies pursued by BRAC 1972–1991', in Edwards, M and Hulme, D (eds) *Making a Difference; NGOs and Development in a Changing World*, Earthscan, London.

Hulme, D and Edwards, M (eds) (1995) *Too Close for Comfort? NGOs, States and Donors*, Macmillan, London.

Hulme, D and Mosley, P (1995) *Finance Against Poverty* (vols 1 and 2), Routledge, London.

ICVA (1991) *Relations between Southern and Northern NGOs: Policy Guidelines*, ICVA, Geneva.

InterAction (1993) *InterAction Private Voluntary Agencies (PVOs) Standards*, Washington DC.

Korten, D (1990) *Getting to the 21st Century: Voluntary Action and the Global Agenda*, Kumarian Press, West Hartford.

LaFond, A (1995) *Sustaining Primary Health Care*, Earthscan/SCF, London.

Lehmann, D (1990) *Democracy and Development in Latin America: Economics, Politics and Religion in the Post-War Period*, Polity Press, Cambridge.

Marsden, D, Oakley, P, and Pratt, B (1994) *Measuring the Process: Guidelines for Evaluating Social Development*, INTRAC, Oxford.

Marzouk, M (1995) 'The Associative Phenomenon in the Arab World: engine of democratization or witness to the crisis?, in Hulme, D and Edwards, M (eds) op cit.

Meyer, C (1992) 'A step back as donors shift institution building from the public to the "private" sector', *World Development*, vol 20, no 8, pp 1115–1126.

Moore, M (1993) 'Good government? Introduction', *IDS Bulletin*, vol 24, no 1, pp 1–6.

OECD (1988) *Development Assistance Committee Report 1987*, OECD, Paris.

OECD (1994) *Development Assistance Committee Report 1993*, OECD, Paris.

OECD (1995) *Development Assistance Committee Report 1994*, OECD, Paris.

Pearce, J (1993) 'NGOs and Social Change: agents or facilitators?', *Development in Practice*, vol 3, no 3, pp 222–227.

Perera, J (1995) 'Unequal Dialogue with Donors: the Sarvodaya Experience', in Hulme, D and Edwards, M (eds) op cit.

Rademacher, A and Tamang, D (1993) *Democracy, Development and NGOs*, SEARCH, Kathmandu.

Riddell, R and Robinson, M (1992) *The impact of NGO poverty-alleviation projects: results of the case study evaluations*, ODI Working Paper no 68, ODI, London.

Robinson, M (1993) 'Governance, Democracy and Conditionality: NGOs and the New Policy Agenda', in Clayton, A (ed) *Governance, Democracy and Conditionality: what role for NGOs?*, INTRAC, Oxford.

Rondinelli, D (1993) *Strategic and Results-based Management in CIDA: reflections on the process*, Canadian International Development Agency, Ottawa.

Salamon, L (1993) *The Global Associational Revolution: The Rise of the Third Sector on the World Scene*, Occasional Paper no 15, Institute for Policy Studies, Johns Hopkins University.

Salamon, L and Anheier, H (1993) *The Third Route: Subsidiarity, Third-Party Government and the Provision of Social Services in the United States and Germany*, report to OECD, Paris.

Smillie, I and Helmich, H (1993) *Non-Governmental Organisations and Governments: Stakeholders for Development*, OECD, Paris.

Smith, B (1990) *More than Altruism: the politics of private foreign aid*, Princeton University Press.

Smith, S and Lipsky, M (1993) *Non profits for hire: the welfare state in the age of contracting*, Harvard University Press.

Tandon, R (1994) 'Civil Society, the State and the Role of NGOs', in Serrano, I (ed) *Civil Society in the Asia-Pacific Region*, CIVICUS, Washington DC.

Tendler, J (1982) *Turning Private Voluntary Organizations into Development Agencies: Questions for Evaluation*, Evaluation Discussion Paper no 10, US Agency for International Development, Washington.

Tendler, J (1983) *Ventures in the Informal Sector and How They Worked out in Brazil*, Evaluation Special Study no 12, US Agency for International Development, Washington.

Tendler, J (1989) 'Whatever Happened to Poverty Alleviation?', *World Development*, vol 17, no 7, pp 1033–1044.

Vivian, J (1994) 'NGOs and Sustainable Development in Zimbabwe: No Magic Bullets', *Development and Change*, vol 25, pp 181–209.

Voorhies, S (1993) *Working with Government using World Bank Funds*, World Vision International Staff, Working Paper no 16.

Wellard, K and Copestake, J (1993) (eds) *NGOs and the State in Africa: Rethinking Roles in Sustainable Agricultural Development*, Routledge, London.

Chapter 2

Bohm, D and Peat, F (1987) *Science, Order and Creativity*, Bantam Books, New York.

Briggs, J P and Peat, F D (1984) *Looking Glass Universe: The Emerging Science of Wholeness*, Simon & Schuster, New York.

Carroll, F (1992) *Intermediary NGOs: The Supporting Link in Grassroots Development*, Kumarian Press, West Hartford.

Edwards, M and Hulme, D (1994) *NGOs and Development: Performance and Account-ability in the 'New World Order'*, background paper for international workshop on NGOs and Development, University of Manchester, 27–29 June.

Esman, M and Uphoff, N (1984) *Local Organizations: Intermediaries in Rural Development*, Cornell University Press, Ithaca, New York.

Fisher, J (1994) 'Is the Iron Law of Oligarchy Rusting Away in the Third World?' *World Development* vol 22, no 2, pp 129–143.

Fox, J (1992) 'Democratic Rural Development: Leadership Accountability in Regional Peasant Associations', *Development and Change*, vol 23, no 2, pp 1–36.

Gell-Mann, M (1994) *The Quark and the Jaguar: Adventures in the Simple and the Complex*, W H Freeman, New York.

Gleick, J (1987) *Chaos: Making a New Science*, Viking Books, New York.

Hunter, G (1969) *Modernizing Peasant Societies*, Oxford University Press, London.

Jantsch, E (1980) *The Self-Organizing Universe: Scientific and Human Implications of the Emerging Paradigm of Evolution*, Pergamon, New York.

Korten, D (1980) 'Community Organization and Rural Development: A Learning Process Approach', *Public Administration Review*, vol 40, no 5, pp 480–511.

Lewin, R (1992) *Complexity: Life at the Edge of Chaos*, Macmillan, New York.

Lipset, M (1956) *Union Democracy: The Internal Politics of the International Typographical Union*, Free Press, Glencoe, Illinois.

Michels, R (1915) *Political Parties*, reprinted by Free Press, Glencoe, Illinois (1959).

Penrose, R (1989) *The Emperor's New Mind: Concerning Computers, Minds, and the Laws of Physics*, Oxford University Press, New York.

Pradhan, P (1983) 'Chhattis Mauja', in *Water Management in Nepal: Proceedings of a Seminar on Water Management Issues*. Agricultural Projects Service Centre, Kathmandu.

Prigogine, I and Stengers, I (1984) *Order Out of Chaos: Man's New Dialogue with Nature*, Bantam Books, New York.

Trochim, W (1992) 'Developing an Evaluation Culture for International Agricultural Research', in *Assessing the Impact of International Agricultural Research for Sustainable Development*, pp 29–49, Cornell International Institute for Food, Agriculture and Development, Ithaca, New York.

Uphoff, N (1986) *Local Institutional Development: An Analytical Sourcebook with Cases*, Kumarian Press, West Hartford.

Uphoff, N (1992) *Learning from Gal Oya: Possibilities for Participatory Development and Post-Newtonian Social Science*, Cornell University Press, Ithaca, New York.

Uphoff (1993) 'Grassroots Organizations and NGOs in Rural Development: Opportunities with Diminishing States and Expanding Markets', *World Development*, vol 21, no 4, pp 607–622.

Uphoff, N (1994) Introduction to *Puzzles of Productivity in Public Organizations: Reinventing Development Administration* (Uphoff, N (ed)), Institute of Contemporary Studies Press, San Francisco.

Waldrop, M (1992) *Complexity: The Emerging Science at the Edge of Order and Chaos*, Simon & Schuster, New York.

Wolf, F (1981) *Taking the Quantum Leap: The New Physics for Non-Scientists*, Harper & Row, San Francisco.

Zukav, G (1979) *The Dancing Wu Li Masters: An Overview of the New Physics*, Bantam Books, New York.

Chapter 3

Biggs, S D and Senaratne S P F (1986) *Who does what research and why: the role and organisation of research in BRAC*, Bangladesh Rural Advancement Committee, Dhaka.

Chambers, R (1992) 'Spreading and self-improving: a strategy for scaling-up', in Edwards, M and Hulme, D (eds) *Making a Difference*, op cit.

Clay, E J and Schaffer, B (eds) (1984) *Room for Manoeuvre: An Exploration of Public Policy in Agricultural and Rural Development*, Heinemann, London.

Dreze, J and Sen, A (1991) 'Public Action for Social Security: Foundations and Strategy', in Ahmad, E, Dreze, J, Hills, J and Sen, A (eds), 1991 *Social Security in Developing Countries*, Clarendon Press, Oxford.

Edwards, M and Hulme, D (eds) (1992) *Making a Difference? NGOs and Development in a Changing World*, Earthscan/SCF, London.

Edwards, M and Hulme, D (1994) *'NGOs and Development: Performance and Accountability in the "New World Order"'*, background paper for the international workshop on NGOs and Development: Performance and Accountability in the New World Order, Save the Children Fund/University of Manchester, 27–29 June 1994.

Fowler, A (1990) 'Doing Better? Where and how NGOs have a comparative advantage in facilitating development', *Bulletin* no 28, pp 11–20, University of Reading Agricultural Extension and Rural Development Department, Reading.

Fowler, A (1992) 'Distant Obligations: Speculations on NGO Funding and the Global Market, in *Review of African Political Economy*, no 55, pp 9–29.

Gershman, J and Bello, W (eds) (1993) 'Struggles for Democracy and Democratic Struggle' in *Re-examining and Renewing the Philippine Progressive Vision*, Forum for Philippine Alternatives (FOPA), c/o CARET, 6 Malinis Street, U P Village, Diliman, Quezon City, Philippines.

Harding, D (1994) 'From Global to Local: Issues and Challenges Facing NGOs', Avocado Series 02/94, Olive Information Service, 23 Acacia Road, Glenwood, Durban 4001, South Africa.

Korten, D (1987) 'Third Generation NGO Strategies: A key to people-centred development', *World Development*, vol 15, supplement, pp 145–159.

Korten, D (1990) *People Versus Government: Restoring Cooperative Democracy through Voluntary Action in Andhra Pradesh, India*, 710 Commonwealth Avenue, Boston, Massachusetts, 02215, USA.

Long, N and Van der Ploeg, J D (1989) 'Demythologizing planned intervention: an actor perspective', *Sociologica Ruralis*, vol 24, no 3/4, pp 226–249.

Marsden, D (1990) *Definitions of Development and the Development of Definitions: Building Models in the Hindu Kush*, Centre for Development Studies, University College of Swansea (mimeo).

Marsden, D and Oakley, P (eds) (1990) *Evaluating Social Development Projects*, Oxfam, Oxford.

Neame, A D (1993) 'The Search for Empowerment in the Philippines: Practitioners or Prophets', unpublished MA dissertation, School of Development Studies, University of East Anglia.

ODA (1992) 'The Process Approach to Projects', *Technical Note* no 4, ODA, London.

Porter, D, Allen, B and Thompson, G (eds) (1991) *Development in Practice: Paved with Good Intentions*, Routledge, London.

Pratt, B and Loizos, P (1992) *Choosing Research Methods: Data Collection For Development Workers*, Oxfam, Oxford.

Schaffer, B (1984) 'Towards responsibility: public policy in concept and practice', in Clay and Schaffer op cit.

Senaratne, S P F (1990) 'The Transformation of the Rural Economy: A Societal Perspective', *Upanathi*, spring.

Starkey, P (1987) *Animal-drawn Wheeled Tool Carriers: Perfected Yet Rejected*, GTZ, Berlin.

Uphoff, N (1993) 'Grassroots Organisations and NGOs in Rural Development: Opportunities with Diminishing States and Expanding Markets', *World Development*, vol 21, no 4, pp 607–622.

Von Pischke, J (1991) *Finance at the Frontier*, World Bank, Washington DC.

White, S (1991) *Evaluating the Impact of NGOs in Rural Poverty Alleviation: Bangladesh Case Study*, Working Paper no 50, Overseas Development Institute, London.

Wood, G and Palmer-Jones, R (1990) *The Water Sellers: A Collective Venture by the Rural Poor*, IT Publications, London.

Chapter 4

Billis, D and Mackeith, J (1993) *Organising NGOs*, Centre for Voluntary Organisation, London School of Economics, London.

Conrad, W R and Glenn, W E (1976) *The Effective Voluntary Board of Directors*, Ohio University Press, Athens.

Edwards, M and Hulme, D (1994) *NGOs and Development: Performance and Account-*

ability in the 'New World Order', background paper to the international workshop at the University of Manchester, 27–29 June 1994.

Tandon, R (1987) *Forms of Organisations: Square Pegs in Round Holes*, PRIA, New Delhi.

Tandon, R (1989) *Management of Voluntary Organisations*, PRIA, New Delhi.

Tandon, R (1991) *NGOs, the State and the Civil Society*, IDR Occasional Paper Series, Boston.

Chapter 5

Bratton, M (1989) 'The Politics of NGO–Government Relations in Africa' *World Development*, vol 17, no 4, pp 569–587.

Edwards, M and Hulme, D (eds) (1992) *Making a Difference: NGOs and Development in a Changing World*, Earthscan, London.

Edwards, M and Hulme, D (1994) *NGOs and Development: Performance and Accountability in the 'New World Order'*, background paper for a workshop of the same title, University of Manchester/Save the Children Fund, June 1994.

Fowler, A (1991) 'The Role of NGOs in Changing State– Society Relations: Perspectives from East and Southern Africa', *Development Policy Review*, vol 9, no 1, 53–84.

Neggers, J and Wils, F (1987) *Self Evaluation among NGDOs and Local Organisations in Third World Countries*, paper presented at the 'Consultation on the Promotion of Autonomous Development', Cebemo, Oegstgeest (Netherlands).

Tendler, J (1987) *Turning Private Voluntary Organizations into Development Agencies: Questions for Evolution*, Evaluation Discussion Papers No 10, USAID, Washington DC.

Wils, F, Madduri, K and Sohoni, N (1993) *AWARE and its Work with Tribals and Harijans in Andhra Pradesh: an Impact Study*, Institute of Social Studies, The Hague.

Wils, F, Lafroce, J, Renaud, P and Zivetz, L (1988–90) *The View from the Field: an analysis and evaluation*, UNDP/NGO Division, New York.

Wils, F, Neggers, J and Beets, N (1988) *Big and Still Beautiful: Enquiry into the efficiency and effectiveness of three big NGOs (BINGOs) in South Asia*, Programme Evaluation Report no 32, Novib Ministry of Development Co-operation, The Hague.

Wils, F, Remmerswaal, J and Neggers, J (1993) *Big NGOs in Latin America: case studies in Peru and Bolivia*, Programme Evaluation Report no 47, Novib Ministry of Development Co-operation, The Hague.

Chapter 6

Biekart, K (1994) *Las Agencias Europeas de Cooperacion No-Gubernmental y La Democratizacion en Centroamerica: lecciones de la decada del ochenta y politicas para las noventa*, TNI/PRISMA, Amsterdam/San Salvador.

Cebemo (1993) *Documento Basico Montevideo*, Cebemo, The Hague.

Danida (1989) *Danish NGO Report*, Ministry of Foreign Affairs, Copenhagen.

Edwards, M and Hulme, D (1992) (eds) *Making a Difference: NGOs and Development in a Changing World*, Earthscan, London.

Finnida (1994) *Strengthening the Partnership: Evaluation of the Finnish NGO Support Programme*, FINNIDA, Helsinki.

Hansen, F (1994) *Coherencia o contradicción?: Las políticas de la Unión Europea, el caso de Centroamérica*, Documento de Trabajo CRIES no 94/4.

Lewis, D (1990) *NGOs and international aid in Central America: the development dialogue between North and South* (paper presented at the CCIC consultation 'NGOs and the North–South Dialogue in the 1990s', Quebec, 8–12 May).

Riddell, R (1990) *Judging Success: Evaluating NGO Approaches to Poverty-Alleviation in Development Countries*, Overseas Development Institute, London.

Riddell, R (1993) *Discerning the Way Together*, report for Christian Aid, ICCO, EZE and Brot fur die Welt.

Visser, E and Wattel, C (1991) *Las relaciones de cooperacion entre la Comunidad Europea y America Central*, in Ruben, R et al, *Mas alla del ajuste: la contribucion europea al desarrollo democratico y duradero de las economias centroamericanas*, DEI, San José.

Chapter 7

Bebbington, A and Riddell, R (1995) 'New Agendas, old problems: governments, NGOs and Myths about direct funding and civil society', in Hulme, D and Edwards, M (eds) op cit.

Carroll, T (1992) *Intermediary NGOs: The Supporting Link in Grassroots Development*, Kumarian Press, West Hartford.

El Taller (1993) *Las ONGs Latinoamericanas frente a la situación actual*, El Taller, Tunis.

Hulme, D and Edwards, M (eds) (1995) *Too Close for Comfort? NGOs, States and Donors*, Macmillan, London.

Lehmann, D (1990) *Democracy and Development in Latin America: Economics, Politics and Religion in the Post-War Period*, Temple University Press.

Misereor (1993) *Seminario sobre Planeación, Monitoreo y Evaluación, Colombia*, Miserior, Aachen.

Noriega, J and Saravia, M (1994) *Peru: Las Organizaciones No Gubernamentales*, Desco, Lima.

Pearce, J (1995) 'NGOs in Latin America: Accountability and Legitimacy', in Hulme, D and Edwards, M op cit.

Richards, M (1985) *The Evaluation of Cultural Action*, Macmillan, London.

Save the Children Fund (1994) *Relatorio de Aviliacao do Projeto Retome Su Vida*, SCF-UK, Recife.

UNDP (1993) *Human Development Report*, UNDP, New York.

Chapter 8

Apnalaya (1993) *Relief and rehabilitation work undertaken in Shivaji Nagar, Govandi, during December 1992 and January 1993*, Bombay: Apnalaya, mimeo.

Apnalaya (1994a) *Report for the Year 1993–94*, Apnalaya, mimeo, Bombay.

Apnalaya (1994b) *Background and Philosophy*, Apnalaya, mimeo, Bombay.

Avina, J (1993) 'The evolutionary life-cycle of non-governmental development organisations', *Public Administration and Development*, vol 13, no 5 (December).

Casley, D J and Lury, D A (1982) *Monitoring and Evaluation of Rural and Agricultural Development Projects*, Johns Hopkins University Press, Baltimore.

Nadkarni, V (1992) *Drug Abuse Demand Reduction: Focus on Community-based Approaches*, Tata Institute of Social Sciences, Bombay.

Chapter 9

UNFPA (1994) *Income Generation and Family Planning for Working Women in the Urban Slums of Madras and Rural Areas of Tamilnadu*, UNFPA/Working Women's Forum, New York/Kancheepuram.

WWF, 1995; original data provided for this publication by the Working Women's Forum.

Chapter 10

Siddiqui, K (1987) *Benefit Packages Received by Functionaries of Government Organisations and NGOs*, ADAB, Dhaka.

White, S (1992) *Evaluating the Impact of NGOs on Rural Poverty Alleviation in Bangladesh*, Overseas Development Institute, London.

Chapter 11

Ahmed, Noman (1994) *NGOs, Atheists and Apostates*, Deshapremik Kishore Sangshad, Dhaka, Bangladesh.

Ahsan, E and Muslim, S N (1994) *Accountability in the Bangladesh Civil Service*, report presented at ASEAN-SAARC Conference on Administrative and Financial Accountability. Dhaka, Bangladesh, 16–20 January 1994 (quoted in the *Daily Star*, 18 January 1994).

Association of Development Agencies in Bangladesh (ADAB) (1993) *Code of ethics*, ADAB, Dhaka, Bangladesh.

Association of Development Agencies in Bangladesh (ADAB) (1994) *The Position Paper* presented at the press conference on 4 June 1994. ADAB, Dhaka, Bangladesh.

Clark, J (1991) *Democratizing development: the role of voluntary organizations*, Kumarian Press, West Hartford.

Edwards, M and Hulme, D (1994) *NGOs and Development: Performance and Accountability in the 'New World Order*, background paper in June for the SCF/IDPM workshop on NGOs and Development, Manchester.

Holloway, R (1994) *Alternatives to donor funds for South Asian NGOs: what do we know and what do we need to know?*, paper presented at the South Asian NGO Research Project Meeting, Dhaka, Bangladesh, 6–10 March 1994.

Impact Monitoring and Evaluation Cell (IMEC, formerly known as Research, Evaluation and Monitoring Cell) and *Horizon Pacific International* (HPI) (1993) *Impact Assessment and Internal Monitoring System of Proshika*, Implementation Report: Stage One, Proshika, Dhaka.

Korten, D C (1990) *Getting to the 21st century*, Kumarian Press, West Hartford.

Mitchell, R et al (1994) *Proshika Manobik Unnayan Kendra, Bangladesh, Phase V (July 1994–June 1999), appraisal*, Proshika, Dhaka.

Muhammad, Anu (1988) *Crisis of development in Bangladesh and NGO model* (in Bengali), Prochinta Prokashani, Dhaka.

NGO Affairs Bureau (NAB) (1992) *NGOs in Bangladesh*. NGO Affairs Bureau, Dhaka, Bangladesh.

NGO Affairs Bureau (NAB) (1993) *Rules and procedures to be followed by all foreign NGOs working in Bangladesh and Bangladeshi NGOs receiving foreign funds* (in Bengali). Prime Minister's Office, Dhaka, Bangladesh.

Rahman, M H (undated) *What the NGOs are doing in the pretext of service provision* (in Bengali), Shibli Prokashani, Dhaka.

Report of the Task Forces on Bangladesh Development Strategies for the 1990s (1991) 'The role of NGOs' in *Managing the Development Process*, vol 2, University Press Limited, Dhaka, Bangladesh.

Smillie, I (1992) *BRAC at 20*, BRAC, Dhaka, Bangladesh.

Tandon, R (1994) 'Civil society, the state and the role of NGOs' in Isagani R Serrano (ed) *Civil society in the Asia-Pacific Region, Washington DC*, CIVICUS, Washington DC.

Umar, Badruddin (1989) 'The vicious circle of bourgeois politics in Bangladesh and what we need to do', in Badruddin Umar *Military rule and politics in Bangladesh* (in Bengali), Protik Prokashana Sangstha, Dhaka.

Umar, Badruddin (1994) 'NGO–GO entente in Bangladesh', in Badruddin Umar, *Economic–political situation in Bangladesh* (in Bengali), Jatio Sahitya Prakashani, Dhaka.

Wood, GD (1994) *Bangladesh: whose ideas, whose interests?*, University Press Limited, Dhaka.

Chapter 12

Barkan, J D, McNulty, M L and Ayeni, M A O (1991) '"Hometown" Voluntary Associations, Local Development, and the Emergency of Civil Society in Western Nigeria', *The Journal of Modern African Studies*, no 29, pp 457–480.

Barnes, S (1975) 'Voluntary Associations in a Metropolis: the case of Lagos', *African Studies Review*, vol 18, no 2, pp 75–87.

Bratton, M (1988) '"Beyond the State": Civil Society and Associational Life in Africa', *World Politics*, vol 41, no 3, pp 407–430.

Bratton, M (1989) 'The Politics of Government–NGO Relations in Africa', *World Development*, vol 17, no 4, pp 560–587.

Carroll, Thomas, F (1992) *Intermediary NGOs: the Supporting Link in Grassroots Development*, Kumarian Press, West Hartford.

Daum, C (1992) *L'immigration ouest-africaine en France: Une dynamique nouvelle dans la vallée du fleuve Sénégal?*, Institut Panos, Paris.

Fowler, A (1993) 'Non-Governmental Organisations as Agents of Democratization: An African Perspective', *Journal of International Development*, vol 5, no 3, pp. 325–339.

Hamad, A Z (1993) 'Dismantling Civil Society: Suppression of Freedom of Association in Sudan', *Censorship News*, no 27, article 19, London.

Jules-Rosette, B (ed) (1979) *The New Religions of Africa*, Ablex Publishing Corporation, Norwood, New Jersey.

Lithman, Y G (1984) 'When tomorrow is today: development as the idiom of routine', *Ethnos*, 3–4, pp 250–265.

Little, K (1965) *West African Urbanization: A Study of Voluntary Associations in Social Change*, Cambridge University Press, Cambridge.

Massaro, R J (1994) *Still Searching for the Missing Link: Tanzanian National Settlement Strategies*, paper presented at the 1994 Annual Meeting of the African Studies Association, Toronto.

Trager, L (1994) *Rural–Urban Linkages and Local 'Development': Whose Agenda? What Impact?*, paper presented at the 1994 Annual Meeting of the African Studies Association, Toronto.

Uphoff, N (1986) *Local Institutional Development*, Kumarian Press, West Hartford.

Chapter 13

Bratton, M (1990) 'Non-Governmental Organisations in Africa: Can they Influence Policy?', *Development and Change*, vol 21, no 1.

Edwards, M and Hulme, D (eds) (1992) *Making a Difference: NGOs and Development in a Changing World*, Earthscan/SCF, London.

Edwards, M and Hulme, D (1994) *NGOs and Development: Performance and Accountability in the 'New World Order'*, background paper, to the workshop of the same title, SCF/University of Manchester, 27–29 June 1994.

Ratter, A and Kwesiga, J B (1994) *Realising the Development Potential of NGOs and Community Groups in Uganda*, a report for the Ministry of Finance and Economic Planning, Kampala.

Chapter 14

Anderson, P, Arrow, J and Pines, D (eds) (1988) *The Economy as an Evolving Complex System*, Addison-Wesley, Redwood (California).

Campbell, P (1990) 'Strengthening Organisations', *NGO Management*, no 18, pp 21–24.

Carlsson, J, Kohlin, G and Ekbom, A (1994) *The Political Economy of Evaluation: International Aid Agencies and the Effectiveness of Aid*. St Martin's Press, London.

Carvalho, S and White, H (1993) *Performance Indicators to Monitor Poverty Reduction*, World Bank, Washington DC.

Cassen, R (1986) *Does Aid Work?* Oxford University Press, Oxford.

Chambers, R (1985) *Normal Professionalism, New Paradigms and Development*, paper for the seminar on Poverty Development and Food: Towards the 21st Century, Institute of Development Studies, University of Sussex, Brighton (mimeo).

Chambers, R (1993) *Challenging the Professions: Frontiers for Rural Development*, Intermediate Technology Development Group, London.

Cracknell, B (1983) *The Evaluation of Aid Projects and Programmes*, proceedings of a conference organised by the Overseas Development Administration in the Institute of Development Studies at the University of Sussex, 7–8 April, Overseas Development Administration, London.

Drucker, P (1990) *Managing the Non Profit Organization: Principles and Practices*, Harper Collins, New York.

Drucker, P (1993) *The Five Most Important Questions You Will Ever Ask About Your NonProfit Organization: Participant's Workbook*, Drucker Foundation/Jossey-Bass, San Francisco.

Edwards, M and Hulme, D (1994) *NGOs and Development: Performance and Accountability in the 'New World Order'*, background paper for the international conference of the same title, Save the Children/University of Manchester, 27–29 June.

Fowler, A (1989) 'Why is Managing Social Development Different?', *NGO Management Newsletter*, no 12, pp 18–20.

Fowler, A (1992a) 'Distant Obligations: Speculations on NGO Funding and the Global Market', *Review of African Political Economy*, no 55, pp 9–29.

Fowler, A (1992b) *Prioritising Institutional Development: A New Role for NGO Centres for Study and Development*, Gate Keeper Series, no 35, International Institute for Environment and Development, London.

Fowler, A, Campbell, P and Pratt, B (1992) *Institutional Development and NGOs in Africa: Policy Perspectives for European Development Agencies*, International NGO Training and Research Centre and Novib, Oxford and the Hague.

Fowler, A (1994a) *The World Bank and its Stakeholders: Who are They and Why?*, discussion paper, Human Resources Vice Presidency, World Bank, Washington DC.

Fowler, A (1994b) 'Capacity Building and NGOs: A Case of Strengthening Ladles for the Global Soup Kitchen?', *Institutional Development*, vol 1, no 1.

Gell-Mann, M (1994) *The Quark and the Jaguar*, Freeman, New York.

Hancock, G (1989) *The Lords of Poverty*, Atlantic Monthly Press, New York.

Hawley, K (1993) *From Grants to Contracts: A Practical Guide for Voluntary Organisations*, National Council of Voluntary Organisations/Directory of Social Change, London.

Herman, R and Heimovics, R (1994) 'A cross-national study of a method for researching non-profit organisational effectiveness', *Voluntas*, vol 5, no 1, pp 86–100.

Howes, M (1992) 'Linking Paradigms and Practice: Key Issues in the Appraisal, Monitoring and Evaluation of British NGO Projects' *Journal of International Development*, vol 4, no 4, pp 375–396.

Hudock, A (1994) *Sustaining Southern NGOs in Resource-Dependent Environments*, paper presented at the Development Studies Association Annual Conference, University of Lancaster, September.

INTRAC/South Research (1994) *A Tool for Project Management and People Driven Development*, reports of a workshop on LFA/OIP, Leuven, International NGO Training and Research Centre/South Research, Oxford/Brussels.

James, R. Strengthening the Capacity of Southern NGO Partners, Occasional Papers Series, vol 1, no 5, 1994, International NGO Training and Research Centre, Oxford.

Kanter, R M (1979) *The Measurement of Organisational Effectiveness, Productivity, Performance and Success: Issues and Dilemmas in Service and Non-Profit Organisations* PONPO Working Paper no 8, Institution for Social and Policy Studies, Yale University.

Korten, D (1991) 'International Assistance: A Problem Posing as a Solution', *Development: Seeds of Change*, no 2/3, Society for International Development, Rome.

Lawrie, A (1993) *Quality of Service: Measuring Performance for Voluntary Organisations*, National Council of Voluntary Organisations/Director of Social Change, London.

Leat, D (1993) *Managing Across Sectors: Similarities and Differences Between For-Profit and Voluntary Non-Profit Organisations*, VOLPROF, City University Business School, London, March.

Lewin, P (1994) *Complexity*, Phoenix, London.

Lewis, J et al (1988) *Strengthening the Poor: What Have We Learned?* Overseas Development Council, US–Third World Policy Perspectives, no 10, Washington DC.

Long, N and Long, A (eds) (1992) *Battlefields of Knowledge: The Interlocking of Theory and Practice in Social Research and Development*, Routledge, London.

Marsden, D and Oakley, P (eds) (1990) *Evaluating Social Development Projects*, Development Guidelines, no 5, Oxfam, Oxford.

Marsden, D, Oakley, P and Pratt, B (eds) (1994) *Measuring the Process: Guidelines for Evaluating Social Development*. International NGO Training and Research Centre, Oxford.

OECD (1993) *Non-Governmental Organisations and Governments: Stakeholders for Development*, Paris.

Oxfam Assembly (1994) *Talking, listening sharing*, Oxfam Assembly Office, Oxfam, Oxford.

Riddell, R and Robinson, M (1992) *The Impact of NGO Poverty Alleviation Projects: Results of the Case Study Evaluations*, working paper, no 68, Overseas Development Institute, London.

Roling, N and de Zeeuw, H (1987) *Improving the Quality of Rural Poverty Alleviation*, final report of the working party on The Small Farmer and Development Co-operation, International Agricultural Centre, Wageningen.

Scott, W (1987) *Organisations: Rational, Natural and Open Systems*, Prentice-Hall, Englewood Cliffs.

Senge, P (1990) *The Fifth Discipline: The Art and Practice of the Learning Organization*, Doubleday, New York.

Smith, S and Lipsky, M (1993) *NonProfits for Hire: The Welfare State in the Age of Contracting*, Harvard University Press, Cambridge, Massachusetts.

Smith, C (1994) 'The New Corporate Philanthropy', *Harvard Business Bureau*, pp 105–116, May–June.

Traidcraft (1994) *Social Audit Report 1993*, Traidcraft Exchange, Newcastle upon Tyne.

UNDP (1993) *Human Development Report*, Oxford University Press, Oxford.

Van Dijk, M (1994) 'The Effectiveness of NGOs: Insights from Danish, British and Dutch Impact Studies' *Schriften des Deutschen Ubersee-Instituts Hamburg*, no 28, pp 27–42.

Waldrop, M (1992) *Complexity: The Emerging Science at the Edge of Order and Chaos*, Simon & Schuster, New York.

White, H and Woestman, L (1994) 'The Quality of Aid: Measuring Trends in Donor Performance', *Development and Change*, vol 25, no 3, pp 527–554.

Wolpert, L (1992) *The Unnatural Nature of Science*, Faber & Faber, London.

World Bank (1994) *The World Bank and Participation*, Operations Policy Department, World Bank, Washington, DC.

Chapter 15

Edwards, M and Hulme, D (1992) (eds) *Making a Difference: NGOs and Development in a Changing World*, Earthscan/SCF-UK, London.

OECD (1988) *Voluntary Aid for Development: the Role of NGOs*, OECD, Paris.

Riddell, R (1990) *Judging Success: Evaluating NGO Approaches to Alleviating Poverty in Developing Countries*, Overseas Development Institute, London.

Salamon, L (1987) 'Partners in Public Service: The Scope and Theory of Government–Nonprofit Relations', in Powell, W (ed) *The Nonprofit Sector: A Research Handbook*, Yale University Press, New Haven.

Singh, B (1987) 'NGO Self-Evaluation: Issues of Concern', *World Development*, vol 15, special supplement on NGOs.

Smillie, I and Helmich, H (1993) *NGOs and Governments: Stakeholders for Development*, OECD, Paris.

Tendler, J (1982) *Turning Private Voluntary Organisations into Development Agencies*, USAID, Washington DC.

UNDP (1993) *Human Development Report*, UNDP, New York.

Chapter 16

Bratton, M (1989) 'Nongovernmental Organizations in Africa: Can They Influence Public Policy?' *Development and Change*, vol 12, no 21, 81–118.

Brown, L D (1991) 'Bridging Organizations and Sustainable Development *Human Relations*, vol 44, no 8, pp 807–831.

Brown, L D (1995) 'Creating Social Capital: Nongovernment Development Organizations and Intersectoral Problem-Solving', Powell, W W and Clemes, E E (eds) *Private Action for the Public Good*, Yale University Press, New Haven.

Brown, L D and Tandon, R (1993) *Multiparty Collaboration for Development in Asia*, United Nations Development Programme, New York.

Carroll, T F (1991) *Tending the Grassroots, Performance of Intermediary Non-Governmental Organizations*, Inter-American Foundation, Washington DC.

Cernea, M (1987) 'Farmer Organizations and Institution Building for Sustainable Agricultural Development', *Regional Development Dialogue*, vol 8, no 2, pp 1–24.

Clark, J (1992) 'Policy Influence, Lobbying and Advocacy', in Edwards, M and Hulme, D (eds), *Making a Difference: NGOs and Development in a Changing World*, Earthscan Publications, London.

Edwards, M and Hulme, D (1994) *NGOs and Development: Performance and Accountability in the 'New World Order'*, background paper for conference by same title, Manchester, England, 27–29 June; Save the Children Fund.

Fox, J (1992) 'Democratic Rural Development: Leadership Accountability in Regional Peasant Organizations', *Development and Change*, vol 23, no 2, pp 1–36.

Hall, A (1992) 'From Victims to Victors: NGOs and the Politics of Empowerment at Itaparica', in Edwards, M and Hulme, D (eds), *Making a Difference: NGOs and Development in a Changing World*, Earthscan Publications, London.

Jenkins, J C (1987) 'Nonprofit Organizations and Policy Advocacy', in Powell, W W *The Nonprofit Sector: A Research Handbook* Yale University Press, New Haven.

Miller, V (1994) *NGOs and Grassroots Policy Influence: What is Success?* IDR Working Paper, vol 11, no 3, Boston.

Chapter 17

Carroll, T (1992) *Intermediary NGOs: the Supporting Link in Grassroots Development*, Kumarian Press, West Hartford.

Edwards, M and Hulme, D (1994) *NGOs and Development: Performance and Accountability in the 'New World Order'*, background paper for the international workshop on NGOs and Development: Performance and Accountability in the New World Order, Manchester, June.

Chapter 18

Clark, J (1991) *Democratising Development: The Role of Voluntary Organisations*, Earthscan, London.

Edwards, M (1993) 'Does the Doormat Influence the Boot? Critical Thoughts on UK NGOs and International Advocacy', *Development in Practice*, vol 3, no 3, pp 163–175.

Edwards, M and Hulme, D (1992) *Making a Difference: NGOs and Development in a Changing World*, Earthscan, London.

Farrington, J and Bebbington, A with Wells, K and Lewis, D (1993) *Reluctant Partners? NGOs, the State and Sustainable Agricultural Development*, Routledge, London.

Fowler, A (1994) 'NGOs and the Globalisation of Social Welfare: Perspectives from East Africa', unpublished.

Gorz, A (1989) *The Death of Economic Reason*, Verso, London.

Hancock, G (1989) 'Lords of Poverty: The Power, Prestige and Corruption of the International Aid Business', *Atlantic Monthly Press*, New York.

Landry, C and Mulgan, G (1994) *The Future of the Charities: Themes and Issues*, Demos, London.

Max-Neef, M (1991) *From the Outside Looking In: Essays in Barefoot Economics*, Das Hammerskjold Foundation, Uppsala.

Traidcraft plc (1993) *Traidcraft plc Social Audit 1992/93*, Traidcraft plc, Gateshead.

Traidcraft plc (1994) *Traidcraft plc Social Audit 1993/94*, Traidcraft plc, Gateshead.

Zadek, S (1994) 'Trading Ethics', *Journal of Economic Issues*, June 1994.

Zadek, S and Evans, R (1993) *Auditing the Market: A Practical Approach to Social Auditing*, Traidcraft/New Economics Foundation, London/Gateshead.

Chapter 19

Bernadas, C N Jr (1991) 'Lessons in upland farmer participation: the case of enriched fallow technology in Jaro, Leyte, Philippines', *Forests, Trees and People Newsletter*, no 14 (October), pp 10–13.

Chambers, R (1994) 'The Origins and Practice of Participatory Rural Appraisal', 'Participatory Rural Appraisal (PRA): Analysis of Experience' and 'Participatory Rural Appraisal (PRA): Challenges, Potentials and Paradigm', *World Development*, respectively, vol 22, no 7, July, pp 953–969; no 9, September, pp 1253–1268; and no 10, October, pp 1437–1454.

GTZ (1988) *ZOPP (an introduction to the method)*, Deutsche Gesellschaft für Technische Zusammenarbet (GTZ) GmbH, Postfach 5180, D-6236 Eschborn 1 bei, Frankfurt am Main.

IDS/IIED (1994) *Participatory Methods and Approaches: Sharing Our Concerns and Looking to the Future*, Institute of Development Studies, University of Sussex, and International Institute for Environment and Development, London (May).

Kochendörter-Lucius, G and Osner, K (1989) *Development Has Got a Face: Lifestories of Thirteen Women in Bangladesh on People's Economy*, results of the International Exposure and Dialogue Programme of the German Commission of Justice and Peace and Grameen Bank in Bangladesh (14–22 October).

Leach, G and Mearns, R (1988) *Beyond the Woodfuel Crisis: People, Land and Trees in Africa*, Earthscan Publications, London.

Mascarenhas, J, Shah, P, Joseph, S, Jayakaran, R, Devavaram, J, Ramachandran, V, Fernandez, A, Chambers, R and Pretty, J (1991) *Proceedings of the February 1991 Bangalore PRA Trainers Workshop, RRA Notes* no 13, IIED, London and MYRADA, Bangalore.

Osner, K, Kochendörfer-Lucius, G, Muller-Glodde, U and Warning, C (1992) *Exposure and Dialogprogramme: Eine Handreichnung fur Teilnehmer under Organisatoren*, Justitia et Pax, Kaiserstrasse 163, 5300 Bonn 1.

Porter, D, Allen, B and Thompson, G (1991) *Development in Practice: Paved with Good Intentions*, Routledge, London and New York.

Pretty, J and Chambers, R (1993) *Towards a Learning Paradigm: New Professionalism and Institutions for Agriculture*, IDS Discussion Paper no 334, Institute of Development Studies, University of Sussex, Brighton (December).

SPWD (1992) *Field Methods Manual Volume I: Diagnostic Tools for Supporting Joint Forest Management Systems*, prepared for the joint Forest Management Support Programme, Society for Promotion of Wastelands Development, 1 Copernicus Marg, New Delhi 110001.

Starkey, P (1988) *Perfected yet Rejected: Animal-drawn Wheeled Toolcarriers*, Friedrich, Vieweg & Sohn, Braunschweig/Wiesbaden.

Chapter 20

Baron, B (1993) *Innovation and Future Directions in East Asian Philanthropy: Strengthening the Public/Private Interface*, Asia Foundation, San Francisco.

Bebbington, A and Riddell, R (1995) 'New Agendas and Old Problems: Issues, Options and Challenges in Direct Funding of Southern NGOs', in Hulme, D and Edwards, M (eds) *Too Close for Comfort?*, Macmillan, London.

Beets, N, Neggers, J and Wils, J (1988) *Big and Still Beautiful: Enquiry in the Efficiency and Effectiveness of Three Big NGOs (BINGOs) in South Asia*, Programme Evaluation NR32, DGIS/Novib.

Carroll, T (1992) *Intermediary NGOs: the Supporting Link in Grassroots Development*, Kumarian Press, West Hartford.

Commins, S (1995) 'Too Close for Comfort?', in Hulme, D and Edwards, M (eds), op cit.

Constantino-David, K (1992) 'The Philippine Experience in Scaling-up', in Edwards, M and Hulme, D (eds) *Making a Difference: NGOs and Development in a Changing World*, Earthscan/SCF, London.

Crombrugghe, G, Douxchamps, F and Stampa, N (1993) *Evaluation of EC–NGO co-financing in relation to institutional support for Grassroots Organisations in Developing Countries*, COTA, Brussels.

Drucker, P (1990) *Managing the Non-Profit Organisation*, Harper Collins, New York.

Edwards, M (1994) 'NGOs in the Age of Information', *IDS Bulletin* (Spring), IDS, Sussex.

Edwards, M and Hulme D, Eds (1992) *Making a Difference: NGOs and Development in a Changing World*, Earthscan/SCF, London.

Fowler, A (1988) *NGOs in Africa: achieving comparative advantages in relief and micro-development*, IDS Discussion Paper 249, IDS, Sussex.

Fowler, A (1991) 'The Role of NGOs in changing state–society relations: perspectives from Eastern and Southern Africa', *Development Policy Review*, vol 9, pp 53–84.

Fowler, A (1993) 'NGOs as agents of democratisation: an African perspective', *Journal of International Development*, vol 5, no 3, pp 325–339.

German, T and Randel, J (1994) 'Trends in Official Aid and the Implications for NGOs', paper presented to the Workshop on NGOs and Development: Performance and Accountability in the New World Order, SCF/IDPM, Manchester, June 27–29 1994.

Hasan, A (1993) *Scaling-up the OPP's low-cost sanitation programme*, OPP/RTI, Karachi.

Hellinger, D, Hellinger, S and O'Rogan, F (1988) *Aid for Just Development*, Lynne Rienner, Boulder and London.

Howes, M and Sattar, M (1992) 'Bigger and better? Scaling-up strategies pursued by BRAC 1972–1991', in Edwards, M and Hulme, D (eds), op cit.

Hulme, D and Edwards, M (eds) (1995) *Too Close for Comfort? NGOs, States and Donors*, Macmillan, London/St Martin's Press, New York.

Keating, M (1994) 'North America's Independent Sector', in CIVICUS, *Citizens Strengthening Global Civil Society*, Washington DC.

Knight, B (1993) *Voluntary Action*, CENTRIS, London.

Korten, D (1990) *Getting to the 21st Century: Voluntary Action and the Global Agenda*, Kumarian Press, West Hartford.

Marsden, D, Oakley, P and Pratt, B (1994) *Measuring the Process: Guidelines for Evaluating Social Development*, INTRAC, Oxford.

Perera, J (1995) 'The case of Sarvodaya', in Hulme, D and Edwards, M (eds) *Too Close for Comfort? NGOs, States and Donors*, Macmillan, London.

Riddell, R and Robinson, M (1992) 'The impact of NGO poverty-alleviation projects: results of the case-study evaluations', ODI Working Paper no 68, ODI, London.

Robinson, M (1995) 'NGOs as Public Service Contractors', in Hulme, D and Edwards, M (eds), op cit.

Rondinelli, D (1993) *Strategic and Results-based Management in CIDA: Reflections on the Process*, Canadian International Development Agency, Ottawa.

Smillie, I (1993) *From Partners to Stakeholders: The CIDA–NGO Challenge*, mimeo, Ottawa.

Uphoff, N (1992) *Learning from Gal Oya: Possibilities for Participatory Development and Post-Newtonian Social Science*, Cornell University Press, Ithaca.

Van der Heijden, H (1987) 'The Reconciliation of NGO Autonomy and Operational Effectiveness with Accountability to Donors', *World Development*, vol 15, supplement, pp 103–112.

Wierdsma, A and Swieringha, J (1992) *Becoming a Learning Organisation*, Addison-Wesley, London.

Wils, F, Maddin, V, Alexander, K and Sohoni, N (1993) *AWARE and its Work with Tribals and Harijans in Andhra Pradesh*, Institute of Social Studies, The Hague.

Glossary

ADAB	Association of Development Agencies in Bangladesh
BINGO	Big NGO
BRAC	Bangladesh Rural Advancement Committee
CBO	Community-based organisation
CIDA	Canadian International Development Agency
CIVICUS	World Alliance for Citizen Participation
FAO	Food and Agriculture Organisation
GRO	Grassroots organisation
NGO	Non-governmental organisation
NNGO	Northern non-governmental organisation
OECD	Organisation for Economic Co-operation and Development
SEWA	Self-Employed Women's Association
SIDA	Swedish International Development Authority
SNGO	Southern non-governmental organisation

Index